A Precarious Balance

A Precarious Balance

Democracy and Economic Reforms
in Eastern Europe
Volume I

Edited by Joan M. Nelson

A Copublication of the

International Center for Economic Growth

and the Overseas Development Council

 **PRESS**

Institute for Contemporary Studies
San Francisco, California

Publication signifies that the International Center for Economic Growth believes a work to be a competent treatment worthy of public consideration. The findings, interpretations, and conclusions of a work are entirely those of the authors and should not be attributed to ICEG, its affiliated organizations, its Board of Overseers, or organizations that support ICEG.

The Overseas Development Council fosters an understanding of how development relates to a much changed U.S. domestic and international policy agenda and helps shape the new course of global development and cooperation. ODC's programs focus on three main issues: the challenge of political and economic transitions and the reform of development assistance programs; the development dimensions of international responses to global problems; and the implications of development for U.S. economic security. ODC is a private nonprofit organization funded by foundations, corporations, governments, and private individuals. The views expressed in this book are those of the authors and do no necessarily represent those of the Overseas Development Council as an organization or of its individual officers or Board, Council, and staff members. Overseas Development Council, 1875 Connecticut Avenue, N.W., Washington, D.C. 20009.

Publication of the publication was made possible by support from the United States Agency for International Development (AID) and the Bank of America.

Inquiries, book orders, and catalog requests should be addressed to ICS Press, Institute for Contemporary Studies, 720 Market Street, San Francisco, California 94102 USA. Telephone: (415) 981-5353; fax: (415) 986-4878; book orders within the continental United States: **(800) 326-0263**.

Editor: Heidi Fritschel; Indexer: Shirley Kessel; Cover designer: Irene Imfeld

Library of Congress Cataloging-in-Publication Data

A Precarious balance/edited by Joan M. Nelson.
    p.   cm.
    Contents: v. 1. Democracy and economic reforms in Eastern Europe
    ISBN 1-55815-322-5
    1. Europe, Eastern—Economic policy—1989– —Case studies.
2. Latin America—Economic policy—Case studies. 3. Latin America—
Economic conditions—1982– —Case studies. 4. Post-communism—
Europe, Eastern—Case studies. 5. Europe, Eastern—Politics and
government—1989– —Case studies. 6. Democracy—Latin America—Case
studies. 7. Latin America—Politics and government—1980– —Case
studies. I. Nelson, Joan M.
HC244.P715 1994
338.947—dc20
                                            94-20970
                                              CIP

Contents

List of Tables and Figures

Tables

Figures

List of Abbreviations

AECD	Agency for Economic Coordination and Development (Bulgaria)
BANU	Bulgarian Agrarian National Union
BBWR	Nonparty Bloc for Reforms (Poland)
BSP	Bulgarian Socialist party
CITUB	Confederation of the Independent Trade Unions of Bulgaria
CMEA	Council for Mutual Economic Assistance
ÉSZT	Association of Unions of Professionals (Hungary)
ÉT	Interest Conciliation Council (Hungary)
FIDESZ	Federation of Young Democrats (Hungary)
FKGP	Smallholder party (Hungary)
GDP	Gross domestic product
GNP	Gross national product
IMF	International Monetary Fund
KDNP	Christian Democratic People's party
KLD	Liberal Democratic Congress (Poland)
KOR	Committee for the Defense of Workers (Poland)
KPN	Confederation for an Independent Poland
LAÉT	Association of People Living under the Poverty Line (Hungary)
MDF	Hungarian Democratic Forum
MGK	Hungarian Economic Chamber
MGYOSZ	National Association of Hungarian Industrialists
MRF	Movement for Rights and Freedoms (Bulgaria)
MSZMP	Hungarian Socialist Workers' party (Communist party)
MSZOSZ	National Association of Hungarian Unions
NBP	National Bank (Poland)
OPZZ	General Polish Confederation of Trade Unions

PC	Center Alliance (Poland)
PL	Peasant Alliance (Poland)
PSL	Polish Peasant party
PZPR	Polish United Workers party
RdR	Movement for the Republic (Poland)
SD	Democratic party (Poland)
SdRP	Social Democracy of the Republic of Poland
SOE	State-owned enterprise
SPA	State Property Agency (Hungary)
SZDSZ	Alliance of Free Democrats (Hungary)
SZEF	Cooperative Forum of Unions (Hungary)
SZOT	National Council of Unions (Hungary)
TDDSZ	Democratic Union of Research Workers (Hungary)
UD	Democratic Union (Poland)
UDF	Union of Democratic Forces (Bulgaria)
UP	Labor Union (Poland)
VOSZ	National Association of Entrepreneurs (Hungary)
ZChN	National Christian Union (Poland)
ZSL	United Peasant party (Poland)

Preface

In the past decade the countries of Eastern Europe and Latin America have taken dramatic steps toward democratic rule and market-oriented reforms in hopes of achieving political freedom and economic prosperity. The ultimate success of these changes, however, is not yet assured. Painful economic reforms and the sometimes messy push and pull of democracy can stimulate nostalgia and even pressure for the security of authoritarian or totalitarian political systems and command economies.

This two-volume study, *A Precarious Balance*, is based on a project of the Overseas Development Council coordinated by Joan M. Nelson in which twelve social scientists look at the interaction of political and economic reforms in six countries to see how they sometimes support and sometimes impede one another. In Eastern Europe, Bulgaria and Poland are attempting simultaneous reform, while Hungary is farther along the road to a market economy. In Latin America, treated in the companion volume to this book, Argentina, Bolivia, and Brazil have slightly more experience with democracy but are still working on liberalizing their economies.

While there are countries that have adopted market reforms under authoritarian systems, the objective of this study is to examine the links between political and economic changes in countries that are pursuing both at once. These links are often elusive, but they will certainly affect the outcome of present reform efforts in Eastern Europe and Latin America. The authors in these two volumes address vital questions: To what extent do democracy and the market go hand-in-hand and to what extent do they conflict? How do reforms affect parties and interest groups and vice versa? How can a broad share of the population be given a stake in the success of the reforms? The answers to these and other such questions will determine the future of the political and economic transitions in Eastern Europe and Latin America.

In this crucial moment of history, a greater understanding of the processes of democratic and market-oriented change is vital, for failure in any one country will have consequences far beyond its borders. The International Center for Economic Growth is pleased to collaborate with the Overseas Development Council to publish this important study, which deserves the attention of policy makers, scholars, and students of development the world over. A companion study of these issues, *Intricate Links: Democratization and Market Reforms in Latin America and Eastern Europe*, focuses on policy issues common to both regions and will be published by the Overseas Development Council in fall 1994.

John W. Sewell
President
Overseas Development Council
Washington, D.C.

Nicolás Ardito-Barletta
General Director
International Center for
Economic Growth
Panama City, Panama

August 1994

Editor's Preface

Two roughly simultaneous trends have emerged in much of the world since the mid-1980s. In almost all of Latin America, in most of what was recently the communist world, and increasingly in sub-Saharan Africa, authoritarian governments have disintegrated or been pushed aside by demands for more free and open political systems. And in much of the world, inward-oriented growth strategies entailing extensive state intervention are being replaced by more open and market-oriented policies and institutions.

This volume, and a companion volume on Latin America, begin to explore how political and economic liberalization interact. There is a massive literature on different aspects of market-oriented economic reform. Transitions from authoritarian to democratic political systems have also been extensively analyzed. But the two trends are usually examined separately. Where they are brought together—for instance, in the growing literature on the politics of market-oriented economic reform—the focus often is on narrow, short-run issues: political obstacles to economic reform and tactics to overcome those obstacles.

The studies in this volume try to move beyond the politics of economic stabilization and market-oriented reforms, to consider how democratic openings and efforts to consolidate democracy interact with deliberate and rapid economic liberalization. We also move beyond the fairly short-run focus of much previous work to consider not only democratic transitions but also the long and delicate process of consolidating democracy, not only initial economic stabilization and liberalization measures but also the slower and more complex structural and institutional reforms.

We do not assume that these two trends automatically or necessarily go together. Indeed, since World War II and outside of Western Europe, strong market-oriented growth strategies or vigorous economic liberalization have more often been pursued by authoritarian than democratic governments: Taiwan, Korea, and Chile are obvious examples. Postcolonial and later democratic transitions seldom triggered a shrinking state economic role; more often heightened democracy was associated with increased state intervention. For a brief moment, after the collapse of communism at the end of the 1980s, it seemed to many that democratic governments and market-oriented economies must go hand-in-hand. But both longer history and more recent experience underscore instead the complex and ambiguous relations between the two processes: each complements and supports the other in some crucial respects, but the two also often conflict not only in the short run but also in more fundamental, often unanticipated, ways.

Nor do we assume that democratization and marketization follow some single trajectory, some roughly similar route in different countries. Quite obviously the starting points—the nature of the economic and political systems before significant reforms—varied greatly. Desired end points also vary: a wide range of specific arrangements are possible within the broad categories of market economies and democratic polities. The specific version that emerges in any country will reflect historical and cultural legacies, not only differing priorities but also the unintended consequences of major choices. It follows that the links between economic and political liberalization are not only complex and problematic but also highly variable. The six country cases explored in this and the companion volume document how unique historic legacies, institutions, and circumstances lead to contrasts in the sequences, pace, and design of political and economic reforms, and in the prospects for sustaining and deepening those reforms. Much more tentatively, they begin to suggest how interactions between market-oriented policies and democratic political processes may shape the particular kinds of market-oriented economies and democratic polities that emerge.

Despite the crucial unique features of each case, however, certain common themes emerge within each region and—to a surprising degree—across both regions. The overviews to this and the companion volume summarize regional themes. Themes and issues common to both Latin America and Eastern Europe are explored in a later volume, *Intricate Links: Democratization and Market Reforms in Latin America and Eastern Europe*, to be published in fall 1994 by the Overseas Development Council.

The country and regional studies are the product of a collegial effort by twelve social scientists, all but one from Latin America or Eastern Europe. The group included economists, economic historians, and political scientists, several with considerable direct policy experience. In addition to those whose work appears in this volume, the group included Adolfo Canitrot, Marcelo Cavarozzi, Eduardo A. Gamarra, Bolívar Lamounier, Silvia Sigal, and Miguel Urrutia. We met initially in June 1992 to develop working concepts and briefly compare country experience. Regional workshops in autumn 1992 and a cross-regional conference in March 1993 provided further opportunities to compare cases and sharpen the analyses.

In Latin America, we analyzed the experience of Argentina, Bolivia, and Brazil; in Eastern Europe we examined Bulgaria, Hungary, and Poland. The choice of cases in Latin America was largely guided by our interest in interactions between roughly simultaneous economic and political liberalization. That focus ruled out the two Latin American countries most advanced in market-oriented reforms: Chile and Mexico. We also decided not to examine several long-established competitive democracies attempting far-reaching economic reforms: most notably Costa Rica and Venezuela. Argentina and Bolivia were obvious candidates: after definitive shifts from military to civilian rule in the early 1980s, both (with lags) pursued dramatic economic stabilization and structural reforms. Brazil was chosen because of its size and importance and because its post-1985 experience underscores the risks of half-hearted reforms that deepen the crisis unleashed by the exhaustion of statist growth strategies. In most of Eastern Europe political and economic openings coincided (although Hungary's history of economic liberalization begins much earlier). Our selection reflected our desire to include at least one country from the Balkans rather than focus solely on Central Europe. Further, we wished to avoid the complications introduced by severe regional and ethnic divisions (as in Czechoslovakia, which had not yet split when the project began).

In each of these cases, the authors sought to capture key characteristics of political and economic transformations and to consider how each transformation affects the other. That inquiry was handicapped by the brevity of the period that has elapsed since political transitions occurred, especially in Eastern Europe. Examining short time periods inevitably spotlights the importance of voluntaristic action: the decisions and behavior of key individuals and small groups, rather than the effects of changes in broader social, economic, or political structures or trends. Moreover, the studies deal with unfinished stories: even while the studies were being written major and quite unexpected events changed the pictures in Bulgaria, Poland, and Brazil.

One important dimension of these transformations is the extent to which they represent sharp breaks from the past. Certainly in Eastern Europe, most observers perceived the changes of 1989 and 1990 as abrupt and unexpected discontinuities. Political and economic shifts were less dramatic, but still major, in our Latin American cases. Yet in both regions, the importance of a wide variety of legacies from the recent and the more distant past has become increasingly evident. The case studies illustrate how different starting points, as well as the ongoing effects of institutions, attitudes, and relationships from the past, shape both market-oriented economic reforms and efforts to consolidate democratic openings.

Above all, these studies attempt to trace the links between the shift to more liberal political institutions and later efforts to consolidate these, on the one hand, and economic measures, including stabilization, liberalization, and structural reforms, on the other. The links are often indirect and elusive. One fairly clear link turns out to be the extent to which political elites and the broader public perceive the need for both economic and political reforms as intertwined, or instead (as in our Latin American cases) initially assume that political transformation will correct economic difficulties without painful economic reforms. A second link also operates through public perceptions: economic and political measures and trends each affect the credibility of the other. Other interactions are mediated through changes in civil society rather than through public opinion. Both political and economic transformations alter the structure, agendas, alliances, and strategies of major interest groups like farmers, labor unions, and business associations. These changes in turn affect both democratic consolidation and further economic reform. Still another linkage flows not through organized interest associations but through shifts in socioeconomic structure: the effects of market-oriented reforms in creating or enlarging groups with strong stakes in the system and, conversely, groups that are excluded.

Some of these and other linkages emerge quickly; others are at best beginning to be visible, and how they will evolve remains unclear. Our authors pushed toward tentative conclusions, aware that the evidence is still limited and that the interactions we want to grasp are inherently extremely complex. Still more elusive, yet extremely important, are the ways in which such linkages may affect the specific character of emerging market systems and democratic politics.

The focus of the case studies is on trends and structures internal to each country. External forces obviously powerfully influence and sometimes largely determine domestic choices and events. The cases discussed here are not independent of each other: especially within each region, events and experience in one country (and especially the countries that started reforms earlier) obviously shape debates and choices in other countries. With respect to economic stabilization, experience in Latin America spilled over regional boundaries to influence thinking in Eastern Europe.

Still more obvious is the importance for internal trends of international political and economic events, such as the Soviet Union's loosened control over Eastern Europe and its own internal disintegration, or the Gulf War. In all of our cases, specific international institutions, particularly the International Monetary Fund (IMF) and the World Bank, creditors' organizations (the Paris and London clubs), and, in Eastern Europe, the European Community played direct and influential roles with regard to economic policy. Yet outside pressures bear differently on different countries, in part reflecting divergent earlier policies and events and in part as a result of varied responses by governments and societies. The purpose of these studies, however, is not primarily to trace and understand the course of economic reforms or democratic consolidation but to explore the linkages between the two processes. Those linkages are intrinsically internal to each country.

This volume and its companion volume on Latin America are products of a collegial research project of the Overseas Development Council. The project as a whole was primarily financed by the Pew Charitable Trusts and the John D. and Catherine T. MacArthur Foundations. The International Center for Economic Growth provided funds for regional workshops in Budapest and Rio de Janeiro to review initial country drafts. The participants in the regional workshops and the later cross-regional conference contributed not only to the individual case studies but to the project as a whole. We would like to thank the Institute of World Economics of the Hungarian Academy of Sciences and the Department of Economics of the Pontifical Catholic University of Rio de Janeiro for hosting the regional workshops. We are also indebted to the participants in those workshops and the cross-regional conference for their many insights and suggestions: they are listed at the end of the volume. Finally, we would like to gratefully acknowledge the ongoing support, resourcefulness, and patience of the staff of the Overseas Development Council and particularly of Stephanie Eglinton.

CHAPTER 1

The Transition in Bulgaria, Hungary, and Poland: An Overview

Jacek Kochanowicz, Kalman Mizsei, and Joan M. Nelson

In 1989, communism collapsed in Eastern Europe.[1] The Polish "Round Table" of August 1989 and Hungary's decision to permit free passage to East German refugees triggered chain reactions. One by one Eastern European communist governments, their legitimacy shattered, let opposition movements surface and ceded their monopoly on power. Emerging elites set as their goal the establishment of market economies and democratic political systems. The collapse was wholly unexpected, and the course of transformation totally uncharted.

This volume analyzes the relationship between market reforms and democratization in three Eastern European countries: Poland, Hungary, and Bulgaria. A considerable body of theory and evidence suggests that, once established, market economies and pluralist politics are mutually supportive. But historically the rise of democratic institutions has been a long and complex process. Few nations have attempted to move simultaneously from command to market economies and from highly authoritarian single-party to democratic multiparty political systems. Therefore there has been very little analysis of how the processes of economic and political liberalization interact when they are undertaken jointly.

On the face of it, such simultaneous transformations look improbable. In the now highly developed countries of Western Europe, markets and capitalism emerged before mass democracy. Much more recently, in the successful newly industrialized countries of Southeast Asia, early phases of industrial

1

development and social modernization took place under authoritarian rule. In contrast, in several Latin American nations early mass political mobilization (often including militant union action) spurred inflation, disrupted emerging markets and industrial development, and ultimately aborted emerging democratic processes.

Eastern European experience between the two world wars reinforces doubts about regional prospects for simultaneous transformation. Parliamentary democratic systems launched after World War I could not contain the inflation of the 1920s or cope with the depression of the 1930s. Most of the countries of the region slid toward authoritarianism while at the same time developing highly statist economies. The beginning of the 1990s shows disconcerting similarities to the earlier era: inflation, recession, and unemployment again test fragile democratic traditions, while reforms must combat the additional obstacles created by forty years of communist authoritarianism and command economy.

Not only historical experience but also the logic of the situation argues that simultaneous market-oriented reforms and consolidation of democratic openings are in sharp tension with each other. Democratic politics are likely to block economic reforms that inflict severe costs on much of the population; struggles over fundamental constitutional issues and the restructuring of party systems and interest groups are likely to divert attention and prevent action on urgent economic measures. And if those reforms are actually carried through, then the resulting economic hardship may well push democracy off course.

Yet, surprisingly, democracy holds and the economic transformation pushes forward in most of the countries of the region. Elections are free, and governments are responsible to legislatures. The media are not censored; civil rights are not abused.[2] Four years after the collapse of communist governments, most prices and much trade are freed of controls. The private sector already accounts for over 40 percent of output in Hungary and at least 45 percent in Poland. Stabilization has been reasonably effective: inflation is falling or has reached manageable levels. Exports have expanded. These gains have come at a heavy price, and the future is far from assured: both points will be discussed in this essay and the case studies that follow. But the striking fact to date is that democracy has held while market reforms have progressed.

What factors have permitted this outcome, confounding apparent tensions and historical experience? Are those factors likely to persist, or are the later stages of the attempt at simultaneous transition likely to take a different course in some or all of the countries of the region?

This study seeks to shed some light on these questions, though it can hardly provide definitive answers: too little time has passed since the collapse of the communist monopoly on power, and three country cases offer only partial evidence. Our comparative approach is further limited by considerable interdependence among the three cases and by the fact that we are examining the initial stages of what will certainly be a long historical process.[3]

Why these three countries? Poland and Hungary are of course among the "Western tier" reformers; Bulgaria represents the Balkan countries, which began their transformation slightly later and have cultural and historical legacies and geographical links different from those of the Western tier. We have selected three fairly homogenous countries in order to screen out the additional complications introduced by ethnic or regional tensions. Bulgaria's relative homogeneity, of course, is not typical of other Balkan nations. Since Yugoslavia was not part of the Soviet Bloc, we have not tried to take into account its experience nor that of its successor units.

The collapse of communism and the transition to a new order is a global process, in which evolution in any given country is related to much wider international economic and political trends and forces. In this volume, however, we focus primarily on internal developments, touching only briefly on the external context.

The events of 1989–1990 in Eastern Europe were startlingly abrupt. Yet the collapse of communism grew out of a long process of the disintegration of the institutions and effectiveness of the command economy and the communist political system. Disintegration started at different times and moved at different rates in our three cases, as well as elsewhere in the region. Post-1989 economic and political reforms obviously do not build on clean slates but on the partial ruins of the former systems. In each country, the nature of the transition itself and later transformation has been powerfully affected by the degree to which old institutions and legitimacy had already decayed.

Where disintegration of the old arrangements started early and was well advanced by 1989, it was followed by the emergence of new economic, political, and social institutions and actors, providing a basis for the far more rapid post-transition emergence of markets and democratic politics. Where disintegration started late and occurred slowly, emergence of new institutions and actors was delayed. Since 1989, a third process has come into play: the redefinition of both communist and anticommunist institutions and actors' roles and strategies. All three processes—disintegration, emergence, and redefinition—continue to unfold in present-day Eastern Europe.

The three processes provide a conceptual framework for summarizing and comparing transitions and transformations in our three case studies. This overview examines each process in turn. The final section suggests some reasons for the compatibility thus far—contrary to both historical experience and logical expectations—of democratic openings and economic reforms and identifies some of the challenges that lie ahead.

First, however, we sketch a few key features of the historical heritage of each of the three countries under review. In each, unique historic, cultural, and social legacies shaped responses to and effects of the communist era. These differences in turn affected the way in which communist economic and political systems eventually disintegrated, the groups and institutions that have emerged to replace communism, and receptivity to Western models of democracy and market economy.

Heritages

The three nations have sharply contrasting historic associations with "West" and "East." Poland and Hungary received Christianity from Rome, while Bulgaria, developing within the shadow of the Byzantine Empire, participated in Eastern Christianity. Bulgaria's isolation from the West was reinforced by a long period of Turkish rule. These contrasting religious and cultural traditions in Poland, Hungary, and Bulgaria shaped social and political evolution and continue to do so today. Poland and Hungary are both dominantly Catholic. Hungary, however, includes a sizable Protestant population. Although the Catholic Church played a lesser role in political affairs in Hungary than in Poland, in both countries the substantially autonomous (and sometimes antagonistic) spheres of church and state created an inherent pluralism, a climate in which the notion of civic associations independent of the state could later emerge. Bulgaria, in contrast, is largely Eastern Orthodox, save for a Muslim minority of roughly 10 percent. The traditional Orthodox fusion of head of state with head of church worked to discourage the idea of pluralism. Poland and Hungary represent, therefore, the Western-oriented part of Eastern Europe (in which Slovakia and the Czech Republic can be included), while Bulgaria exemplifies the Balkan countries.

These different traditions affected the countries' pre–World War II patterns of modernization and their reaction to communism after the war and to its collapse some forty years later. Bulgarians were sympathetic toward Russia both because they had religious and linguistic ties to that country and because Russia helped Bulgaria shed the Turkish yoke at the end of the nineteenth century. Hungary, in contrast, looked west: it was part of the Hapsburg Empire and was long strongly influenced by German culture. Poland was more complex on this score: rural and urban segments of society were deeply divided socially and culturally. An important stratum of intelligentsia and a powerful, elitist "high culture" tradition survived both war and Stalinism. While most Poles tended to be both anti-German and anti-Russian (reflecting their unhappy national history), intellectual elites were pro-Western not only throughout the nineteenth and early twentieth centuries, but even under communism.

Despite some broad parallels, the three nations' political histories, including their experience with independence and democracy, also varied in ways that affected more recent events. All were independent states for periods during the Middle Ages and in the early modern period, but each came under the domination of larger empires or states—Russian, Prussian (later, the German Reich), Hapsburg, and Turkish—before they had begun to evolve into modern nations. Therefore all started to develop the institutions and traditions of independent modern states relatively late: Hungary (within the dual monarchy), after 1867; Bulgaria, with the end of the Turkish occupation early in this century; and Poland, after World War I. Current efforts to revamp the structures of the state, the economy, and the political system can draw on only limited prior experience with independent government.

With respect to economic and social patterns, compared with Western Europe all three countries were peasant societies until World War II. Much of the population was at best only partly engaged in the market economy. In each, the state played an important role in early steps toward modernization and economic development. The metaphor of "returning to Europe," so fashionable now in Poland, misses the point: Eastern Europe, save perhaps the Czech lands, lagged considerably behind Western Europe, and this lag had deep historical roots (see Chirot 1989). Among the three, Bulgaria was the most rural and egalitarian, while Hungary had the strongest "petite bourgeoisie" tradition.

All three countries went through the harsh experience of World War II (Poland on the side of the Allies, the other countries on the Axis side), and communism was established after the Red Army overran their territories in 1944. Poland was most devastated, and its social structures were shattered by the war. The Holocaust, the shift of territory to the West, and the postwar expulsion of Germans from the acquired territories also left Poland much more ethnically homogeneous than it had been before the war.

The initial period of communism was probably harsher in Hungary than in Poland or Bulgaria: terror and repression were freely used both in the early years and after the attempted uprising of 1956. Paradoxically, Hungary after 1956 went furthest in "domesticating" the communist system, developing its own unique modifications that would later ease the market and democratic transitions. In Poland, in contrast, strong social tensions emerged in later years. In Bulgaria, communism was more readily assimilated, owing to traditional social egalitarianism, pro-Russian feelings, and perhaps also the paternalistic Orthodox cultural legacy with its lack of emphasis on individual freedom. In all three countries, the communist era brought profound changes—most dramatic in Bulgaria and least dramatic in Hungary—converting largely peasant societies into substantially urban and industrial ones. In Bulgaria in particular, many of these changes were widely seen as positive.

In short, varying cultural and historical legacies produced important variations in the impact of and responses to the imposition of communist systems. The lowest degree of political acceptance was in Poland, the highest in

Bulgaria. These contrasts strongly influenced differences in the timing, nature, and sequencing of the disintegration of communism in the three countries, and the emergence of new political and economic institutions and groups.

Disintegration

Communism's final collapse in 1989 was preceded by a long process of decomposition of all aspects of the system—economic, social, and political. In Hungary and Poland in the later years, disintegration was accelerated in some respects by deliberate reforms. After 1989, of course, the dismantling of communist economic and political institutions intensified. But the process is still far from complete.

Analyzed with a perspective of several decades, communism had its own life cycle of growth and decay. Initially, totalitarian regimes generated high rates of economic growth by using political mobilization techniques; drawing on easily obtainable manpower, energy, and raw materials; and disregarding ecological consequences. These advantages initially offset the inherent inefficiency of command economies (low output-input ratios) and their inability to innovate. Societies atomized by war and revolution were responsive to political mobilization; rapid upward mobility for some segments of society also generated political support.

By the late 1950s, however, difficulties were emerging: new social structures began to become more rigid and resources less readily available. Despite attempts at autarky and the rapid reduction of trade outside of the communist bloc, communist economies became dependent on technology transfers from the West. Nor could initial efforts at cultural isolation be maintained: partial openings to the West after the mid-1950s spurred rising consumer demands.

In Poland and especially in Hungary, partial reforms eased the first round of difficulties. When similar problems reemerged in the 1970s, they were temporarily offset by foreign borrowing. But by the late 1970s and the 1980s, the communist system throughout the region was less and less able to face the challenge of international economic and military competition, especially accelerating technological change. Nor could it meet the consumer and political aspirations of its own societies. Welfare achievements—cheap housing and food, free health and education—deteriorated. By the beginning of the 1980s, at least the more enlightened segments of ruling elites realized that the system was in fundamental crisis. Within the constraints of the system, however, they were not able to put forward credible policies of adaptation.

Economic disintegration was paralleled by a decay of totalitarian political structures. Powerful lobbies arose within various regions and industries, eroding central economic control. The dedicated, even fanatical, party cadres of the 1950s gave way to the petty realists of the 1960s, and they in turn to the corrupt and cynical bureaucrats of the 1970s. Only lip service was paid to Marxist-Leninist ideology, particularly in more liberal Hungary and Poland. An implicit bargain replaced earlier political mobilization: political quiescence in exchange for economic security and progress. Growing inability to deliver progress thus struck directly at the basis of fragile legitimacy. Perestroika in the Soviet Union delivered the final blow.

Variation among Countries in Patterns of Disintegration

Within these broadly similar trends, the specifics differed in each of the three countries. De-Stalinization (the dismantling of the techniques of political mobilization of the entire society) in the 1950s was handled quite differently in Hungary and in Poland; in Bulgaria it never really occurred. The revolutionary sixteen months of Solidarity's emergence in Poland in 1980–1981 has no counterpart in Hungary or Bulgaria: that period essentially destroyed the morale of the ruling elite and fatally wounded the Leninist "transmission belt" role of labor unions in Poland.

Paradoxically, the harsh terror imposed in Hungary after 1956 paved the way for a later process of pragmatic change imposed from above in response to economic problems, coupled with a policy of coopting the intellectuals. After 1956 Premier János Kádár repressed both left- and right-wing opposition and initiated a long series of gradual, relatively successful market-oriented reforms. A sizable circle of economists became familiar with Western theories and analysis. The reforms produced reasonably efficient systems of resource allocation and product distribution, avoiding both severe shortages and repressed inflation. Foreign trade was more diversified than elsewhere in the region. Agriculture was organized in collectives, but part of the land was rented out to the collective farmers, who lived in successful symbiosis with the profit-oriented cooperative units. In Hungary one could almost discern a silent but deliberate dismantling of the command economy, to a degree unique in the region. Nonetheless, Hungary could not wholly escape the gradual disintegration common to the region, since the reforms fell far short of a fundamental change in system.

Poland, in contrast, went through repeated cycles of attempted reforms and reaction. Władysław Gomułka neither wished nor was able to follow the Kádárist centrist path after the disturbances of 1956 in Hungary. Instead, partial and ineffective reforms were introduced during the late 1950s, the 1970s, and the 1980s. These failed to avert increasingly severe economic crises, leading by 1988 to acute shortages and in 1989 to near hyperinflation. That situation called for the harsh "shock therapy" instituted by Leszek Balcerowicz. The failure of earlier partial reforms also left more severe structural problems than those in Hungary. Poland depended more heavily on trade within the Council for

Mutual Economic Assistance (CMEA) area, and many state-owned enterprises were extremely hard hit by its collapse. Agriculture was almost wholly private, but most farms were small and technically backward. And because of policies pursued during the 1970s, both the size and structure of external debt were extremely burdensome.

As we noted earlier, Bulgaria was far more receptive to both communism and Russian influence, though repression of intellectuals and other critics of the regime was also harsher. Clear signs of disintegration, including acute shortages and inflation, did not emerge until relatively late in the 1980s. The command system was left virtually intact until the very end; growing difficulties prompted frequent reorganizations of the management hierarchies that fell short of meaningful reforms. Bulgarian industry was highly concentrated in large state enterprises; likewise, agriculture was dominated by immense collectives. Bulgarian trade depended overwhelmingly on the CMEA; the Soviet Union accounted for as much as two-thirds of Bulgaria's foreign trade. Therefore the collapse of the socialist international trade system left Bulgaria one of the most isolated countries in the region. The Yugoslav conflict next door further aggravated the country's physical isolation from the developed parts of Europe.

Post-1989 Dismantling

After 1989, of course, deliberate dismantling greatly speeded the disintegration of the old system throughout the region. Stabilization policies, introduced by the postcommunist governments with the backing of the International Monetary Fund (IMF), and the collapse of CMEA trade spurred the processes of disintegration. Of the countries in the region, only Hungary and Czechoslovakia had relatively stable macroeconomic situations that made shock therapy unnecessary. But Hungary shared with the other countries a sharp drop in output, as state enterprises proved much less adaptable to market rules than the mushrooming (but still mainly small) private firms.

The accelerated dismantling of the old system dramatically altered the situation of many major social groups. Workers in state enterprises faced sharp declines in real income and the possibility of unemployment. The intelligentsia had been employed under communism as managers of state enterprises and staffs of public sector cultural, educational, and political institutions. The protracted and severe fiscal crisis compressed their incomes and undercut their security. Despite the contrasts among the three countries in the property structure and organization of agriculture, farmers in all three felt the consequences of the collapse of guaranteed prices, import competition from the European Community, and the reduction of state subsidies for agricultural inputs.

Whereas before 1989 recessions had usually been transformed into inflation and shortages, in the new economic order the fall in output and revenues and macroeconomic imbalances produced severe fiscal crisis in each of the three countries.[4] Fiscal strain in turn accelerated the disintegration of the inefficient but pervasive welfare systems (health, education, housing, and pensions). The consequences were particularly painful in the context of falling real wages and rising unemployment. Not only social services, but the entire range of state functions and services continued to deteriorate, in part as a result of fiscal pressures and in part because of the disruption, confusion, and demoralization of abrupt changes. Bureaucrats' behavior could hardly be expected to change overnight. Moreover, most are poorly paid and easily corrupted by the new temptations of the emerging market economy.

The process of disintegration will continue for some years, since the role of large state enterprises in the economy is still much too great and social values still reflect four decades of communism in the region. Moreover, the capacity of most public institutions continues to decline. Eastern European societies will have to struggle with the legacy of communism for a long while.

Emergence

Parallel to the unraveling of the old systems and in direct proportion to their disintegration, market institutions and elements of civil society started to emerge. This emergence was clearest in Poland and Hungary. Of course, the events of 1989 mattered. But in these two countries there was also considerable continuity; the political collapse of communism was perhaps most important as a symbol. It also helped to bring in foreign political backing and, with it, capital and foreign expertise. In Bulgaria, in contrast, elements of civil society and market institutions began to emerge only in the late 1980s, and the collapse of communist control was essential before serious economic reform could begin.

Emerging Elements of Future Market Systems

Economic reforms in Hungary and Poland before 1989 have already been discussed as responses to disintegration. Some of these reforms also contributed to the emergence of markets, gradually introducing market mechanisms within the command economy by shifting allocative decisions from central authorities to state enterprises. This shift allowed directors of those enterprises, especially in Hungary, to learn Western-style management, financial, and marketing techniques.

Not only the contrasting nature and degree of communist economic reforms, but also differences in the influence of workers in Poland and Hungary contributed to different degrees of "market learning" in the two countries. In Hungary, workers' opposition to the communist regime was less powerful than in Poland, in part because of memories of the brutal crushing of the Hungarian uprising of 1956. Therefore consumer prices could be kept comparatively high, and consumer markets remained in equilibrium. Shortages were less acute and frequent, and all economic actors received more social training in market behavior. In Poland, in contrast, workers' pressures held down consumer prices, directly causing recurrent severe shortages and indirectly interfering with learning about market principles.

Alongside limited market-oriented changes in the organization and operations of the official sectors in Poland and Hungary, the shadow or second economy was emerging well before 1989. Flourishing particularly in services, technically illegal but tolerated shadow economy activities helped to fill the gaps in the official distribution network, increased family incomes, and provided experience in entrepreneurship.

Both countries also permitted a limited amount of officially sanctioned private economic activity. As already noted, Poland's agriculture remained almost entirely in private hands, while in Hungary private plots were permitted within the larger structure of agricultural collectives. In both countries there were also a fair number of legal family-sized enterprises in retail trade and crafts. In Poland by the second half of the 1980s, as antiprivate property ideology diminished, restrictions on the size of enterprises were lifted and foreign capital was permitted to enter. The result was the growth of somewhat larger private businesses. The private sector expanded continuously from the late 1970s on, while the output of the state sector shrank considerably. Private sector growth was still inhibited, however, by lack of capital, skills and expertise, infrastructure, and confidence that the new policy changes would be sustained. In Hungary the pattern and timing of emerging private sector activity was similar to that in Poland in spite of marked differences in the patterns of dismantling the communist system. In the final years of the communist era, informal privatization of state enterprises also gained ground in Hungary.

Hungary and Poland's loosening of the command economy was unique within the Soviet Bloc. Bulgaria, in contrast to these two but in common with the rest of the bloc, had very little private sector (legal or shadow) and virtually no experience with marketlike incentives and constraints within the all-encompassing state sector. The most rural of the three countries, Bulgaria had an agricultural sector dominated by immense Soviet-style state and kolkhoz farms.

The political transitions of 1989 sharply accelerated the emergence of small and medium-size private sector firms. By March 1993, private sector activity was estimated to account for at least 45 percent of gross domestic product (GDP) in Poland (and the sector employed almost three-fifths of the labor force); 40–42 percent of 1992 GDP in Hungary; and roughly 20 percent of GDP in Bulgaria.

The way in which different postcommunist countries stabilized their macroeconomic situations influenced private sector formation. In Poland the Balcerowicz plan squeezed the large state trading organizations; accompanied by a conscious policy promoting small privatization, this tactic caused a rapid takeover of virtually the whole retail market by small private entrepreneurs. Bulgaria's lag reflects not only the absence of private or marketlike experience before 1989, but also macroeconomic policies somewhat less vigorous than Poland's. As a result, its state-owned trading companies have been less energetically pushed out of operation. In Hungary the small-scale private sector grew rapidly, but this increase was a continuation of earlier trends. András Körösényi's discussion of Hungary in this volume emphasizes the strong continuity of economic reforms in Hungary in the late 1980s.

In all three countries, however, it has proved more difficult and slower to revise old and create new legal and financial institutions appropriate for market economies than to encourage small private firms. Again, both in Poland and in Hungary there had been some modest steps to develop such institutions in the last years of the communist period. Legal regulations had been amended and financial markets (such as banks and stock exchanges) introduced and reorganized. Still, despite the efforts of postcommunist governments and parliaments, these reforms are lagging behind the needs of the burgeoning business sector. For example, financial intermediaries able to channel private savings into investment remain extremely weak.

Transformation of the large state-owned enterprises has proved much more difficult than small-scale privatization. In most of the region, with the exception of Hungary, most large enterprises have not changed status. However, piecemeal and inevitably experimental privatization policies, coupled with "spontaneous" behavior by managers and others, are under way in most countries and have gone particularly far in Hungary, which has also pressed official privatization programs more rapidly than other countries. The process is producing layered, complex, and often obscure networks of property rights. For instance, managers of state-owned firms may spin off assets to new satellites that are legally limited liability firms; the old firm remains the dominant owner, while suppliers and banks (still state-owned) are also major shareholders. It may be difficult to develop and apply appropriate regulation for these unanticipated and poorly understood ownership networks. More broadly, the emerging patterns defy conventional distinctions between public and private sectors. The effects on productivity, investment, taxation, and other crucial aspects of economic performance remain to be seen.

Unhealthy side effects of the emerging market are also quickly appearing: tax evasion, corruption of officials, and mafia-type illegal economic activities.

These effects are exacerbated by the general weakness and disintegration of the state already mentioned. Side effects are partly a result of lags in legal and financial reforms. The temptation is also huge: no accepted moral code guides businesses and state officials, and privatization and easy access to the money of state banks generate large-scale corruption. Such phenomena, which appear almost universally in the early stages of capitalism, are probably unavoidable. They are nevertheless dangerous, posing both a direct threat to private and public sectors and a more indirect risk that criminal structures, once brought to life, will petrify.

New Social Stratification

New social groups are emerging parallel to the development of markets. In Hungary and Poland an embryonic entrepreneurial class, present throughout the entire communist period, expanded considerably during the 1980s. Still small compared with that in Western societies, this middle class is growing rapidly. A tiny group of very wealthy people is also appearing. Income differences (which, contrary to the official propaganda, never disappeared under "real socialism") have become much more conspicuous. In Bulgaria, restitution of urban property to precommunist owners has created a small but politically influential class of property owners. The short-run effects of the measure in stimulating entrepreneurship remain uncertain.

At the other end of the social scale, one of the unfortunate outcomes of reduced real wages and growing unemployment is the emergence of an "underclass" of people, who, for various reasons (such as age, social and ethnic characteristics, and lack of education or skills), are unable to compete in the new system. In Poland, the emerging underclass includes many low-income, poorly educated rural people, as well as unskilled manual workers in urban areas. It is also beginning to include even some skilled employees of state enterprises, who, for lack of housing elsewhere, cannot move out of regions particularly hard hit by unemployment and recession. Undereducated young people from working-class urban backgrounds pose particularly urgent social problems. Gypsies in many countries of the region confront special problems of combined ethnic and social prejudice. Among the cases studied here Hungary is the most affected by the problems of Gypsies. The social situation of Turks and of Gypsies is difficult in Bulgaria as well, while Poland is the most ethnically homogeneous country in the region.

The Emergence of Civil Society and Political Opposition

Critical groups—embryonic political opposition—had also started to emerge in Poland and Hungary long before communism collapsed. While economic reforms proceeded furthest before 1989 in Hungary, political opposition was most developed in Poland. Bulgaria, in the political as in the economic sphere, had the least experience with opposition before 1989. It needed the external impulse of perestroika in the late 1980s to give birth to a modest environmental movement and to the autonomous trade union federation Podkrepa.

In Poland, the emergence of critical groups independent of the state owed much to the Roman Catholic church. Historically, the church had maintained its autonomy; under communism it played the role of a "public sphere" both in its own right and as the vehicle for covert but ardent nationalist sentiments. Since at least 1976, there had also been a tolerated open opposition, reinforced by the sixteen months of mass participation through Solidarity in 1980–1981. Workers' councils were also comparatively numerous and influential in their own enterprises. Economic structure—specifically, the relative importance of heavy industries where workers' organizations tend to be strong—contributed to the political importance of unions and workers' councils in Poland. In Hungary, in contrast, the church played very little political role. Nor, after 1956, was there significant mass-based opposition; criticism was more intellectual in character. In both countries, since the harness of ideology and censorship was relatively loose, the authorities tolerated considerable independent activity within academia and the arts. Through teaching, movies, cabarets, essays, books and translations, cartoons, and rock music, independent ideas were diffused to a wider public. "Homo sovieticus" was disappearing, and elements of civil society clearly emerged in Hungary and Poland before the major political shakeup.

Even within the very core of communism, the party itself, independent tendencies were not unknown in Hungary and Poland, although in neither country did internal criticism reach the level of that in 1968 in Czechoslovakia, when the Communist party was briefly the main proponent of radical reform. In Poland in 1980–1981 there were unprecedented attempts to institutionalize such tendencies, but the more general tendency was to exclude dissenters. In contrast, in Hungary after 1956, the Kádár regime followed a strategy of trying to coopt dissenters. As a result, the political transition in Poland was fundamentally confrontational and entailed mass mobilization, while the Hungarian transition was negotiated among political elites and involved rather little mass participation. In Bulgaria, doubts and divisions within the party surfaced only just before the moment of transition and were generated largely by events in the Soviet Union. The transition began as a "palace coup" by reformers seeking to introduce perestroika. Moreover, the Communist party maintained broad popular support, as its victory in the first competitive election demonstrated. These contrasting dynamics of political transition in turn shaped the patterns of post-transition politics.

Another important aspect of the emergence of civil society consisted of constitutional and statutory changes under communism that expanded the role of the judiciary and the rule of law. For example, administrative and labor courts were established in Poland in the 1970s and constitutional and state tribunals and the office of the ombudsman in the 1980s.

After the collapse of communism, all three countries rapidly started to build new constitutional and political orders—a process that is still just beginning. Civil society, so important in the final abolition of communism, turned out to be only partially prepared for this new task. Social structures are in flux, as they reorient themselves to new economic and political rules of the game. New social groups are not yet well organized; indeed, it is hard even to define and articulate interests in the context of rapid change. Nevertheless, certain groups have managed to develop or retain some capacity to influence government policies. The clearest illustrations are probably the former Communist and Solidarity labor federations in Poland and the dramatically growing Podkrepa federation in Bulgaria. Business associations in all three countries have also emerged rapidly. In Poland some agricultural interests have maintained strong associations to pursue their goals, and all three countries have organized (or revived pre-Communist) agrarian political parties. More generally, however, the opposition elites that emerged in the last years of the communist era and gained experience in civil disobedience and passive resistance had no practical knowledge of open, competitive democratic electoral politics. Especially in Poland and Bulgaria, parties were often little more than personalist factions, emerging almost accidentally and with little social basis, often uniting under symbols from the past or from abroad. Only more recently have they started to search for constituencies.

In Poland, opposition to communism was powerfully united under the umbrella of Solidarity. But Solidarity started to crumble within a few months after the Communist government was displaced. The negotiated transition entailed a lengthy period of coalition government that included the discredited Communists; in the first free elections electoral arrangements produced a badly fragmented legislature. This result contributed to ongoing tension between the president, the government, and the legislature. New electoral laws adopted in 1992 produced a much less fragmented outcome in the elections of September 1993. It remains to be seen whether the decisive leftward swing of those elections will produce a more coherent legislature.

In Hungary and Czechoslovakia, more workable party structures emerged in the campaigns for the first democratic elections in 1990. In Hungary the six-party system, fostered by electoral laws discouraging fragmentation, has turned out to be surprisingly stable, adding to the overall stability and gradual progress of the country. But even in Hungary, and more clearly in Poland and Bulgaria, there is a danger that the parties emerging from the transition period may fail to build broad social bases; much of the public may then become alienated, perceiving politicians and legislators as a new political class playing their own game, divorced from citizens' concerns.

In Bulgaria, the emergence of a new competitive party system took a different path. In Poland and Hungary, the disintegration of the Communist party led to splits and fairly low—though not trivial—popular support in the first competitive elections. In Bulgaria, however, more of the population supported at least aspects of the communist system, and organized opposition emerged only shortly before the transition. As already noted, the former Communist party won the first election, which discouraged both splintering and reform from within the party. The continued strength of the ex-Communists fostered the growing dominance of the most ardent right-wing groups within the variegated democratic opposition. As Ekaterina Nikova describes vividly in her chapter, politics and parties were temporarily frozen in intense polarization.

By the end of 1992, however, the Bulgarian parties showed signs of the pattern traced earlier in Central Europe: the anti-Communist coalition splintered, while the former Communists somewhat reoriented their stance. Moderate democratic groups became alienated or were pushed out of the anti-Communist coalition. The right-wing elements, still bearing the name of the original broad coalition, won a razor-thin majority in the second round of elections in October 1991 and formed a coalition government with the party representing Bulgaria's Muslim population. Within one year, however, the uncompromising rightist government had managed to alienate almost all groups within society, including its coalition partner, and was brought down by a vote of no confidence. The new government formed in the last days of 1992 is a centrist coalition of moderates from the Socialist (ex-Communist) party and the Muslims, with support from some of the original anti-Communist groups. The coalition has not proved very effective, and new elections are likely in late 1994. Bulgaria's electoral laws will discourage fragmentation similar to Poland's, but it remains an open question how the party system will evolve.

Redefinition

The collapse of communism was not only an event of great historical importance, but it was also amazingly nonviolent in most of the bloc. Nor did the transition involve any major physical dislocations: towns and factories were not destroyed; people were not forced to move from their homes. With the broad physical framework and much of the social system intact, the political transition did not entail destruction but rather redefinition of social roles.

The process of redefinition is most visible in the case of the former nomenklatura, those party apparatchiks who played the most important political roles in the old order. In Hungary, as Körösenyi suggests, the nomenklatura had already partly redefined their role by the 1970s, emphasizing technical and managerial skills rather than ideological roles. The nonrevolutionary and negotiated character of the transition spared members of the nomenklatura both physical danger and, at least initially, legal threats. In Poland and Hungary shortly before 1989, many of them had tried to prepare fallback positions. Many turned their political capital into economic capital, converting skills and connections acquired under the old system into marketable assets under the new one. Former party apparatchiks, high officials, and state enterprise managers started early to establish private companies, often privatizing state enterprises or finding jobs as representatives of Western corporations. In short, state officials redefined themselves as capitalists. This transformation happened much more easily in Poland and especially in Hungary than in Bulgaria.

A similar process took place in politics. Communist parties reorganized and changed names, usually calling themselves "social democrats" and claiming adherence to democratic principles. In Hungary the party split in 1989; the reformist wing successfully capitalized on its liberal credentials and is now a well-established part of the Hungarian competitive party system. From 8.5 percent of the seats in the 1990 Parliament, its popularity has risen to the point that it may well run first or second in the elections of spring 1994. In Poland the former Communists won over 10 percent of the popular vote in the 1991 parliamentary elections; within the fragmented Polish Sejm they formed the largest parliamentary caucus. In September 1993 the Democratic Left Alliance, a coalition dominated by the direct successor to the Communist party, finished first with more than 20 percent of the vote, and the left-leaning Polish Peasant party won an additional 15.3 percent. Together the two will control two-thirds of the seats in the Sejm. In Bulgaria, however, reorientation of the former ruling party was slowed precisely by its initial victory (with 47 percent of the vote) in the free elections of 1990; only more recently have some reformist elements split from the party to form separate groups. More generally, in the Central European or Western tier countries of the region, the renamed and to varying degrees reoriented Communists have not been able to capture more than 15 percent in elections, while their counterparts have done considerably better in Bulgaria or Romania.

Trade unions have also had to reorient their structure, agendas, and alliances. In Poland, Solidarity had been a union more in name than in fact, being in reality a political opposition movement. Since 1989 it has had to become a more typical labor union federation. The former Communist unions have also had to reorient their role and have proved surprisingly effective in so doing. Under communism they were corporatist institutions, uniting managers and workers within industries and trying to transmit party policies to the shop floor. Now they organize industrial actions much as Solidarity does. A similar remodeling of the unions is under way in the whole region. Many of the officials of the old unions, perhaps especially the younger among them, are more skillful and disciplined in the day-to-day realities of politics than are most leaders of the newer unions and parties. In Poland and Bulgaria, the reorienting of the former Communist unions has been accelerated by competition with strong new autonomous trade union federations. But more recently that rivalry itself has been redefined: in Poland, at least at the level of some firms, and in Bulgaria, at higher levels, there has been clear collaboration between ex-Communist and anti-Communist unions. Nikova's suggestion regarding Bulgaria applies to Poland as well: union influence is enhanced by the relative weakness of parties. In Hungary, unions in general have long been less influential, and the new anti-Communist unions have thus far been weak. The ex-Communist unions have very cautiously, step-by-step, gained some legitimacy among the employees by actions designed to demonstrate their services, but they have not yet challenged government decisions over the economy. They are, however, open and strong allies of the Socialist party in the 1994 elections.

Within the not yet fully emerged competitive party systems discussed in the previous section, anti-Communist politicians and groups have also had to redefine their roles, since many of them are now part of the new political elite. At the same time, state institutions have been redefined politically, shedding the Marxist ideological legitimization and often donning more nationalistic garb, sometimes—as in Poland—with religious overtones.

Economic and Political Transformation: How Closely Linked?

Even our small sample of cases displays sharp contrasts in pre-Communist heritage and wide variation in the timing and speed of the disintegration of communism and the emergence of new, more market-oriented or democratic actors and institutions. Yet despite considerable differences in the course of economic and political reforms since 1989, the three countries show a number of broad similarities with respect to the nature of the economic measures adopted, the impact of those measures, the slower and more difficult progress of institutional and legal reforms, resistance to large-scale privatization, and the dissolution and restructuring of both former Communist and anti-Communist political coalitions. Since our main interest is the linkages between economic reform and consolidation of political openings, one similarity is particularly interesting: broadly, painful economic reforms have not been blocked by democratic politics (despite considerable protest, particularly in Poland and Bulgaria), nor have unexpectedly severe economic declines thus far derailed democratic consolidation. What factors explain that pattern? Can it be expected to continue?

One set of factors is of course the shared external context. The collapse of the Soviet Union and the CMEA and the Gulf War combined with long-festering domestic economic troubles to create an absolutely overwhelming economic crisis. At the same time, events in the Soviet Union destroyed any remaining credibility of statist economic strategies, while both intellectual currents and real-world events elsewhere around the globe seemed to point to the inevitable triumph of market-oriented economic strategies and democratic political systems. For many in the Soviet Bloc, that triumph not only seemed inevitable but also was ardently desired: both the consumer goods and the political and cultural freedom of the West were magnets. Most clearly in Central Europe, but also in the Balkans, the desire to "belong to Europe" influenced both political behavior and economic policies.

The very severity of the economic crisis also forced rapid imposition of drastic economic measures; the nature of the crisis left little room for maneuver. The international financial community, mainly but not exclusively the IMF, urged tough stabilization measures except in Czechoslovakia (before its division) and in Hungary, where severe imbalances had been avoided.

The depth and drama of the recession also captured public opinion. Initially the public in our three countries (and more broadly in Eastern Europe) was prepared for temporary sacrifice, if not because the old system was despised (as it was in some but not all cases) then because of the glittering lure of Western standards of living. Yet most people probably were not prepared for some of the more drastic aspects of the adjustment, including soaring unemployment rates. An intense debate has emerged among specialists regarding the real impact of the transitions on living standards, taking into account not only nominal wage and price trends but also less easily quantifiable positive and negative trends such as reduced scarcities, the burgeoning and undercounted small-scale private sector, and eroding standards of public services. Popular reactions probably depend less on the balance of objective gains and losses than on hopes, fears, and perceived alternatives. It is worth noting that in Bulgaria—the country in our sample least disaffected from communism—the United Democratic Front won the elections of September 1991 after seven months of supporting acute austerity measures, while the architect of the measures, Ivan Kostov, was returned to the legislature with a strong majority. Still more clear-cut is the popularity among Czechs of Prime Minister Vaclav Klaus, the architect (as former minister of finance) of rapid and sweeping economic reforms.

A fourth common factor that helps to explain the initial compatibility between economic reform and democratic consolidation was the weakness of the potential opposition groups. For the most part, former Communist parties and unions were discredited and in disarray, while newer groups that would later advocate alternative economic approaches or less-than-democratic political philosophies were not yet organized.

Moreover, the democratic consolidation agenda was substantially independent of the economic reform agenda. Intense debates over issues as fundamental as new constitutional frameworks, or as apparently frivolous and superficial as the design of the flag or other symbols, absorbed a great deal of time and attention. So did political maneuvering and planning, as both Communist parties and anti-Communist coalitions crumbled and new parties emerged. Unclear relationships between heads of state, heads of government, and legislatures caused considerable tension; so did issues such as control of the media and the military and, in Poland, relations between church and state.

All of these factors contributed to the somewhat surprising compatibility of initial economic reforms and democratic openings. But links and strains between the two processes may well increase in the near future. To the degree that the macroeconomic crisis has been eased and inflation contained, the sense of potential catastrophe has been reduced. Public tolerance for further sacrifice is dwindling, while the immense task of restructuring the large state enterprises and banks remains to be addressed. The size and dynamism of the private sector, hence its capacity to absorb workers from the state-owned firms, may prove crucial in determining the pace of politically sustainable reform. Opposition groups of the left and right are emerging and are likely to pose more of a threat than in the early post-transition period. Finally, as some of the big issues of initial democratic consolidation are at least temporarily resolved, both the public and policy makers will be freer to turn their attention more fully to economic questions.

As the shared circumstances that dominated the early post-transition stages fade, the contrasts in different countries' heritages from precommunist and communist eras may well exercise more influence on the pace and pattern of economic reform and on political trends. Clearly those countries where disintegration had gone least far and market-relevant experience and institutions had not emerged are at a disadvantage as they now try to encourage market behavior. Creation of new institutions and opportunities may not be able to outpace the destructive effects of dismantling the old arrangements. On the political side, the advantages of an early start may be less clear: it depends what "lessons" were learned regarding effective political behavior. The lessons learned in Hungary, both by elites and by the public, stress elite negotiations and downplay popular participation. In Poland much of the population learned lessons regarding mass political opposition but little about compromise. The turbulent politics of the first years after 1989, however, seem to have produced at least a tacit agreement not to pursue differences to the point of paralysis or breakdown and a somewhat increased capacity for compromise.

Thus far we have discussed the relationship between economic reform and democratic consolidation in terms of short-run effects on the sustainability of economic policies and open politics. But the two processes also interact in more specific and disaggregated ways, some of which are likely to have long-run effects on the pace and pattern of economic and political evolution. For instance, Körösényi points to the replacement of old forms of Communist patronage and clientelism by new patterns of allocation of privatized assets to build political support, while Nikova notes that the second Bulgarian land reform law was motivated far more by the desire to weaken ex-Communist control in rural areas than by the desire to establish more efficient agricultural production. Changing class structure will also of course have powerful effects and indeed may pose one of the long-run challenges to the viability of both aspects of the double transformation. It is to these challenges that we now turn.

Challenges

The processes of disintegration and dismantling, emergence and redefinition are far from over, and the picture is still unclear. Throughout the region, a long road remains to fully fledged market economies and stable democracies.

Challenges to both goals stem in part from the international economic and political setting: international competition is strong; the global economy is in flux; and the regional and world political order is undergoing recomposition after the collapse of the Soviet Empire. Prospects for Eastern European recovery and growth depend on the ability of those countries to compete in world markets. Unfortunately, protectionist impulses have revived in many Western nations with the end of the Cold War threat and as a result of current domestic economic problems. Although the European Community and other Western nations have partially opened their markets to Eastern European goods, the broader goal of integration—more likely for the Central European nations than for the Balkans—will clearly be slowed by fears regarding inflows of cheap imports and anxiety regarding massive labor migration. External debts are a further burden: repayment cuts into funds for domestic investment, while attempts to renegotiate or delay payment reduce credibility with foreign investors. For Bulgaria (among our cases) and several other Balkan countries, the civil war in parts of former Yugoslavia has increased geographic isolation while the international embargo on trade with Serbia has imposed heavy costs. The largest unknown is the future of the successor states of the Soviet Union, which are likely—whatever the course of events—to draw attention and resources away from Eastern Europe.

In addition to the uncertainties and problems of the external context, Eastern European nations face an array of challenges stemming from internal trends. The first of these is the possible rise of antimarket forces. Major social groups are threatened by changes already accomplished or planned, and many people are unprepared to face life in a competitive, market system. Voices for more intervention, for more state protection, for a return to the cozy welfarism of bureaucratic paternalism easily gain popularity among state enterprise workers who fear layoffs, among the growing marginalized underclass, and among the many pensioners. Doubts about the desirability of a largely market economy may extend to other groups as well, particularly in Bulgaria (among our cases) and elsewhere in the Balkans.

This challenge, plus less fundamental but still formidable technical and economic obstacles, thus far has prevented more than modest progress in privatizing or restructuring the massive, inefficient, largely technically obsolete state industries that still make up a large (although in Poland rapidly decreasing) share of the economy and employ a high proportion of the labor force. Hungary's economic and political situation has permitted somewhat better though still partial progress. Any rapid resolution of this issue seems unlikely; considerable state intervention might well occur, reflecting growing demands for some sort of industrial policy to keep potentially viable industries alive.

Aside from the restructuring of state enterprises, the biggest structural challenge the Eastern European countries face is budget reform. In each of these countries, welfare and social spending considerably exceeds that of market economies with comparable per capita income. Yet budget restructuring is a highly complex and politically sensitive operation. Failure to reform in this field would mean that high marginal tax rates will prevail, leading businesses to conceal many of their activities. That outcome would generate much higher inequalities than if radical budget reform could be carried through.

The evolution of political systems also poses challenges. In all three countries (most clearly, thus far, in Hungary and Poland) there are signals of possible right-wing movements of a nationalist or religious character. Such groups feel their national identity is threatened by the changes brought about by the market and democratization and by the cultural homogenization resulting from globalization of markets and political openness. These groups are marginal in both countries. Yet prolonged and widespread hardship could increase their social support. Such tendencies raise questions about the future character of Eastern European societies and states: will they be open and based on liberal ideas and rule of law, or will they instead be defined in ethnic and religious terms?

Clashes over these fundamental political values, as well as over economic goals and means, will affect how still-fluid party systems evolve and how unresolved constitutional questions are managed. In our three countries, only Hungary appears to have evolved a workable party structure; the Polish party system remains fragmented (though less so after the elections of autumn 1993), and the polarized Bulgarian parties seem to be starting a process of crumbling and regrouping. The challenge is not only to create party systems capable of producing stable and effective governments, but also to develop ties between the political class and social constituencies that can counter the growing trend toward cynicism and apathy among the public.

Basic constitutional issues, including the division of power between presidents, governments, and legislatures also must be defined or fine-tuned. Until these issues are resolved, already overburdened governments will be further hampered by uncertainty and controversy.

Consolidating democratic transitions poses a further challenge of incorporating emerging interest groups (themselves still very much in flux) into the decision-making process. Labor unions present a particularly acute challenge. Both their institutional interests and the welfare of many of their members are perceived to be directly threatened by aspects of market-oriented reform, including measures (still largely in the future) to increase the flexibility of labor markets and to reduce the role of unions as channels of social benefits. Unions are likely to resist such reforms, yet they cannot be left out of democratic decision-making processes. Moreover, enlisting some degree of their cooperation may prove crucial for successfully implementing key economic reforms.

Both economic and political challenges converge on a third set of issues: redefining the role of the state itself. Here all postcommunist states are in a dilemma, because they need much less of the state and yet more of the state at the same time. Two overlapping sets of issues demand attention. First, while a market-friendly environment demands less state intervention in the economy, the state must act in many ways as the architect of the transition. The state sector is still considerable, and the government must both introduce privatization and manage those enterprises that, for the time being, will remain in public control. A different but equally crucial state role during the transition period is to provide a safety net adequate to protect both basic welfare and the political sustainability of the reforms. The second set of issues concerns the long term, not the transitional period. Even in a largely market economy the state must serve key functions, including tax administration and enforcement, a fair and efficient judicial system, and the kinds of appropriate market regulations that characterize established market systems. Permanent state functions also include substantial roles in education, health, and social security—but current structures are both inefficient and financially unsustainable. Consolidating market reforms and democratic politics will require reversing the ongoing disintegration of basic state functions, while resolving the extraordinarily contentious questions of the boundaries and goals of those functions.

Despite challenges and anxieties, however, considerable progress has been made on the road to market societies and democratic systems. Whatever the shortcomings of institutional arrangements, the ideas of democracy and markets prevail throughout the region. In contrast with the interwar period, people—by and large—do not seek answers to their problems in strong leaders and authoritarian solutions, and self-appointed "strongmen" have not emerged. It is too early to give any definitive answers why this is so, but certain factors are likely to matter.

First, there is a "snowball effect." The trend toward democracy is global. There is a zeitgeist of which democracy and human rights are part—as totalitarianism and authoritarianism were part of a zeitgeist in the 1930s. Moreover, societies are affected by developments elsewhere much more than in the past. The media—television in particular—play an enormous, unprecedented role, and it is difficult to isolate people from what is going on in other countries. The feeling is overwhelming in the world that statist economies and authoritarian political systems are outmoded and ineffective systems.

Second, there is the enormous appeal of the global mass consumer society. When one looks at young people in a Warsaw disco, in a McDonald's, or in a music shop, it is hard to imagine them in the red ties of the communist youth movement. Blue jeans, cars, washing machines, and videocassette recorders are parts of an open, market society.

Third, in Eastern Europe specifically, the proximity of the European Community has enormous influence. Elites in Eastern Europe know that the values of Western Europe cannot be easily dismissed if a given country does not want to be reduced to the role of a pariah.

Democracy and market reforms thus far have held. These factors improve the chances that they will—against the historical odds—be consolidated.

CHAPTER 2

The Transition to the Market and Democratization in Poland

Jacek Kochanowicz

The final collapse of communism has been one of the most important—and surprising—events of the late twentieth century. The transformation, however, did not start in 1989. Communism, like any social system, was never completely rigid.[1] It evolved over time; it adjusted to external and internal challenges; it was even reformed from above. It also had—in each nation—its own color and flavor. The transformation taking place now is different in each country, as each faces the universal challenges with its particular social, cultural, and intellectual heritage.

In Poland the transition to democracy and a market economy has been a long-term process, and it has been determined not only by global political change—the end of the Soviet Empire—and by the logic of stabilization and liberalization measures, but also by the social and cultural heritage of Polish society. I am convinced—unlike those who advocate swift transition—that this process, generally, must be gradual (although one can argue about the degree of gradualism), since the learning capacities of society are limited and since it is the culture as well as the economy that must change. The process of change produces many unwanted, but perhaps unavoidable, results that are potentially dangerous for the stability of democratic institutions and even for the continuation of market reforms. Of these results, the most important seems to me to be social exclusion, leaving considerable segments of society outside the modernizing sectors, as potential sources of frustration and aggression. The success of the transition, therefore, calls for taking provisions against these dangers. It also calls for the state's playing a considerable role in managing the transition—a requirement that is not easy to meet, since the weakness of the state itself is part and parcel of the process under review.

Since I consider the transition a long-term process, I start my analysis with a review of three overlapping processes: the disintegration of communism, the emergence of civil society, and the emergence of the market. All three processes started well before 1989, and the disintegration of the old order is not yet complete. The "shock therapy" of 1989 and the institutional changes following it accelerated them dramatically, leading to structural changes in the economy and to shifts in the composition of society. After looking at them, I move to a review of the new patterns of politics, which developed after the collapse of communism. Since I consider the state of particular importance in managing the transition because of the deficiency of civil society, I conclude the chapter by reviewing the main challenges facing the state and the contradictions connected with possibilities of answering these challenges.

Crisis and the Decay of Communism

Crisis and the final disintegration of the communist social system were caused by the system's inner logic and by its inability to answer the challenges of the late twentieth century in technological, economic, military, and social spheres. Initially, however, communism had its own measure of accomplishments.

In the Polish case, communism in its purest, Stalinist form was a short-term phenomenon, lasting from 1949 to 1956. Even then the peasantry remained uncollectivized,[2] the Roman Catholic Church independent, and terror relatively mild. During these years, the basic elements of the communist economic system were put in place: state enterprises; "planning" (or rather coordination) in the form of balancing flows of inputs and outputs, usually measured in physical terms; money as a device only for technical calculation; primitive banking strictly subject to state control; administered prices; state monopoly of foreign trade; and partial rationing of consumer goods and services.

During the 1950s and early 1960s, the Communists achieved considerable economic and social success: massive industrialization and urbanization, improvement in standards of living and welfare for large segments of society, and educational advancement. The command economy, combined with total political control, permitted resources to be mobilized and channeled according to state plans. Factors of production (especially labor and energy) were easy to obtain at low cost, while relatively primitive technologies were not incompatible with crude, administrative methods of coordination. Environmental costs were considered to be zero.

Viewed in a longer historical perspective, the statist economy established by the Communists cannot be treated as a complete aberration. Because of the insufficiency of local capital and bourgeoisie, statism in one form or another was always strong in this part of Europe, answering the social and national aspirations of local elites and wider segments of society.

Communism (and World War II) dramatically changed the social structure of Polish society and allowed for considerable advancement by its lower segments. During the 1950s, industrialization and urbanization moved masses of rural people geographically and socially. Over the course of two decades, these processes led to the creation of a "communist middle class" (Kurczewski 1992, Jezierski 1992), consisting of high-level blue-collar workers, white-collar workers (including middle-level apparatchiks), and—in the late stage of the system—modern, commercial farmers, and small businessmen. Membership in the Communist party was not a necessary condition of advancement in each and every case, but it obviously helped. The middle class, while a product of the communist industrialization, was a powerful force leading to its disintegration. The material aspirations of this class—and of the working classes in the widest sense—were strictly consumerist, which made devoting resources to investment increasingly difficult for the state planners.

The stability of communism rested on its ability to provide welfare and security. Employment was full; education and health care were free; food, energy, and housing were subsidized. Workplaces served functions that were far from strictly productive purposes. Through them housing, health care, and even organization of leisure were provided. Pay systems included benefits not related to work performance. The workplace became the most important institution of social affiliation for each person, as well as each person's most important link with the state. Communism, in fact, was a corporatist society (Chirot 1980, Ost 1989). Trade unions included both workers and managers and were organized along main branches of the economy. They were fully subject to party control and played a role—characteristic for corporatist societies—as channels through which those in power could be in touch with substantial segments of the population.

The command economy, however, was essentially inefficient (as measured by output-input ratios).[3] This weakness became visible and painful once the cheap factors of production were exhausted and political control was relaxed. Inefficiency, combined with the growing burden of welfare obligations, lies at the root of the long-term crisis of the communist system. Declining rates of growth (see Figures 2.1 and 2.2), rising capital-output ratios, chronic shortages, latent or open inflation, and periodic political crises became evident as early as the mid-1960s, perhaps still earlier. Informal actors appeared: powerful regional and industrial lobbies, trying—through political channels—to gain access to investment resources, and black marketeers, evolving slowly into a parallel, shadow economy, often living in symbiosis with political protectors.

During the 1960s, the Polish government sought improvement through economic reforms, consisting of injections of certain doses of market structures and incentives. Managers of enterprises were given some (though limited) autonomy over the mix of products and factors of production. Salaries

FIGURE 2.1

Index of National Income in Poland, 1971–1990 (constant 1970 prices, 1970 = 100)

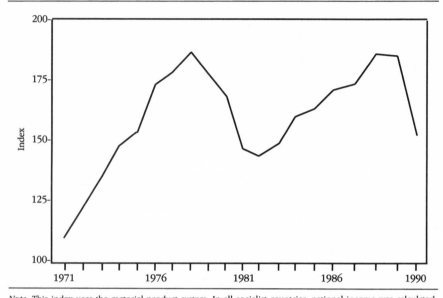

Note: This index uses the material product system. In all socialist countries, national income was calculated as a sum of new value within the so-called sphere of material production, that is, without services. (However, trade and transportation were included as so-called material services.)
Source: Central Statistical Office, *Podstawowe dane statystczne o Polsce 1946–1990* (Basic statistical data about Poland) (Warsaw, 1992), pp. 4–5.

and wages were linked with performance. Periodic shortage crises produced more tolerance of the small, family-size private sector. This sector never disappeared completely, but outside of agriculture it was limited to trade and crafts.

During the 1970s, the government tried another strategy: a leap forward through the introduction of modern, Western technologies bought on credit. As it turned out, the possibilities of absorption in a rational way were limited. Edward Gierek, who led the party at that time, tried to buy social peace through stable prices and a relative abundance of consumer goods, also bought on credit. That strategy led Poland into a debt trap: foreign debt rose from US$8.4 billion in 1975 to US$26.0 billion in 1980 to US$40.8 billion in 1989 (Polish Policy Research Group 1991). The Polish economy proved incapable of repaying credits with higher exports (though one must remember that raising exports was not easy in the 1970s, which were a period of world recession, rising oil prices, and growing exports by newly industrializing

FIGURE 2.2
Index of National Income in Poland, 1975–1990 (constant prices, previous year = 100)

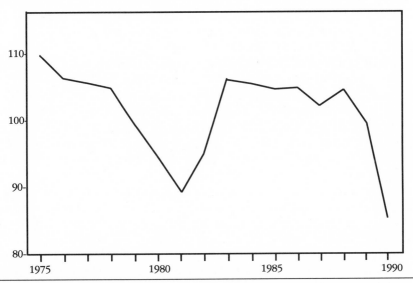

Source: Central Statistical Office, *Rocznik statystczny 1987* (Statistical yearbook 1987) (Warsaw, 1987), pp. 22–23, and *Rocznik statystczny 1990* (Statistical yearbook 1990) (Warsaw, 1990), pp. 24–25.

countries). In 1978, output started to fall, and heavily indebted Poland entered the phase of not only declining rates of growth but also declining output.

The Communist party, controlling all aspects of public life, also went through a process of evolution and ultimately corruption. Before and during World War II those joining the party were idealists. During the Stalinist period, the party was forged into an instrument of totalitarian control. Later, it gradually became a ladder of promotion, joined out of pragmatic or opportunist motives, with disregard to its ideological creed. The late 1960s brought about the end of the appeal of the Marxist doctrine. During the Gierek decade, quite a different type of justification of the system was introduced—modernization and the ideological and moral unity of the nation.

The Beginnings of Civil Society

Elements of both a market economy and an autonomous civil society started to emerge well before the collapse of the communist system. Despite party attempts to totally control social life, there were always spheres that partially or entirely escaped this control. Universities, some weekly newspapers, cabarets and films, and clubs and associations served as forums for open and critical debate. The Roman Catholic Church was never subject to state control. Not only did it remain a spiritually independent corporation with a powerful voice, but it also offered a refuge for lay intellectuals and teachers. Pressures for more political and cultural freedom were closely connected with social change within Poland and with geopolitical changes in the world. The educated middle classes felt more and more blocked in their aspirations because of the stagnant economy. From the 1960s onward, the country became relatively open to ideas coming from outside. Even within official structures, there were shifts toward a certain separation of powers: at the end of the 1970s, administrative and labor courts were established, removing important spheres of social life from the discretionary power of the administration.

The turning point in the creation of a "public sphere" independent of official power was 1976. After a wave of reprisals against participants in labor protests, the Committee for the Defense of Workers (KOR) was founded in Warsaw and attracted respected literary and scholarly figures.[4] KOR was the first independent civic initiative acting openly and thus challenging the Communist monopoly of power. KOR gave birth to a whole set of semi-open opposition activities, of which the most important were *samizdat* publications and educational activities. In the latter, the Church was instrumental, providing a premise for meetings, seminars, and lectures. KOR had a symbolic meaning, but it by no means monopolized opposition activity. There were also other organizations with different ideological inclinations, stressing, like the Confederation for Independent Poland (KPN), nationalist and independence goals. There was also a movement for independent trade unions, in which Lech Wałęsa was active.

Of particular importance for the emergence of civil society were the sixteen months from August 1980 to December 1981 during which Solidarity, the organization of independent trade unions, acted legally.[5] Legalizing Solidarity ended the monopoly of the Communist party. Speaking about this period, one is tempted to use the term "revolution" (Ash 1989), or perhaps "self-limiting revolution" (Staniszkis 1984). There was no violence, but the existing political system and its ideological justification were challenged by a mass social movement that gathered together all possible elements of discontent. Revolutionary tactics—meetings, demonstrations, leaflets, strikes, rhetoric— reached all corners of the country. This emotional atmosphere catalyzed new attitudes and new ideas. The representatives of the old order, especially those on the lower levels, felt paralyzed, and the power structure of communism began to disintegrate. With the growing strength of the regional chapters of Solidarity, a dual power structure emerged.

In the political sphere, one undoubtedly great achievement was freedom of expression. Ideologically, communism became "secularized." Previously, the most important element of the tacit ideology of the system had been that it was almost natural, impossible to change; the sixteen months of Solidarity destroyed that illusion. People realized that social pressure could bend the system almost to the point of collapse. There were now no doubts in the social consciousness that without the Soviet Union, Communist control in Poland would be finished. The population learned that changes can be achieved in a nonviolent way. A whole mass of activists and experts went through an accelerated school of political mobilization, organization, and negotiation techniques.

The imposition of martial law in 1981 did not erase this new civil society. Martial law was introduced by the moderate, reforming faction inside the Communist establishment, and reprisals were relatively mild. Whatever the particular cases of abuse and brutality, the aim of the architects of martial law was to paralyze the opposition, not to destroy it. Wojciech Jaruzelski and his collaborators did not legitimize their rule in terms of a return to a "true" socialism. Rather, they acknowledged that the system—as it existed before Solidarity—had exhausted its possibilities and recognized that reforms were necessary. The system they were trying to construct was an enlightened authoritarianism, declaring intentions of change from above. Their language was a rhetoric of reform. They introduced constitutional changes, further strengthening the rule of law: the State Tribunal, the Constitutional Tribunal, and the office of ombudsman were established (in 1982, 1985, and 1987 respectively). Still more interesting, Jaruzelski desperately tried to build some forms of cooperation with the society, including the Patriotic Movement for National Revival (1982) and the Consultative Economic Council (1982), a group of economists quite critical of the government. Yet another body, the Consultative Council (1986) brought together prominent intellectuals who criticized many aspects of government policies. The Government Committee on Economic Reform, founded in 1981, did not stop its work.

The final demise of communism in 1989 was a product of the impasse in which Polish society found itself in the second half of the 1980s. Gorbachev, glasnost, and perestroika were catalytic in breaking the deadlock. In this atmosphere, after the amnesty for political prisoners in 1986, both those close to Jaruzelski and the leaders of Solidarity started to look for possibilities of negotiating change. After months of cautious circling, round-table talks—opposed by hardline party factions and not attended by radical opposition groups—started in February 1989. Agreements signed on April 5 led to the legalization of Solidarity and introduced a "contract" providing for semifree elections and establishing the office of president.[6]

The elections, which turned into a plebiscite over Communist rule, brought success for the opposition—a success that was completely unexpected by both sides. As a witness of these events noted, "almost the day before anyone who had predicted these events would have been considered . . . a lunatic" (Ash 1990:29). After General Czesław Kiszczak, the interior minister and the architect of the round table talks, tried unsuccessfully to form a coalition government, two satellite parties, the United Peasant party (ZSL) and the Democratic party (SD), abandoned the Communists and joined Solidarity, opening the door to the creation of the first non-Communist cabinet.

The demise of communism in Poland was, therefore, the product of a long-term buildup of the civil society. That process was understood, though hardly welcomed, by the more enlightened circles of Communists. Poland is probably the most advanced case of the development of civil society among the countries formerly dominated by the Soviet Union. One should not be misled, however, into thinking that civil society in Poland is comparable to that in the West. Civil society under communism developed in response to particular pressures and challenges, enabling individuals and groups to gain more space to breathe and move and in the final phase—owing to a lucky set of coincidences—to shatter the rusty structure of oppression. That does not mean, however, that these forms of civil society were well prepared to meet a different set of challenges—those produced by market institutions, capitalism, and political pluralism. Here new forms of voluntary cooperation must develop, and that will take time.

The Emergence of a Market Economy

Market mechanisms never disappeared completely in Poland. The agricultural sector remained in private hands. Some family businesses existed, and the shadow economy was thriving. Several halfhearted attempts were made at reforming the state enterprise sector.

During the sixteen months of Solidarity in 1980–1981, demands for economic reform were answered by the creation of a special government committee that included Solidarity observers. Discussions at that time, however, excluded any talk of private property; proposals were limited to variants of market socialism. Solidarity had an ambiguous attitude toward reforms, well summarized by the banner of strikers in Łódź in 1980: "Economic reform yes, price rises no." The movement was born, among other things, out of discontent with the increasing difficulty of life, including constant shortages. There was also a strong egalitarian streak, directed against the real or imagined privileges of nomenklatura. One of the important demands of strikers in Gdańsk in 1980 was introduction of the rationing of meat, a commodity particularly hard to get. Rationing of everyday necessities was, in fact, introduced at that time and became even more widespread during the early 1980s.[7]

During the debates on the organization of the economy, the idea of employee councils was raised. The idea was popular among political activists of a social-democratic orientation, but it also was supported by many professional economists, who, even if they had some reservations about the efficiency of such management solutions in the abstract, treated councils as a politically feasible substitute for private property.

The idea of councils was first put forward by the Communist party, which probably hoped to control them and create a counterbalance to Solidarity within the enterprises. In a new parliamentary act on state enterprises, employee councils were given considerable power. In many cases, however, Solidarity succeeded in capturing control of the councils. The so-called network of councils soon became a powerful parallel structure. Councils were not outlawed during martial law and continued to play an important economic and political role during the 1980s.

After martial law was introduced, the government initially regained control over the economy through "operational programs": physical targets were set for enterprises, but contracts, not coercion, were used to enforce them. Administrative allocation and rationing were introduced. Attempts to pursue liberalizing economic reforms, however, continued (Kemme 1991). In 1982 the autonomy of enterprises was increased, employee councils were given the right to hire managers, decisions concerning production and investment were decentralized, and many prices were left to negotiations between the enterprises and the buyers (trade companies). Formal limits on wages and employment were lifted, and state economic plans were reduced to guidelines. Although foreign trade remained a state monopoly, enterprises could obtain licenses to trade directly, while an active currency exchange policy stimulated enterprises' interest in exporting.[8] One of the most painful elements of these reforms was a rise in consumer prices (Figure 2.3), no doubt facilitated by martial law. Never before, in fact, had the Communist state in Poland successfully imposed such massive price rises; similar attempts in 1970 and 1976 had triggered mass protests.

Liberalization did not extend, however, to allocation of fuels and primary materials, especially those that were imported; these remained centrally controlled. Branch ministries still played important roles as controllers and "founders" of enterprises. Many enterprises and products were heavily subsidized, and the subvention system was very unclear.

The next wave of reforming activity came in the second half of the 1980s. In official discourse, the idea of a market economy was now more often suggested. Among intellectual elites, there was also a considerable shift from ideas of "market socialism" to proposals for a full-fledged market economy. In 1987 a new Independent Economic Society, dedicated to development of a private sector, was allowed to register. For the first time the idea of a capital market within the state economy was raised (Iwanek and Święcicki 1987). Meanwhile, efforts to link the Polish economy with the West also intensified.[9] In 1986

FIGURE 2.3
Retail Price Index in Poland, 1981–1991 (previous year = 100)

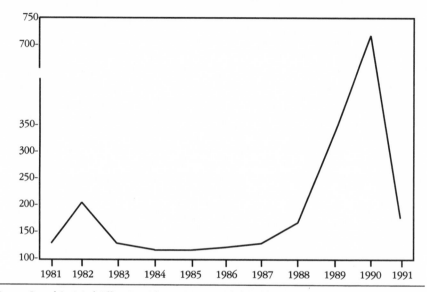

Source: Central Statistical Office, *Rocznik statystczny 1987* (Statistical yearbook 1987) (Warsaw, 1987), p. 413; *Rocznik statystczny 1991* (Statistical yearbook 1991) (Warsaw, 1991), p. 179; *Mały rocznik statystczny 1992* (Concise statistical yearbook 1992) (Warsaw, 1992), p. 104.

Poland joined the International Monetary Fund (IMF) and the World Bank. In the same year a bill on joint ventures was passed.

The pace of market-oriented reforms accelerated under the last Communist government of Mieczysław Rakowski (September 1988).[10] Rakowski's policies were symbolized by the appointment of Mieczysław Wilczek, a successful private businessman, as a minister of industry. A bill on economic activity substantially facilitated the founding of private enterprises. Limits on the number of employees in private firms were removed, opening the way for large-scale private enterprises. Revalidation of the Polish prewar commercial code allowed for the registration of limited liability companies. That step led to a highly politicized controversy about so-called nomenklatura companies. According to new legal rules, it was possible to register companies in which one partner was a state enterprise and a second partner was a private person (often one of the state company managers). Allegedly, this arrangement could lead to a transfer of public resources to private persons.

Under the last Communist cabinet, attempts were also made to end rationing. Currency exchange for individuals was legalized, which immediately led to a mushrooming of private exchange bureaus. (Poland had had, until then, a substantial black market for foreign exchange.) Finally, during the summer of 1989 Rakowski made a desperate gesture that considerably eased the situation of the next government. After a month of a total price freeze, his cabinet decided to free all food prices on the first day of August. Since indexation, won by the opposition during the round-table talks was in operation, this move obviously led to instant inflation. When Leszek Balcerowicz started his anti-inflation policies, after January 1990, the post-Communist government had considerable trouble reverting to indexation.

In retrospect, during these final years of communism, no one believed any longer that the command economy could survive. The moderate factions within the party moved step-by-step toward introducing markets, and even capitalism. These reforms were pursued, however, in a social vacuum, without links to social groups and without their support. Neither authoritarian measures nor attempts to build links with society from above worked. Though market structures emerged, they were only partial and lacked proper political and cultural underpinnings.

Shock Therapy

On August 23, 1989, Tadeusz Mazowiecki took over as Poland's first non-Communist prime minister.[11] Solidarity was not prepared to take power and had not expected to get it. It had no program, no political experience, and no people to nominate for administrative posts. Victory in the semifree parliamentary elections, however, forced Solidarity to take power.

Mazowiecki, though, had enormous support from much of the public, who were united against communism. Thanks to this support, his government (consisting partially of Solidarity people, partially of Communists and their former allies) was able to push the country through a painful economic change. During the implementation of initial reforms, this support waned. A little more than a year later, on November 25, 1990, Mazowiecki was defeated in a presidential election not only by Lech Wałęsa, but also by a previously unknown populist, Stanisław Tymiński, gaining only 18 percent of the vote. The elections signaled the end of unconditional social support for radical reforms.

Solidarity took power at a moment of economic crisis: Poland was suffering from shortages; high foreign debt; and inflation, bordering on hyperinflation, caused by the deregulation of prices by the previous government and by the indexation of wages agreed on during the round-table negotiations. Mazowiecki's advisers started to look for "a Polish Ludwig Erhard"—an architect of radical economic reform. Leszek Balcerowicz—a man whose name later became a symbol of the Polish "shock therapy"—was suggested.

Balcerowicz was a theoretician rather than a man of practical experience.[12] He had already made his name as the author of a radical proposal for market reform as early as 1981. In 1990 he was given a double post of deputy prime minister, responsible for the economy, and finance minister. He served in the Mazowiecki and then the Janusz Bielecki cabinets until Bielecki stepped down after the parliamentary elections of November 1991. He behaved as a technocrat rather than as a politician, trying to stay as far out of political infighting as possible and reducing his public appearances to a necessary minimum (he did not aspire to a parliamentary seat during the 1991 elections). Fluent in English and German, he had good relations with representatives of foreign governments and international institutions, which helped him during his constant campaign for the reduction of the Polish debt. Without doubt a strong believer in democracy, he nevertheless pointed out after his resignation that strong governments do have higher chances of succeeding with stabilization measures, while at the same time remarking somewhat naively that he had thought that Solidarity political camp unity would hold together longer (Balcerowicz 1992:102–3).

Blueprints for reform were quickly drafted, to be introduced as of January 1, 1990. Advice was given by foreign experts. One of them, Jeffrey Sachs—very visible in various Western forums as well as in the Polish media—was later treated almost as the father of the Polish reforms.[13] His involvement helped sell the project to politicians and to the wider public; reforms were presented as the advice of an impartial, brilliant, and successful foreigner who was pushing for a market transition but was critical of IMF conditionalities.

The Balcerowicz team was guided by the neoclassical, neoliberal vision of economic order. The team openly opposed any version of a so-called third way between capitalism and socialism and repeatedly stressed that the system to be built should be one that was tested and proved efficient—that is, Western capitalism. Balcerowicz gave first priority to the fight against inflation, and for this purpose he considered shock therapy preferable to a gradual approach. The containment of inflation was also a condition of agreements with the IMF and other Western financial institutions designed to ease Poland's foreign debt and facilitate its gradual integration into the international economy.

It is often forgotten when notions of shock therapy and "big bang" are mentioned that when Balcerowicz took office, the process of economic change was quite advanced. The economic policy of the Mazowiecki government was sold to the public, however, as a dramatic change from an unpopular and inefficient old order to a new, logical system that in due course would lead to an improvement of living conditions. What is called the "Balcerowicz plan" consisted mainly of stabilization and liberalization measures. These measures had to be painful—in fact, they were probably more painful than was initially expected.

A series of preliminary steps was taken during the second half of 1989. The dollar value of the zloty was devalued almost fourfold; prices of coal, energy, and steel were sharply increased; prices of many commodities were freed; the growth of credit was curtailed; and the wage indexation formula was modified. These steps were followed, on January 1, 1990, with the announcement of a package of measures approved by the Parliament four days earlier aimed at reducing the fiscal deficit from 7.5 percent of gross national product (GNP) to 1 percent. In January all remaining food and agricultural subsidies were eliminated, and coal and energy subsidies were drastically curtailed (to be further reduced gradually in the future). Budgetary expenditures were to fall, revenues were expected to rise, and treasury notes were introduced to finance the remaining deficit. To encourage saving and achieve a positive real interest rate, the National Bank was to adjust its discount rate at monthly intervals. Foreign exchange was made available for importers (this was the so-called internal convertibility of the zloty), while the official rate of exchange of the zloty was set using the parallel market as an indication. The zloty was initially undervalued in order to promote exports and reduce imports, while at the same time it was assumed that inflation would correct the underdevaluation. A group of Western countries provided a fund of US$1 billion to guarantee the stability of the zloty; this fund was one of the main anchors of the program. The range of administered prices was considerably reduced, but the prices of energy, fuel, transportation, and rents remained regulated (Wellisz 1991:9). The wage indexation system was retained, but changes in the cost of living became a maximum rather than a minimum guide for wage increases.

The tight monetary policies introduced in 1989–1990 were continued throughout Balcerowicz's term of office (until the end of 1991) and were retained during the next cabinets. Nevertheless, the conditions required by the IMF were met only until July 1991. Thereafter, a dramatic budgetary gap started to open—owing not to increased expenditures but to dwindling revenues. The zloty was devalued several times and later also linked to a basket of foreign currencies instead of solely to the dollar.

As a result of these measures, demand-pull inflation caused by subsidies to consumer goods and wage pressure was reduced (Figures 2.3 and 2.4) but was replaced by corrective inflation caused initially by increased energy prices. In fact, the initial increase of prices in January 1990 was twice as high as expected. After two months of very high inflation (almost 80 percent in January, almost 25 percent in February), price rises slowed in March 1991 to slightly over 4 percent. Thereafter through mid-1993, inflation has been kept to roughly 3–4 percent per month, with slight variations. It has not been possible to further reduce inflation, partly because of periodical increases in official prices of

FIGURE 2.4
Monthly Retail Price Index in Poland, 1990–1992 (previous month = 100)

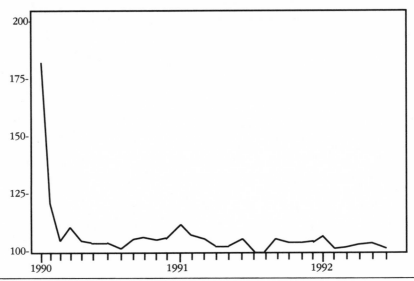

Source: Central Statistical Office, *Biuletyn statystczny* (Statistical Bulletin) 36, no. 6 (July 1992), p. 82; *Mały rocznik statystczny 1992* (Concise statistical yearbook 1992) (Warsaw, 1992), p. 105.

energy and partly because of the gradual internationalization of the Polish economy and the accompanying rise in the prices of tradables to the world level (Wellisz 1991). Monopoly practices of the state-owned enterprises may also contribute somewhat to continued, though quite low, inflation.

The extent of the impact of tight monetary policies on the standard of living is open to debate. Real money incomes fell about 20 percent in 1990 but remained almost unchanged the following year (Figure 2.5). The initial drop was caused not only by decreased real wages, but also by unemployment, which had not existed under the previous system and began to emerge at the end of 1990. Nonmonetary incomes fell owing to the reduction of benefits. In 1992, average real incomes decreased significantly. As a result of the growing income differences, consumption of food by lower-income groups decreased considerably in 1992 and 1993.

The introduction of stabilization measures, however, reduced shortages. The mere existence of shortages makes comparisons with real incomes in Poland before 1990 slightly misleading, since the earlier indexes were based on controlled prices of goods that were in fact unavailable. The liquidation of

FIGURE 2.5
Index of Real Incomes in Poland, 1981–1990 (previous year = 100)

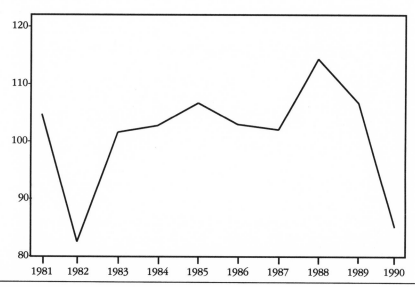

Source: Central Statistical Office, *Rocznik statystczny 1991* (Statistical yearbook 1991) (Warsaw, 1991), p. 194;
Mały rocznik statystczny 1992 (Concise statistical yearbook 1992) (Warsaw, 1992), p. 85.

shortages itself was an important improvement in welfare. While the gain is difficult to measure, anecdotal evidence and everyday observation leaves no doubt that goods previously impossible to buy were now available, and less time and energy were spent for shopping. The reduction of shortages was made possible both by reduced demand and by the supply reaction of the quickly expanding trade sector (about which more later) and increased consumer imports.

It was not, unfortunately, caused by an increase in the output of the manufacturing sector. On the contrary, stabilization spurred a recession in industrial output—a much more serious one than had been forecast (Figure 2.6 and Table 2.1)—mainly among the large state-owned enterprises (see Dąbrowski et al. n.d.). Their initial situation was basically good: they had reserves of stocks and currencies dating from the past and were able to realize good profits. But from early 1991, difficulties developed in connection with the dollarization of Council for Mutual Economic Assistance (CMEA) trade and the later collapse of the Soviet market. According to some estimates, the loss of the Soviet market accounts for about 35 percent of the output loss (Gelb

FIGURE 2.6
Index of Industrial Output in Poland, 1986–1991 (previous year = 100)

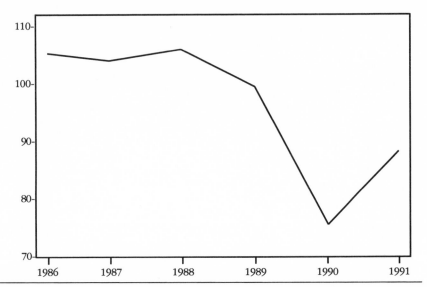

Source: Central Statistical Office, *Rocznik statystczny 1991* (Statistical yearbook 1991) (Warsaw, 1991), pp. 26–27; *Mały rocznik statystczny 1992* (Concise statistical yearbook 1992) (Warsaw, 1992), p. 177.

1992:11). At the same time, there was an apparent increase of output in the private manufacturing sector.

The state enterprises' difficulties were the most important cause of increased unemployment. By mid-1992 over 2 million workers, or about 10 percent of the labor force, were unemployed (Table 2.2). The exact figures are debatable, but there is no doubt regarding the overall tendency.

Institutional Reforms and the Infrastructure of Markets

The Balcerowicz team is sometimes criticized for not advancing institutional reforms as vigorously as they fought inflation (Moskwa and Wilkin 1991:12, Balcerowicz 1992:101). It is true that they were intellectually better prepared for dealing with strictly economic issues on a macroeconomic level than with legal and institutional matters. The team probably also tended to underestimate the significance of institutional issues. They were overwhelmed by an

TABLE 2.1

Index of Industrial Output in Poland, 1991–1993
(monthly average for 1990 = 100)

Year and month	Total	Mining	Manufacturing
1991 January–December[a]	88.1	94.6	87.7
1992 January–December[a]	91.8	94.0	91.8
1991 June	79.9	90.8	79.2
July	78.7	93.2	77.7
August	78.1	84.1	77.7
September	80.4	87.6	79.8
October	87.7	94.3	87.3
November	80.9	91.8	80.2
December	84.0	92.4	83.4
1992 January	82.2	98.8	80.8
February	78.4	95.4	77.0
March	90.8	100.4	102.4
April	86.3	94.5	85.7
May	81.4	84.1	81.6
June	86.2	84.1	86.7
July	86.3	87.3	86.6
August	84.0	83.2	84.2
September	91.0	93.5	91.0
October	95.2	97.8	95.1
November	91.1	93.1	91.2
December	95.9	79.9	97.7
1993 January	86.5	95.9	85.8
February	84.5	97.6	83.5
March	97.0	100.5	96.9

[a]Monthly average.

Source: *Biuletyn statystyczny* (Statistical Bulletin) 36, no. 8 (September 1992), p. 94; *Biuletyn statystyczny* (Statistical Bulletin) 37, no. 3 (April 1993), p. 100.

enormous task and by political resistance connected with implementing the stabilization plan, and they had tremendous problems finding capable and skilled people. Over time, it became more and more difficult to push the necessary legislation through the Parliament. Finally, since the market economy was at a rather primitive stage at first and was also rapidly evolving, policy makers often noticed the need for legal changes only later. By and large, the team continued the process of transition to an economy based on private property by passing new laws and amending existing ones, although this ongoing process of piecemeal change was veiled in the rhetoric of a drastic and radical break with the communist past.

Indeed, the political change and the new rhetoric facilitated this process. In the media and in the language of politicians, market institutions and behavior were now prized as a blessing. Individual entrepreneurship became

TABLE 2.2
Unemployment in Poland, 1990–1993
(in thousands)

Year and month	Number	% of labor force
1990		
March	266.6	1.5
June	568.2	3.1
December	1,126.1	6.1
1991		
June	1,574.1	8.6
December	2,155.6	11.8
1992		
June	2,296.7	12.6
December	2,509.3	13.6
1993		
March	2,648.7	14.2

Source: Central Statistical Office, *Rocznik statystyczny 1991* (Statistical yearbook 1991) (Warsaw, 1991), p. 106; *Mały rocznik statystyczny 1992* (Concise statistical yearbook 1992) (Warsaw, 1992), p. 157; *Biuletyn statystyczny* (Statistical Bulletin) 36, no. 7 (August 1992), p. 30; *Biuletyn statystyczny* (Statistical Bulletin) 36, no. 3 (March 1993), p. 32.

a basic virtue, by which a person could win social approval. A new culture of business—however superficial and naive—started to shape the everyday life of Poles.

In the legal sphere, freedom of economic activity was being gradually broadened (see Gray 1991). The law on economic activity, passed in 1988, abolished ceilings on employment and the size of enterprises. Laws on establishing firms were amended and relaxed. To a degree, this process consisted of a return to the precommunist past. New private limited liability and joint stock companies are now being founded according to the Polish prewar commercial code of 1934, revived under the Rakowski government and later amended. Bankruptcy laws dating from 1934 were amended in 1990, but few bankruptcies thus far have been allowed to test these regulations, and both creditors and debtors lack experience with bankruptcy proceedings. Antimonopoly laws were introduced (Iwanek and Ordower 1991).

Rules governing foreign capital were relaxed (Moskwa 1991). The new law equalized conditions for foreign and local investors. Indeed, foreigners now even enjoy certain privileges, such as tax holidays, if they bring in substantial capital[14] or new technologies, or they export over 20 percent of the value of sales. Foreign firms operate under the Polish commercial code, and permits are required only if a company operates in specified areas such as seaports or airports. All profits can be transferred abroad.

The government started dismantling the state monopoly in foreign trade at the end of 1987 (Michałek 1991:4ff.), but trade liberalization gained real significance only after the changes in foreign exchange policy of January 1990. Since then any economic agent is free to export or import, and a permit is needed only for a few goods such as military or radioactive products (Michałek 1991:12).

The basic task of institutional reform has been to improve the functioning of markets. If one looks at the market for consumer goods, there is no doubt that the sheer easing of restrictions on economic activity and macroeconomic stabilization worked in a positive direction. Various institutions of the consumer goods market—street peddlers, bazaars, then private shops, and even malls—developed quickly, and the range of easily obtainable goods and services became incomparably wider. Advertisements and "yellow pages" in telephone directories started to make these markets more transparent. On the other hand, the stability of newly established shops is not very high, the quality of many products and the authenticity of trademarks are often dubious, and there are problems with post-sale service and replacement of defective goods. Service in shops or restaurants, although incomparably better than in communist times, still leaves much room for improvement.

The market for producer goods has became basically free, with the elimination of the last remaining elements of central allocation of intermediate goods (Balcerowicz 1992:52).

The labor market is still far too inflexible. There is no correlation between unemployment and wage restraint (Socha and Sztanderska 1992:14). Wage and employment rigidities have many causes, including the passive state policy toward safety-net measures (which are overly redistributive), stagnation of vocational training and retraining, and the inefficient housing market. These factors are coupled with established institutional arrangements for wage bargaining and employment policy. Collective bargaining tends to be pursued under the pressure of strikes or strike threats and in a highly uncoordinated manner. Average wages in the economy—but not productivity, prices, and wage rates for specific enterprises—have been a standard reference point in labor disputes.

Capital and financial markets have developed slowly. A stock exchange was created in Warsaw but still has limited significance, since only a few companies are listed. A second, more important step is the development of the banking system. Until the late 1980s, almost all banking services were provided by the National Bank (NBP).[15] In 1988, the State Saving Bank (PKO), previously part of the NBP, was made independent; at the beginning of 1989 local branches of the NBP were changed into nine independent state banks. In April 1993, the first of these was privatized. Only then did the NBP start to act like a Western-style central bank. At the end of 1989, rediscount credit was introduced by the NBP as a form of refinancing for the state banks.

Private banks started to be established beginning in early 1990. In 1990 and 1991 around eighty licenses were granted for the establishment of new banks, most of them private, some with foreign participation. The new banks are being founded according to rules similar to German traditions of universal banking; most are commercial but are allowed to engage in investment financing.

Despite this quantitative growth, the banking system remains inadequate, and banks are undercapitalized. Improvements in rules regarding capital adequacy are needed, as well as development of deposit insurance, credit guarantees, and banking supervision. Banks are short of skilled and experienced personnel, and they lack expertise in granting credit. Clearing has still not been introduced, and the telecommunications system is not up to the task. Banks are notoriously burdened with bad debts owed by state-owned enterprises.

Property rights are still not well defined and protected within the Polish economy. Amendments to the Constitution and the Civil Code have removed the distinction between so-called social and private property, but further legislation and court action are needed to make the protection of property rights effective. There are difficult, politicized issues of reprivatization of real estate and enterprises nationalized or confiscated under communism. Voices are sometimes raised against former members of the *nomenklatura*, who allegedly gained capital at the end of the communist period through their access to the sources of power.

Contracts are based on the Civil Code, modeled on the French *code civil* and introduced under communism in 1964. It has been amended several times recently.

Intellectual property was, by and large, relatively well protected under communism. Poland has laws protecting copyrights, trademarks, and patents. The protection of software, however, is still not resolved, and there are problems with audio- and videotapes.

Privatization

Privatization has been one of the main aims of the reformers. "Small privatization"—the selling or leasing of shop space, pharmacies, apartments, plots of land, and the like—was relatively easy. Existing legal regulations allowed certain measures in this respect as early as 1989. There was a barrier in access to shop space, since state users were privileged, but the privatization law of July 1990 equalized state and nonstate users, giving the latter an equal opportunity to rent space and allowing them to buy state property. The level of rents, however, now decontrolled, has emerged as a new obstacle.

Privatization of large state-owned enterprises (SOEs) is another matter.

It is a hot political issue, and debates are full of high rhetoric. Advocates present privatization as an obvious road to economic prosperity and attack those who have doubts as closet believers in statism. Opponents attack privatization with accusations ranging from sheer demagoguery (a sellout of public property at ridiculous prices, a submission of the Polish economy to foreign capital, or mere corruption and theft) to more serious arguments suggesting that privatization is being used as a substitute for industrial policies and structural reforms or as an excuse for not reforming management of SOEs. Many also argue that the social and political costs of privatization are being neglected.

Leaving aside political haggles between various parties, the issue now seems to be not so much whether to privatize or not to privatize—there are no proponents of a statist economy—but whether the process of privatization should have a "shock" or instead a more organic character. Advocates of the first approach propose schemes of mass privatization and rapid liquidation of the public sector. Adherents of more organic approaches stress the importance of the gradual rise of new private firms (to absorb workers displaced from the failing SOEs) and point out the need to establish good management of SOEs to make them more attractive to prospective buyers. They regard as inevitable a rather long cohabitation of private and public sectors in Poland. According to this approach, privatization should be treated not as a precondition to but rather as a part of the restructuring of state-owned firms. Ownership restructuring would then be one aspect of the process, which would also involve the restructuring of production, finances, and management of enterprises. Whether privatization should begin or end this process should be decided not a priori, but according to the circumstances of each case.[16]

The task of privatization is enormous, since Poland has about seven thousand SOEs. Various approaches were proposed, including the public sale of profitable, well-managed enterprises; the sale or distribution of shares to employees; or the free distribution of shares to all citizens (see Lewandowski and Szomburg 1990). A hot exchange developed over the so-called enfranchisement of the nomenklatura, an alleged semilegal acquisition of state property by well-connected former members of the top establishment. Another debate focused on the reprivatization of assets nationalized or confiscated under Communist rule in and after 1944.

In February 1991, Parliament approved a privatization program calling for converting half of all state enterprises to private firms over three years. Selected profitable enterprises were to be privatized using a case-by-case method, after valuation by consulting firms; large blocks of shares were to be sold to core investors (preferably foreign). The governments of Mazowiecki, Bielecki, and later Hanna Suchocka tried to foster images as architects of effective privatization, while the cabinet of Jan Olszewski in practice slowed the process.

As of mid-1993, an enterprise can be privatized either through the sale of stocks or through legal liquidation and the sale of physical assets. Parliament debated an alternative method—a program of mass privatization—several times during the first half of 1993. As proposed by the Suchocka government, the scheme would create several state investment funds, which would own shares of selected profitable state firms, starting with an initial group of 600. Shares in the funds, in turn, would be sold at nominal prices to all willing citizens.[17] This plan was heavily criticized. Critics feared a massive sellout of shares by poorer citizens, which might lead to the collapse of financial markets and might also concentrate shares in a few hands through speculative schemes. Many also doubted that the investment funds would prove good managers of enterprises. The initial version of the program was rejected by the Sejm. A scaled-down version was approved at the end of April 1993. The consequences remain to be seen.

Conventional privatization through a sale of stocks is long and costly, and it is difficult to establish the value of assets. Foreign firms can be hired to appraise value, but this procedure often leads to accusations of adding unnecessary additional costs. It is hard to establish the prospects of a particular enterprise. Profitability in the usual sense does not mean much, because most SOEs are heavily in debt, owed partly to banks and partly to other enterprises. (Massive interenterprise debt came to be one of the most important characteristics of state industry in the last years of communism and during the transition.) More than half of state-owned enterprises have large accumulated debts. As a result of these difficulties, by June 1992 only a little over three hundred state firms had been legally converted from SOEs managed by employee councils into state-owned corporations, as a first legal step toward privatization (see Table 2.3).[18] Of these four hundred, the stocks of about forty had been sold to private owners (Kostrz-Kostecka 1992).

TABLE 2.3
Number of Corporatized
("Commercialized") State-owned
Enterprises in Poland, 1992

Total corporatized companies	308
Types of companies	
Joint stock	251
Privatized	24
Limited liability	57
Privatized	6

Source: Central Statistical Office, *Mały rocznik statystyczny 1992* (Concise statistical yearbook 1992) (Warsaw, 1992), p. 277.

A second possible route to privatization is to liquidate the firm in a legal sense and sell its physical assets (Table 2.4). As of June 1992, 271 enterprises had ended in this way, and another 336 had started this process. Finally, as of the same date, 754 other enterprises had started the process of bankruptcy, which also leads to legal termination of their existence and channels their physical assets into private hands.

The process of terminating an enterprise, through bankruptcy or other means, is usually slow, since it is difficult to sell old machinery. The process also usually means that the workers lose their jobs. Relatively more enterprises are liquidated in such a way in the less-industrialized regions, which aggravates the problem of unemployment.

A close look at cases of firms preparing for privatization often does not leave much room for optimism. A china factory in southwestern Poland had in the past employed up to 2,500 workers but according to Western consultants needs fewer than 900. Another company in the region, a linen factory, should reduce employment from 800 to 250 workers; in addition its survival depends on a heavy injection of investment. A new private cotton company reduced employment from 2,000 to 580 and had orders through the end of 1992 but lacks backing from local authorities in its efforts to get credit for supplies. A corporatized and well-equipped children's garment company would like to sell its office building and a nursery, but nobody wants to buy them.[19] (Many SOEs are burdened with resort houses, nurseries, and other facilities that were parts of their welfare programs; now they can neither afford to maintain them nor sell them.) The government has not analyzed the fate of enterprises that have changed hands and seems to assume that privatization automatically leads to improvement.

That privatization of larger SOEs is difficult is not surprising. Many (if not most) of these firms have obsolete machinery. The 1970s were a period of heavy (though misdirected) investment and of technology imports. The next

TABLE 2.4
The Liquidation of State-owned Enterprises in Poland, through June 1992

Type of liquidation	Begun	Terminated
Privatization	607	271
Bankruptcy	754	78

Source: Ada Kostrz-Kostecka, "Prywatyzacja po polsku" (A Polish way of privatization), *Rzeczpospolita* (September 3, 1992).

decade, especially the second half, reversed this tendency (Figure 2.7), and therefore new owners usually must be prepared for substantial additional investments. Many enterprises are seriously in debt. Some sectors such as armaments, mining, and metallurgy are in a particularly difficult situation; the government has started to work on long-term plans to downsize them. In general, SOEs are overmanned, by Western standards. The workers usually have mixed or negative feelings about privatization and vague ideas about what a capitalist enterprise is all about.[20] In short, the Polish SOE does not seem to be a particularly attractive piece of property, and neither local nor foreign investors have rushed to buy.

Structural Changes and Economic Performance

Poland's stabilization program and institutional reforms have stimulated major structural changes, both welcome and unwelcome. The share of the private sector in the number of firms and in output is rising, thanks more to the

FIGURE 2.7
Rate of Investment in Poland, 1970–1990

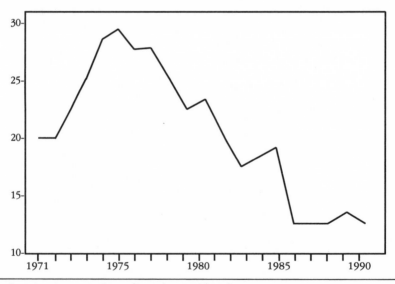

Note: These data are computed according to the material product system.
Source: Central Statistical Office, *Podstawowe dane statystczne o Polsce 1946–1990* (Basic statistical data about Poland, 1946–1990) (Warsaw, 1992), pp. 6–7.

emergence of new enterprises than to privatization. Employment is shifting toward the private sector; as of December 1991, more than half of all workers are employed in the private sector (Table 2.5).

In the first half of 1990, small-scale, bazaar-type entrepreneurs, both registered and unregistered, became an everyday fact of life throughout the country. Street peddlers appeared in every neighborhood, selling their wares from open suitcases, camp beds, or vans. Meat and toilet paper—proverbial symbols of shortage—became abundant. Surprisingly, during the next several months this type of trade became better organized, as local authorities introduced regulations and traders moved into shop space, leased or bought under the provisions of the "small privatization" program.

Much small-scale commercial and manufacturing activity is not registered. Apart from the tax evasion tactics of new firms, the Central Statistical Office is unable to capture activities of firms employing fewer than five workers. Still, the official data record considerable growth. Already in 1989, the non-agricultural private sector provided 7.5 percent of gross domestic product (GDP), twice as much as in 1980 (Grabowski and Kulawczyk 1992:13). After January 1990, private sector employment, contribution to GDP, and number of firms all grew considerably (Tables 2.5, 2.6, and 2.7). But while very small firms have multiplied, far fewer medium-sized firms have emerged, and there tends to be a gap between small (mainly private) and large (usually state) units.

According to a detailed study of a sample of 300 firms (Grabowski and Kulawczyk 1992), the new companies have been established by relatively well-educated people (almost 65 percent with college or higher educations). Most were previously managers or employees in the state sector, but quite a number had some experience in private business. They usually started with a small sum of capital, coming from savings accumulated in Poland, earned abroad, or borrowed from friends and family. (Only in 12 percent of cases was a bank the source of initial capital.) The new entrepreneurs were motivated more by a desire for an independent source of income than by dreams of a big fortune (see Bednarski 1991). Growth of capital was faster in smaller companies than in

TABLE 2.5

Employment by Sector in Poland, 1990 and 1991 (thousands of employees)

Sector	December 1990	December 1991
Public	8,243.4	7,046.0
Private	8,230.6	8,815.2

Source: Central Statistical Office, *Mały rocznik statystyczny 1992* (Concise statistical yearbook 1992) (Warsaw, 1992), p. 267.

TABLE 2.6

Number of Individual Businesses in Poland, 1989–1992 (thousands of businesses)

1989	December	813.5
1990	December	1,135.5
1991	March	1,162.9
	June	1,272.4
	September	1,365.6
	December	1,420.0
1992	March	1,430.2
	June	1,523.4
	December	1,630.6

Note: These data are for very small businesses, not companies.
Source: Central Statistical Office, *Rocznik statystyczny 1991* (Statistical yearbook 1991) (Warsaw, 1991), pp. 21–22; *Biuletyn statystyczny* (Statistical Bulletin) 36, no. 8 (September 1992), p. 90; *Biuletyn statystyczny* (Statistical Bulletin) 37, no. 3 (April 1993), p. 96.

TABLE 2.7

Types of Economic Units in Poland, 1990–1993

		Commercial law companies		
Year and month[a]	SOEs	Belonging to the Treasury	Joint ventures[b]	Privately owned
1990					
December	8,453	248	1,645	29,650	6,416
1991					
March	8,578	282	2,290	34,642	7,168
June	8,591	283	2,840	38,516	7,698
September	8,419	308	3,512	41,450	8,103
December	8,228	376	4,796	45,077	8,676
1992					
March	8,273	504	6,187	48,404	9,236
June	8,180	650	7,648	51,174	9,759
December	7,342	764	10,131	47,690[c]	9,182[c]
1993					
March	6,838	792	11,473	61,437[c]	11,787[c]

Note: Cooperatives, establishments belonging to organizations, and foundations are not included.
[a]Data are for the last day of the month.
[b]These companies are partly state owned and partly foreign owned.
[c]Different concept than in previous rows.
Source: *Biuletyn statystyczny* (Statistical Bulletin) 36, no. 6 (July 1992), p. 89; *Biuletyn statystyczny* (Statistical Bulletin) 37, no. 3 (April 1993), p. 95.

those of medium size. Small firms usually operated locally. Initially services predominated; more recently small manufacturers have become increasingly common. Demand is the most important barrier (the new entrepreneurs fear the competition of the parallel economy much more than that of the state enterprises), but at the same time their marketing and advertising are inadequate. Manufacturers often depend on a single buyer. Small sector firms still lack adequate institutional support: banking, consulting, information. Managerial experience is limited.

Despite the growth of the private sector, both GDP and industrial output fell dramatically in 1991 and 1992—in fact, much more than had been forecast at the beginning of the Balcerowicz plan (Figures 2.6 and 2.8). This phenomenon is common to all postcommunist countries.[21] Among the causes were monopolies, higher costs of inputs, demand barriers caused by stabilization measures, dollarization and then loss of the Soviet markets, and loss of markets for armaments and inputs to socialized agriculture (Kuczyński 1992). This

---

FIGURE 2.8
Index of Gross Domestic Product at Constant Prices in Poland, 1981–1991 (1980 = 100)

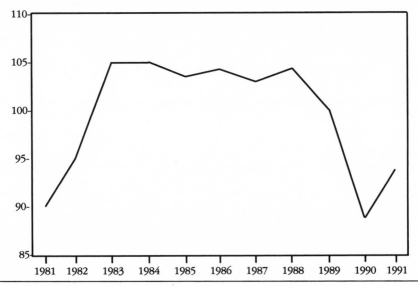

Note: Since 1980 Poland has computed national income statistics according to the "Western" method, including services.
Source: Central Statistical Office, *Rocznik statystczny 1990* (Statistical yearbook 1990) (Warsaw, 1990), p. 113; *Rocznik statystczny 1991* (Statistical yearbook 1991) (Warsaw, 1991), p. 118; *Mały rocznik statystczny 1992* (Concise statistical yearbook 1992) (Warsaw, 1992), p. 247.

severe recession began to reverse in the second half of 1992 (Table 2.1). In early 1994, GDP growth for 1993 was estimated to have been 4 percent. Exports are high (limited domestic demand is often cited as an explanation), and the balance of payments is positive.

Of course, the behavior of the economy is still generally determined by the large state-owned enterprises, which dominate mining and manufacturing. From the beginning of the transition, policy makers assumed that the SOEs were not likely to adjust well to the new circumstances; therefore they perceived privatization as crucial. In addition to problems discussed earlier, the legal situation of the SOEs hampers efficient behavior. Property rights are unclear. Part of SOE capital belongs to the state; part (accumulated from earned profits) to the enterprise itself. State firms are additionally constrained by two special taxes not applied to the private sector: the dividend (a tax on capital assets) and the PPWW, a punitive tax on excessive wage increases. The PPWW was introduced because it is assumed that SOEs lack the incentives for wage restraint of a private owner.

Managerial responsibility is complex. An enterprise is partly responsible to a "founding organ," one of the branch ministries. At the same time it is governed by the employee council, which hires managers and has broad decision-making authority. In many enterprises, there are competing trade unions. Managers are quite weak relative to workers, and traditionally they were as interested as the employees in pressing the state for subventions. Their experience concerns organizing production, securing supplies (a constant problem in shortage economies), and managing social relations; they lack experience with finance, quality control, cost containment, and marketing. Relying on their political power, state enterprises only recently have begun to be afraid of possible bankruptcy.

Initially, both managers and workers tended to operate within a short time horizon, maximizing wages and trying to maintain employment levels. Their actions were understandable, bearing in mind high inflation, unstable political conditions, unclear legal prospects for any given firm, and a historical tendency for the state to bail out failing firms. Several studies, however, suggest that a significant number of SOEs may be able to adjust to the new situation (OECD 1992, Pinto et al. 1992). These firms have become more efficient in using factors of production, have maintained productivity, and have showed restraint in borrowing and in setting wages. Their management was able to change the product mix to increase sales. These managers have learned the lesson of three years of reforms: they do not count on government bailouts and have lengthened their time horizons. They identify with their firms, knowing that if a firm has a good standing, they have a chance to keep their jobs after the firm is privatized or can count on participation in the privatization process. Both good and bad firms exist in all sectors of the economy.

None of the post-transition Polish cabinets have had a genuine industrial policy. Under political pressure, however, governments developed certain measures, apart from privatization programs, to deal with SOEs. One of the most important is the restructuring plan. The stabilization fund (originally provided to anchor the 1991 stabilization effort but never drawn on for that purpose) is to be used to recapitalize banks, which in turn would help profitable enterprises to clear their books. A second proposed element of the industrial policy (broadly interpreted) is the pact on state enterprises. The pact allows those enterprises that decide to become corporations to choose their preferred route to privatization. Enterprises selected for mass privatization are excluded. The pact also provides for probable removal of the much-resented PPWW, the punitive tax on "excess" wage hikes, and easy access to shares in privatized firms for workers.

Agriculture poses a separate problem. Poland is not particularly well endowed for agricultural production. Infrastructure is underdeveloped; farms are small and undercapitalized. Out of 2.1 million private farms, only a few hundred are modern commercial enterprises, while the rest operate on a semisubsistence basis. Reforms hit the commercial farms hard, however, since farmers lost guaranteed prices and a secure state market for their products, as well as cheap, administratively allocated production inputs, while trade liberalization exposes them to Western competition. Many of the commercial farmers are skillful entrepreneurs, however, and there are signs they will be able to adapt, provided infrastructure is improved and the local food processing industry develops. On the other hand, hidden unemployment will increase, since agriculture as a whole will have to act as an employment buffer (Kwieciński and Leopold 1991:18–19).

Apart from the changes in the official, recorded sphere of the economy, the parallel sphere has also changed. Since systematic studies do not exist, I can offer only a few words of a hypothetical character based on partial, anecdotal evidence. With the transition, two main reasons for the shadow economy in the communist era—shortages and overregulation of economic activity—disappeared. The shadow economy has become more like that in the West, comprising a whole range of activities from tax evasion to mafialike corruption schemes to drug trade. Opportunities for such activities seem to be considerable, since the underdeveloped new legal infrastructure leaves gaps that are filled by "grey" activities and since government regulatory capacities are not up to the task of monitoring the quickly emerging private sector. To a certain extent, these illegal activities have a role in the process of "primitive accumulation of capital" unfolding in Poland. In addition, the disintegrating structures of the Soviet empire have produced considerable criminal activity, ranging from the depths of the Commonwealth of Independent States (CIS) to Germany. For example, smuggling stolen cars from Germany to the CIS became a major business for Polish mafias. Polish police, frontier, and customs services are ill prepared to deal with these new problems.

Social Structure, Conflicts, and Interests

The social structure that emerged under communism is undoubtedly disintegrating. But it is still difficult to say anything definite about the crystallization of a new class structure. Statistics are imprecise, but even a cursory observation suggests a considerable increase in income differences and much new wealth (including cars, villas, consumer imports). There are also new, visible signs of poverty: beggars, people collecting trash, and homeless.[22] Social structures are affected by the decline of average recorded real income, loss of job security, and shifts in the structure of incomes. Cheap housing, medical care, education, and other benefits obtained through either employers or general programs are dwindling owing to the disintegration of the institutions that provided them. The relative importance of money income has increased, and life has became much more "marketized."

High-ranking members of the nomenklatura have lost their privileges, although some former dignitaries became successful businessmen. Because of their skills and connections, they have more opportunities for positions in foreign firms (joint ventures) or on the boards of directors of corporatized state enterprises or newly founded banks. The rising new "high bourgeoisie" is statistically insignificant. More important is the middle class. White-collar employees in the so-called budgetary sphere (teachers, doctors, middle-level administrative officials, and others in state services) are significantly worse off: the fiscal crisis has steadily eroded real salaries, while cost of education (particularly valued by this group as they seek to educate their children for similar jobs) has risen. This segment of the population gained a great deal from the political opening but mostly in the form of nonmaterial benefits. It remains to be seen whether public and private white-collar workers will acquire the status of the Western middle class. More enterprising members of this group are now leaving the public sector. The situation of highly skilled blue-collar workers greatly depends on their ability to find new employment. And as noted earlier, commercial farmers face difficulties due to rising prices of inputs, competition from imported foods, and increased interest rates.

The crucial question is whether a classical middle class, based on property and business, is emerging. There is—as I noted above—a considerable growth in small and medium-sized business: now about 1.5 million enterprises are registered. Many of these businesses, however, are not only small but also unstable. One of the dreams of the authors of mass privatization schemes was the creation of a class of owners. Even if this were to succeed, however, it would be a long wait for the results. This emerging middle class does not have any visible political representation at the moment.

Members of the lower classes are, not surprisingly, in the worst situation, especially in regions with high unemployment. Data show that those without skills are first to be fired. Of particular importance is the fate of unemployed youth, who can be permanently marginalized. The possible social effects are easily seen in U.S. inner cities or, closer at hand, in the former German Democratic Republic. Unfortunately, there are already signs of the emergence of an underclass of unskilled, undereducated people who have difficulty finding a place in the new society. There is, in consequence, a rise in extremist sociopolitical subcultures. Some Polish skinheads are attracted by extremist anarchism. Others are joining the Polish National Community, a far right anti-German and anti-Semitic movement whose members—dressed similarly to Nazi stormtroopers—demand "Poland for the Poles." Analysts warn about the possibility of a rise of an underclass of "structural victims of market reforms" (Grabowska et al. 1991:74). If one looks for threats to democracy, this marginalization is obviously one of the most important.

The transition to a market economy produces a cultural shock. People must cross the "valley of tears" (Dahrendorf 1990) before things improve and they learn a new way of life. Cultural shock is therefore as important as the measurable changes in the standard of living. Shock is produced by rapid and unexpected social change. It is worth remembering that workers in Gdańsk rebelled in 1980 against the imperfections of the communist welfare state and not in favor of capitalism. To the extent that they looked to the West, they were attracted to consumerism, not to the discipline of the marketplace. Now, however, the communist welfare state has disintegrated, destroying institutions that were taken for granted. Income differences and unemployment, previously unknown, are growing. Free travel is now possible, but there is also an inflow of poor immigrants. Goods and services are available in a range and quality unknown in the past, but there is little money. Western mass culture is omnipresent, bringing foreign food, loud music, praise of violence, and pornography. The shock poses an ideological challenge. There were promises that the end of communism would bring "normalcy." However—as the writer Jacek Bocheński remarked recently—people are starting to discover that this "normal" capitalism is not so nice. "Nobody had warned us that capitalism would come," comments Bocheński ironically (Bocheński 1992). Ideological responses can easily be adverse to the market, democracy, and open society. They can easily praise nationalism, xenophobia, and authoritarianism as defenses against the dangers of the market economy and the hedonistic values of the West.

Can we say anything precise about the emergence of new types of conflicts and the crystallization of new interests? If we are to judge from the types of protests prevailing, those that dominate still reflect the patterns of the old system. The two most visible types of protests are those of farmers and those of workers in big state-owned enterprises. As early as 1990, an analyst noted growing frustration among workers because of blocked economic aspirations not balanced by expanded liberties (Wnuk-Lipiński 1991:34). There have been several waves of strikes in big public enterprises, often accompanied by hunger protests, demanding higher wages and government assistance in reconstructing specific branches of the economy. The most recent of these waves occurred in the first half of 1993 in the Silesia mining sector, among textile workers in Łódź. In both cases protesters demanded some form of government intervention on their behalf.

Protesters often justify their actions with talk of price rises, the decline of the level of living, and the loss of security. Justifications often refer to a "right" to a certain level of living and to a dignified life. Observers with more liberal orientations often respond that it is not possible to pursue a dialogue with the protestors in terms of economic arguments such as the need to link wages to productivity. The government tries to avoid becoming a party to these conflicts, but the protesters perceive the state as having an active role—which is not surprising, since most industrial firms still belong to the state and the government claim that the enterprise management should make decisions sounds unduly meek. Workers are still convinced that they have a justified claim against the state concerning their level of living; they are strongly influenced by their collective experience of a form of protest that proved effective in the 1970s and in particular during 1980–1981.

State enterprise workers have lost their benefits, and in many cases their incomes have fallen dramatically. They are threatened with unemployment, and the newly emerging private sector is still too weak to offer many jobs or rising standards of living. Moreover, thus far conditions of workers for private employers are not very attractive. State workers therefore see few opportunities for themselves in the process of privatization. Leftist ideas are currently unpopular, but these conditions create fertile ground for populist attitudes and policies (Grabowska et al. 1991:74).

The rural population is also hard hit by the changes. Over 30 percent of the population lives in the countryside, and about 25 percent of the active population is employed in agriculture. It is important to distinguish, however, between the small strata of highly commercialized entrepreneurs and the vast mass of semisubsistence peasants. Under communism, many of the latter could find supplementary employment in state industries, but now that opportunity is gone. In some regions there are also agricultural workers on dying state farms. Agricultural workers and peasants are in a particularly hard situation, since they lack both capital and skills necessary for the "market game." The rural population is generally older and less educated than that in the cities. This frustrated segment of society is another potential client of demagogic populist politicians.

Various farmers' movements, some of them extremist in nature, have organized protests opposing cuts in subsidies and demanding guaranteed prices and protection from market forces (especially imports). Such protests have been mainly organized by heavily indebted commercial rural entrepreneurs.

New Politics

Political change in Poland is still more abrupt and unexpected than economic change. The new political order is far from crystallized. The nature and positions of old actors are changing rapidly; still more dramatic is the emergence of a large number of new parties and other politically relevant groups. Parties and parliamentary clubs frequently rename and regroup. Politics is fragmented and opaque, and institutional and procedural settings are changing and unclear.

The initial transformation took place under the banner of a unified society opposing the Communist authorities, who were allegedly totally alienated from the public and held power thanks only to Soviet protection. The sudden collapse of communism in Eastern Europe seems to support such a thesis. Nevertheless, the real composition of forces was more complicated, and the rapid subsequent dissolution of Solidarity demonstrates that the notion of social unity was somewhat idyllic.

The Polish Parliament elected in October 1991, with its twenty-nine parties, has been the most fragmented in Eastern Europe. This fragmentation results from the negotiated political transition in Poland: Round-table talks were held between the representatives of the Communist government and part of the opposition united under the umbrella of Solidarity. Later Solidarity began to disintegrate. This process of disintegration was accompanied by an institutionalization of groups that were neither Communist nor aligned with Solidarity and a reintegration of the postcommunist left (Wasilewski 1992:275). As the 1991 parliamentary elections showed (Table 2.8), the former Communists retain considerable support and so does the Polish Peasant party, a communist ally before 1989. The post-Communist trade unions now have more members than the Solidarity trade union federation.

The new parties have neither clear social bases nor much practice in communicating with the public. The public, in turn, is not particularly interested in parties. Abstention during the 1991 elections was alarmingly high; the national average turnout was only 43 percent. Polls show rising distaste with politics. Debates on abortion and waves of accusations of politicians for their alleged involvement either in corruption scandals or with the Communist security services reinforce the decline in the authority of politicians. One of the unfortunate results is the rising preference for authoritarian solutions shown by some polls.[23]

Because of weak links between the elites and the rest of the society, Polish politics and state making mainly involve "the political class" consisting of politicians, union leaders, prominent journalists, some civil servants, and outspoken academics.[24] This elite is in fact "the state," being perhaps more important than official structures. The core of this class was formed during the last ten to twenty years of opposition to communism. Except for former

TABLE 2.8
Results of November 1991
Parliamentary Election in
Poland (percentage)

Party	Sejm	Senate
SLD	13.0	1.1
UD	12.3	13.3
WAK	10.7	3.6
PSL	10.4	1.5
KPN	10.0	3.2
PC	9.6	7.8
KLD	8.0	3.0
PL	6.1	1.5
Solidarity[a]	5.1	9.1
Other	12.8	12.7

Note: SLD = SDRP and other former Communists; WAK = ZChN and other Catholics.
[a]Solidarity put forward its own election
list.
Source: Central Statistical Office, *Mały
rocznik statystyczny 1992* (Concise statistical yearbook 1992) (Warsaw, 1992), p. 63.

Communists, most members of the class were associated with Solidarity. Now they have been joined by many aspiring politicians who do not have a record of fighting against communism.

The political experience of the majority of this class comes from participation in a civil rights movement rather than in a modern democracy. Professional experience is mostly academic or journalistic. By and large, members of the new elite are not skilled in using the media or in organizing electoral support. Experienced in the "discourse of values," they are only now learning how to practice open politics. Much of politics is highly personalized, with open personal animosities. Politicians tend to lose contact with their power base, in part because their social and material status has improved while large segments of society instead feel a decrease in their standard of living.

Experience with running the government is also recent and limited. Many new ministers have been university professors or journalists who rarely managed organizations larger than several people. Their organizational experience as participants in a semilegal opposition movement was also different from what is needed for running large formal agencies. In consequence, the everyday practice of bureaucracy is often incompetent, as learning takes time. With the exception of people who worked for international organizations, members of this class also have little practical knowledge of Western developed societies (and still less of developing countries). Logistical support—such as think tanks, researchers, and office staff—is inadequate.

The Parliament, a principal forum for the most important parties, has considerable constitutional powers, as one would expect in a parliamentary democracy. A Polish sociologist responded to the question "Who governs Poland?" with the answer "The leadership of parliamentary parties" (Śpiewak 1993:37).

Parliamentary politics is in practice often a matter of veto power. Fragmented parties make formation of cabinets difficult. Apart from the first cabinet, under Mazowiecki, each of the next three had only limited or shaky support in the legislature (see the Appendix). The cabinet of Hanna Suchocka was formed in July 1992 by an improbable coalition of seven parties, of which the Democratic Union and the National Christians were the pillars. The partners agreed only on limited areas. The Suchocka government initially drew part of its strength from the patronage of Lech Wałęsa. It could not, however, survive a withdrawal of the Solidarity parliamentary faction support and as a result was voted out of office in June 1993—which prompted Wałęsa to dissolve the Parliament.[25] An undoubtedly positive aspect of the Suchocka government record was its ability to continue not only the economic, but also the foreign policy, of the three previous cabinets. (Krzysztof Skubiszewski held the post of foreign minister from the very beginning). Poland has good relations with all emerging post-Communist states. There have been constant efforts to forge links with the European Community (EC) and the North Atlantic Treaty Organization (NATO) on many levels, including mutual treaties and harmonization of Polish laws with EC norms. Cross-pressured by the various members of the coalition, the Suchocka government faced far greater difficulties with economic policy.

The division of power between the Parliament, the government, and the head of state is unclear and in flux. Constitutionally, the president—although elected by a general vote—has limited powers. However, Lech Wałęsa's personality and historic role make him an important player in his own right. Wałęsa defies easy description. The man became a living legend during the sixteen months of Solidarity: an electrician with no formal education beyond technical school became the leader of a movement that shook the Soviet empire. Interned under martial law and—after his release—declared by the authorities "an ordinary citizen," he remained a symbol of Solidarity and nonviolent revolution against totalitarian rule and was recognized as such with a Nobel Peace Prize. During the round-table talks, he proved to be a skilled and flexible but tough negotiator. Ambitious and vain, he ran for and won the presidency. A skilled orator (despite the fact that he uses language that makes grammarians shudder), he is metaphorical, cryptic, and often self-contradictory. Wałęsa is accused of having no clear policies and of concentrating power by playing various segments of the political elite against each other.

Wałęsa's long-term objective is to strengthen the constitutional powers of the president relative to the Parliament and the cabinet—which is not surprising, taking into consideration both the nature of Polish politics and his personality. In early 1993, his office submitted to Parliament a radical proposal for a new constitution. Personally, Wałęsa is authoritarian, but at the same time he defends democracy and the rule of law, as his recent proposal for a bill of rights suggests. Despite the lack of a "presidential party," he is a mighty power broker. Twice he managed to resolve a constitutional crisis by playing various forces against each other. For the time being, his tactics consist more in fragmenting the political scene than consolidating it. His overall popularity, measured by polls, is declining, and he has strong opponents. Still, the fragility of most cabinets to date and the fragmentation of the political scene raise the real possibility of presidential rule.

The Church, which played such an important role in building civil society under communism, is now trying to consolidate its power. It has pressed for abolition of the right to abortion and won the introduction of religious instruction in the public schools. Its overall popularity, however, as measured by opinion polls, is diminishing. Initially the most popular institution in the post-transition arena, the Church slipped more recently to third place after the army and police! In one poll 85 percent of respondents opposed a major role for the Church in state affairs.[26]

The formal structure of the state remains undefined. Poland still has no new constitution. The Communist one was amended several times, declaring Poland "a democratic state under the rule of law." Political and ideological debates over the future constitution, which will define the state, and over several major statutory laws can be summarized under three headings: the character of national identity and in particular the place and role of religion; attitudes toward the communist past; and the extent of state responsibility for the welfare of its citizens.

National identity and tradition—identified with catholicism—are stressed by many who feel uneasy with new developments and are afraid of the influence of secular, Western culture. In the idea of joining Europe, they see more danger than promise. Populist parties clearly play upon this feeling. There are also forces in Poland (represented mostly by National Christians) that would like to define the Polish state in terms of Christian values and national identity. These ideas are viewed with sympathy by some factions of the Roman Catholic Church, although the hierarchy is careful not to commit itself too much to actual political positions. These forces are hostile to the liberal idea of separation of state and religion and to the concept of an ideologically neutral state. Several recent developments offer evidence of this tendency, including a Senate proposal to start the Constitution with the words "In the name of Almighty God," a bill regarding radio and television that demands that all stations respect "Christian values," and a law severely restricting abortion. There is also considerable hostility toward victims of AIDS.

The abortion law has wide significance, since it touches broader issues of personal liberty and the basic values upon which the state is founded. The issue of definition of the state will not disappear easily. On the contrary, one may expect in the future a repetition of this debate on various occasions. There are deep historical reasons for these debates. In the sixteenth to eighteenth centuries Poland was a multiethnic, multicultural, and multireligious state. During the nineteenth century, the era of modernization and nation building, Poland lost its independence. Therefore, the basic cultural identity of the modern Polish nation then emerging was organized not around its own territorial state, but around two values: language and the Roman Catholic religion. The stereotype of the Pole-Catholic was constructed at that time and helped to organize elites against the powers partitioning Poland. Later this concept helped to preserve cultural autonomy under the communist system. There is no doubt that this interpretation of tradition and cultural identity will be hard to reconcile with more civic forms of national identification and with the liberal values prevailing in much of Western Europe, which also have a powerful hold over parts of Polish society.

The issue of the communist past is also of tremendous importance. The basic question is whether and to what extent the present state is a continuation of the communist one. The new elites legitimize themselves in terms of regained independence and a radical, almost revolutionary break with the past. In everyday parlance, the present situation is referred to as the "third Republic," the second one being prewar Poland. Ideologically, the communist Polish People's Republic is dismissed as an insignificant historical episode. The transition, however, was nonviolent, and the basic structures of the communist state were reformed rather than abolished and replaced. For all practical purposes (starting with international treaties and ending in everyday issues of high school diplomas and civil court sentences), the present state is a continuation of the previous one. This fact, however, makes the ideological rationalization of the new order difficult.[27] This debate ranges over many specific issues. Some propose so-called decommunization (banning former party activists from government jobs) or at least a lustration (a similar ban for informers and functionaries of the communist security apparatus).[28] Allegations of involvement in the Communist system are often invoked in political arguments. Accusations of collaboration with the Communist political police were raised against the closest advisers of the president and even against Wałęsa himself. The debate also touches economic issues, since the question arises of reprivatizing assets seized by the state under communism.

Finally, there is the issue of the degree of state responsibility for the welfare of its citizens. The question can be stated in shorthand: Is Poland to become capitalist, or should it instead adopt a "social market economy" with a social democratic character and with ample welfare provisions? Put another way, should Polish capitalism imitate the libertarian Anglo-Saxon model or the more interventionist Western and Northern European models? This is a serious issue not only for ideological reasons, but also on practical grounds. The heritage of the communist experience encouraged dependency on the state. Moreover, Poland still lacks nongovernmental public organizations and social insurance schemes that might buffer raw market forces. During the hardships of transition this issue will not be easy to solve.

Because of a lack of agreement on these fundamental matters, constitutional problems have been addressed through temporary solutions. On August 1, 1992, the Sejm approved a so-called little, or provisional, Constitution, which laid out rules concerning the separation of powers among Parliament, the president, and the cabinet, mainly focusing on provisions to prevent or resolve crises produced by the fragmented Polish political scene. Recently, the president proposed a permanent bill of rights, which would establish limits on state rights over citizens and legal means for citizens to defend themselves against the state. The proposal solves the problem of social rights in an interesting way: the government is obliged to formulate social programs and to report on their implementation, but citizens cannot have recourse to the courts to demand those rights. The issue of the final constitution—and, consequently, the shape of the state—will be further discussed and probably will be determined by the relative strength of the main players. The same factors will shape electoral laws, which still call for proportional representation. Only with difficulty did Parliament approve a new 5 percent threshold for party representation in the legislature.

Apart from the ideological and constitutional definitions of the state, there are also problems concerning its practical functioning, caused partly by the character of the civil service. Under communism, the whole structure of bureaucracy was tailored to the needs of the command economy and authoritarian state. As it stood, the existing apparatus was politically and organizationally not up to the task of transition and especially not up to the task of building market institutions. It could not, however, simply be dismantled and replaced. Each of the four post-transition cabinets has tried to reorganize the central administration to some degree, but no overall plan has been tried. Whatever was achieved, the bureaucracy is still not capable of implementing the various urgent institutional reforms. The pool of prospective entrants to the service is inadequate; the pay, in comparison with that in the private sector, is too low; and the prestige of work for the state is low as well. The crisis of the bureaucracy is connected with the constitutional issues, since the parties try to influence every level of government. Rules of recruitment are unhealthy, and the higher posts in the civil service are regularly filled on the basis of personal acquaintance and political relationships. Twice, when cabinets changed, much of the experience gained by new officials was lost in the shake-ups.

The unclear character of the Polish state, the fragmented political scene, the raw and intellectually primitive character of political debate, and the inefficient civil service may prompt speculation about a lack of stability of Polish democracy. It certainly cannot be characterized as deep rooted and well crystallized. On the other hand, no violence is being used; no political actors declare intentions to introduce an authoritarian system; the media—in particular, printed media—are free; and there are dailies and weeklies of all imaginable political colors. State television and radio are not totally independent, but controls consist mostly of informal pressures by various segments of the power elite. One by one, however, new private radio and television stations are emerging. All this does not mean that there are no dangers. The challenges to Polish democracy, however, lie elsewhere: They are connected with the great shifts in social structure. The emerging underclass and the endangered situation of the workers from large, inefficient state enterprises are clearly the most distressing signs.

Challenges Facing the State

Broadly speaking, transformation of former communist systems requires reducing the role of the state. A closer look, however, reveals that transition also calls for redefining the state's role. The way the state was shaped under communism does not fit the role it must play in relation to the emerging market economy. In general, in market-oriented systems government must formulate and manage macroeconomic and social policies, regulate markets to minimize external diseconomies (such as environmental damage, unfair competitive practices, and consumer deception), invest in infrastructure, and promote research and development as well as general education. In all postcommunist countries there are additional reasons for a considerable, albeit transitional role of the state.

1. In the developed countries, the institutional infrastructure of markets and capitalism developed in the course of a long historical process, to a certain degree "organically." In Eastern Europe, this process must be accelerated, and apparently the state will be its main agent. Markets cannot be constructed instantly and the state must act, for the time being, as an "artificial limb" (Modzelewski 1992).

2. In the communist countries there were very limited possibilities for voluntary associations or nonprofit institutions that, in the West, fill the space between the state and the private sector, supporting the latter and

meeting those needs the market cannot satisfy. Chambers of commerce, mutual insurance, educational organizations, professional societies, co-operatives, charities, and clubs—all these institutions, so vital for modern society, had almost no place under communism. Before they are able to grow organically, the state—which performed many of their functions—cannot simply shed all responsibility.

3. It is imperative to create a new type of social safety net. Under communism (which was, in fact, one type of corporatist society), welfare was provided partly through the state enterprises and partly through the state bureaucracy, financed directly from the state budget. Now a new system must be built to care for the unemployed and socially weak in a different, more efficient, and more flexible way. This task cannot be postponed, not only for humanitarian reasons, but also because postponement might be politically explosive and might destabilize the process of reform itself.

4. Postcommunist countries shoulder a heavy burden of state-owned enterprises. Influenced by a simplified doctrine of the "invisible hand," the state initially left the enterprises to their own devices, which in fact meant turning them into abandoned property. Although there are good arguments that in the long run they should be privatized, the short-run prospects for privatization are limited. Therefore, the problem of managing and restructuring the state enterprises must be addressed in a more comprehensive way.

5. Where there is heavy foreign debt, the state will have to collect resources to repay it. There are also two other implicit sorts of debts which must be repaid: ecological debt and the costs of maintaining and upgrading infrastructure. Both debts have been neglected for years.

6. Finally, there is the question of whether postcommunist countries—relative latecomers in the field of international competition—should pursue more active industrial policies in order to help specific firms (rather than sectors) that show prospects of viability but face difficulties stemming from systemic changes. Industrial policies might also facilitate growth of small and medium-sized manufacturing firms.[29]

Two major obstacles hamper the state in undertaking these tasks of transition. The first set of obstacles consists of the political and bureaucratic contradictions and shortcomings mentioned in the previous section. It should be stressed that not only political stability but also an efficient civil service is indispensable to the process of reform, since it is the state administrative apparatus that prepares materials for and implements policy decisions. Even the best ideas have no chance of realization without such a civil service. In order to be effective and efficient, this civil service must be insulated from politics (recruited and promoted on the basis of merit) and from business. Therefore civil servants should be relatively well paid, while not necessarily numerous.[30]

The second obstacle to an efficient state is fiscal. In fact, almost all the problems of transformation are reflected in budgetary issues.[31] At present, Poland redistributes around 40 percent of GDP through the central and local budgets and extrabudgetary funds. Although not excessive as it stands, this share is likely to increase, given the challenges facing the state. In 1989 the Polish budget deficit was 7 percent of GDP. There was a surplus of 1 percent in 1990, but in 1991 the deficit rose to 4 percent.

The stabilization plan of 1990 balanced the budget mostly by dramatically slashing subsidies. The revenue system, however, remained basically unchanged, mainly drawing on the turnover and profit taxes from state-owned enterprises. The *dywidenda* (a tax on SOE assets) and the PPWW (a tax on excessive wage increases in SOEs) were added in 1989 as transitional measures, to stabilize state revenues and to discipline nonprivate enterprises.

In 1991 a grave fiscal crisis started that has not yet been resolved. Budget problems stemmed from the declining output and profitability of the state enterprises.[32] Finding themselves in a difficult situation, many enterprises stopped paying taxes and making contributions to the state pension fund. They often preferred to increase wages, gambling that the government would bail them out. The turnover tax, which worked well under the command economy, became hard to collect from the growing retail and distribution sector. The fiscal administration is inefficient in collecting taxes from the emerging private sector, and by and large, the tax contribution of the private sector is disproportionately low. In 1991, the government tried to stabilize the budget by further cutting public sector real wages and retirement benefits, but these moves were resisted by the constitutional court. The government also cut investments in the public sphere, especially in infrastructure.

The reform process separated national and local finances. Now the *gminas* (cities and towns) control their own finances, partly supported by the national budget. Two other important aspects of fiscal reform are the personal income tax, which began to be collected in 1992, and the value added tax, which was introduced in 1993. The VAT has the advantages of being the most stable source of revenue and being able to reach expanding private sectors. On the other hand, introducing the new systems will entail considerable learning costs.

Reforms are also needed on the expenditures side, and here progress is modest (if one leaves aside the brutal slashes already made). As mentioned earlier, welfare schemes, in particular pensions and health care, must be restructured. Until now the budget has continued to subsidize pension funds, and it finances health care almost entirely. Thus far only initial steps have been taken; they might be better described as debates rather than reforms. There are also specific transitional problems such as an absence of budget funds to supplement current pension contributions. Generally, as Crombrugghe (1992) notes, Poland still favors care (health and pensions) over opportunities (education and infrastructure).[33]

A three-year perspective on the budget shows that politically Poland was able to take big initial cuts but has barely been able to sustain them. Unfortunately, but not surprisingly, the current political pressure on the budget usually pushes away from the desired reforms. These pressures seek to help failing enterprises, appease farmers, keep housing subsidies and welfare benefits, and index public sector pensions and salaries. Such pressures make it difficult to allocate money to infrastructure and education, and the growth of government borrowing reduces the availability of capital for private investment. The possibility of a high budget deficit in the future forestalls negotiations with the IMF, the Paris Club, and the London Club regarding Poland's external debt. Indirectly, fiscal pressure makes Poland less attractive to foreign capital.

Concluding Remarks

Poland has advanced considerably on the road toward a market economy and an open society since 1989. Polish society was probably better prepared to meet the new challenges than some other postcommunist countries. Still, the changes are painful. For considerable segments of society they have produced a decline in the standard and security of living and the cultural shock of a new way of life. There is a powerful attraction to freedom and democracy but also a disillusionment with how nasty, brutal, and inefficient market economies and competitive politics can be. Confidence in politicians and institutions is declining, although there are no voices arguing for authoritarian rule at the moment. Democracy, although not contested, is far from being well established. The institutions and traditions of civil society and the rule of law are weak. Competing forces try to define the state, and there are no guarantees regarding the outcome.

Put briefly, there are at least two social projects proposed. One is clear and logical: the idealized Western society, with the rule of law, democracy, and a market economy. The trouble is that for many this social project is not attractive, because it carries risks of losing national and religious identity. Many others feel that there is little room for them in a world organized according to these principles, since they have neither the experience nor the skills to enter the new game. For them, other projects are proposed, more vague, but perhaps more appealing: a stronger executive, more state paternalism, more safety, and more regard for moral values and historical identity.

The long-term process of decay of the communist system and the recent acceleration of change have generated new conflicts and new interests. However, the process of decomposition of the old order still dominates. The new private sector is developing organically, but the large state enterprises are difficult to remove from the stage—and they still support 4 million workers and their families. It is questionable whether market forces should be left as the sole means to restructure those enterprises and whether, under the existing circumstances, immediate privatization is appropriate for all of them.

Among the new trends, the rise of unemployment is the most distressing. Concentrated in less-developed regions, touching less-educated, less-skilled, less-enterprising, and younger people, it may easily contribute to a process of social exclusion, to the emergence of an underclass of those unable to find a place for themselves in a new competitive order, and therefore disappointed with the new way of things. Together with segments of the rural population and frustrated workers of decaying public factories, they might easily produce the electorate for populist, authoritarian demagogues.[34]

How fast the transformation should proceed is ardently debated. Some argue for the advantages of shock therapy. Under the political and economic circumstances of 1989, shock therapy was an appropriate choice, as it helped to end definitively the previous political regime. It is an open question, however, whether the whole process of transition can be treated in the same way. The adherents of such an approach are rightly accused of proposing a new, liberal utopia in place of a communist one. There is a strong argument for a gradualist approach, for Popperian "piecemeal social engineering" (Murrell 1992). In the West, market economies took centuries to develop; it would be unwise to expect that they can be built instantly in Eastern Europe.[35] As an adherent of this position, I would like to add that the pace of transition is constrained by the human resources available—by the supply of managers, administrators, and politicians capable of operating well in the new system. The transformation is an enormous social learning process, and learning takes time. It is obvious that it is impossible to produce, say, a pianist or an army general instantly. Such is also the case with a corporate lawyer, an accountant, a bank manager, or even a parliamentarian. But the transformation is also a social learning process in a larger sense, touching each and every citizen. This larger process requires each person to learn to take responsibility for his or her own life and to live in an open but competitive society. This sort of learning also takes time,[36] and trying to accelerate it too much may produce dislocations that are difficult for the society to absorb.

Transformation produces conflicts over the role the state should play. Some oppose its active role, convinced by neoliberal arguments and recent trends in the West, afraid of the danger of inflation and even of a slide to some form of statist system. Others, however, call for progrowth policies and a substantial state-organized social safety net (or a "social market economy"). This conflict has a deeper meaning: Is a self-regulating market a possibility or utopia? It is not easy to balance these arguments, but—for reasons developed in the previous section—I would argue that the state must inevitably play a considerable role in the transition, while redefining its character and retargeting its role toward providing opportunities rather than care. Only by smoothing the road and opening new possibilities for large groups of society can the dangers to democracy and future market reforms be reduced.

Appendix to Chapter 2
Basic Indicators and Chronology for Poland

TABLE A2.1
Basic Economic and Social Data for Poland

Population (mid-1991)	38.2 million
Urban population	62 percent
Life expectancy at birth	66.1 male
	75.3 female
GDP per capita (1990)	US$1,790
	US$4,980[a]
Index of GDP growth (previous year = 100)	
1989	100.2
1990	89.8
1991	92.4
GDP from manufacturing (1990)	44.1 percent
GDP from agriculture (1990)	11.8 percent
Inflation (consumer price index, previous year = 100)	
1989	364.6
1990	660.9
1991	159.4
Foreign debt (1989)	US$40.8 billion

[a]Based on purchasing power parity.
Sources: Central Statistical Office, *Rocznik Statystyczny 1991* (Statistical Yearbook 1991) (Warsaw, 1992); World Bank, *World Development Report 1991* (New York: Oxford University Press, 1991); "The Polish Economy and Politics since the Solidarity Take-over: Chronology of Events and Major Statistical Indicators," *PPRG Discussion Papers*. no. 6 (Warsaw: Polish Policy Research Group, 1991).

TABLE A2.2

Chronology of Events in Poland, 1956–1993

1956	Destalinization and economic reforms take place; these are later mostly aborted. Władysław Gomułka takes power under the banner of the "Polish road to socialism."
1968	Student protests are followed by repression. Official anti-Semitism and anti-intellectualism exist. There is a practical end to Marxism.
1970	Edward Gierek takes power and tries to modernize the economy with Western technologies, causing a debt crisis.
1976	After food riots, the Committee for the Defense of Workers (KOR) is formed; this is the beginning of open opposition.
1979	Pope John Paul II visits Poland.
1980	The Solidarity trade union is formed, and sixteen months of pluralist politics follow.
1981	Martial law is introduced on December 13 (ended July 1983). The Wojciech Jaruzelski team tries reforms and seeks ways to communicate with society—but without giving any powers to the opposition. Various regulations "freeing" the economy are passed during the next years.
1982	Prices are partially deregulated.
1985	Poland joins the IMF and the World Bank.
1986	An amnesty for political prisoners opens the way for informal contacts with the opposition.
1987	The so-called "second stage" of economic reform takes place.
1988	The government gives the first official hints about the possibility of round-table talks.
1989	Round-table talks take place in February and March. In June elections, Solidarity wins all but one mandate for the Senate and all mandates allotted to the opposition for the Sejm, the lower house (35 percent). In July Jaruzelski becomes president. In August Tadeusz Mazowiecki forms the first non-Communist government. There are still Communist ministers in his cabinet.
1990	The Balcerowicz plan (shock therapy) begins to be implemented in January. The Communist party dissolves itself. In July the last ministers associated closely with the Communist regime leave the government. In the second half of the year the split in the Solidarity camp becomes visible; in the next couple of years it will lead to the creation of PC, UD, and an independent Solidarity parliamentary platform. Jaruzelski steps down as president. In the first round of presidential elections in November, Mazowiecki loses to unknown populist Stan Tymínski and announces his resignation from the post of prime minister. In December Lech Wałęsa is elected president.
1991	Jan Krzysztof Bielecki (KLD) becomes prime minister of a predominantly liberal government in January. In August the Moscow coup occurs, and the Soviet Union dissolves. October parliamentary elections (40 percent of people vote) produce a split legislature (twenty-nine parties). Jan Olszewski becomes prime minister, supported by PC, ZChN, KPN, PL, and KLD.
1992	After a "file crisis" (an attempt by the government to complete a list of politicians who were political police informers under communism), the Olszewski cabinet is voted out in June. Wałęsa asks Waldemar Pawlak, the PSL leader, to form a new government. The mission fails. Hanna Suchocka (UD) forms a cabinet, consisting of a coalition of seven parties, of which the UD and the ZChN are pillars. Solidarity supports Suchocka.
1993	In April a "mass privatization" program is voted in. In June the Suchocka government, after loss of Solidarity support, is voted out of office by the Sejm (lower house); the Parliament (both houses) is dissolved by the president; Suchocka cabinet stays in caretaker capacity. New elections are scheduled in September.

Source: Author.

Demobilization and Gradualism: The Political Economy of the Hungarian Transition, 1987–1992

András Körösényi

Observers around the world were fascinated by the parallel moves toward democratization and market-oriented economic reform in Latin America and Eastern Europe during the 1980s and 1990s. Political scientists and economists, however, were skeptical about the feasibility of this double transition. Many of these experts assumed that the necessary economic stabilization measures and adjustment policies would weaken political stability and undermine the new democratic regimes. Others emphasized that the peculiarity of this third wave of democratization is that it is accompanied by an unprecedented mass belief in the free market economy (Huntington 1991). Political scientists have now turned their attention to the links between economic and political factors and to the ways in which the transition might be phased.

In Hungary, initially, there was no direct short- or medium-term relationship between the economic and political transitions. Each sphere had substantial autonomy. First, the economic transition began without any political change. The 1987–1988 economic liberalization was inspired by crises in the economy, particularly balance of payments problems and serious indebtedness. Paradoxically, the appointment of a hard-line Communist politician, Károly Grósz, to the premiership brought changes in economic policy, but Grósz had no intention of widening the liberalization to the sphere of politics. He represented the first version of reformism: economic liberalization under an authoritarian political system. Reforms were designed to establish a market economy but not capitalism (in other words, Hungary maintained the socialist ideological preference for public ownership).

Next came changes on the political scene. The split within Hungary's Socialist Workers' party (MSZMP) between liberalizers and hard-liners, the emergence of opposition groups, and the rising pressure for political reforms had mainly, but not exclusively, political causes. Political changes were also partly connected to economic causes. By 1985–1986 the failure of the economic reforms that had been adopted in the first half of the 1980s disappointed the reformist groups of MSZMP members and economic technocrats. They lost their faith in the possibility of pure economic reform and widened the scope of their thinking to the sphere of politics. The emerging pressure for political change can therefore be partly explained by the crises of the socialist economy.

By 1989–1990, the political transition had become independent from economic processes and was rooted mainly in political factors. The victory of the nonsocialist parties in the 1990 parliamentary elections, however, also pushed the economic transition forward. The need to create not only a market but also a capitalist economy was accepted by the nonsocialist majority. The character of the economic transition (methods, speed, and preferences) was, however, shaped very much by political factors.

I will begin this chapter by giving a short overview of the prehistory of the transition, emphasizing the role of previous cycles of market-oriented reform in the Hungarian economy. I will then focus on the economic transition: the major incentives behind the transition, the key areas of stabilization policy and structural changes, and the social costs. The next section reviews the political transition: the major political parties and interest groups, the constitutional changes, and the institutional setting of the new parliamentary regime. The following section focuses on the politics of the transition in economic and political spheres. Differentiating between two types of political-economic games, I will propose a model for analyzing the strategies of the key actors. In the final section I will try to describe the links between economic transformation and democratic consolidation and offer cautious prospects for the future.

Prehistory: The Heritage of Economic Reforms

Hungary, which has an industrialized economy (see Table 3.1), had a less rigid economic system than the other countries of the Council for Mutual Economic Assistance (CMEA). Dissatisfaction with the planned economy has had a long tradition in Hungary, and various cycles of economic reform have aimed to improve the economic mechanism of the Communist regime and create a socialist market economy. Hungary has had a strong tradition of reformist thinking in economics, and the "reform economists" acquired a quasi-political role beginning in the late 1960s.

Three waves of market-oriented economic reforms have taken place: 1968,

TABLE 3.1
The Macroeconomic Structure of the Hungarian
Economy: Sources of GDP and Distribution of
Employment, 1989 and 1991 (percentage)

Economic sector	GDP, 1989	Employment, 1991[a]
Industry	35.2	29.7
Construction industry	6.6	7.0
Agriculture and forestry	20.8	16.1
Traffic, post, and telecommunication	9.5	9.0
Trade	8.7	12.0
Others	19.2	26.2
Total	100.0	100.0

[a]As of January 1.
Source: GDP data are from A. Gyulavári, "Gazdaság," in R. Andorka, T. Kolosi, and G. Vukovich, eds., *Társadalmi Riport, 1990* (Budapest: TÅRKI, 1991), p. 64. Employment data are from Central Statistical Office, *Magyarország 1991* (Budapest, 1992), p. 7.

1981–1984, and 1987 to the present. These waves of reform have resulted in a "bargaining economy," a system in which enterprises and ministries negotiated on prices, subsidies, taxes, tariffs, and other economic regulations. The 1968 reform abolished the planned economy (the system of compulsory directives) and made possible the emergence of labor and commodity markets. The direct links between the state-owned enterprises and the planning authorities (the ministries) were eliminated, and in the "neither planned nor market economy"[1] of the 1970s and 1980s the managers of small- and medium-scale enterprises became more or less autonomous actors on the market. The distribution of economic resources was controlled by government agencies and by the Hungarian Central Bank (by commercial banks since 1987), but market forces became stronger and partly determined the decisions of most economic actors by the 1980s.

Most Hungarians became familiar with economic calculation and with supply and demand through the spread of the shadow economy, which was a source of additional income for approximately 75 percent of the population (Andorka 1990). Analysts often characterize the effect of the massive shadow economy as an "underground" embourgeoisement of society (Hankiss 1990, Szelényi 1988).

The Political and Cultural Heritage of the Kádár Regime

After the political earthquake of the 1956 anti-Communist revolution, the Communist leadership, under Premier János Kádár, established a more moderate authoritarian regime. Between the mid-1960s and mid-1980s the main feature of Kádárism was its attempt to conciliate society. The political leadership searched for a social consensus by offering material benefits in exchange for political acceptance and passivity. Using a kind of bargaining politics with informal (nonorganized) interest groups, the regime achieved a tacit consensus with the intelligentsia, professionals, blue-collar workers, and the peasantry. The regime gave people room to achieve individual material and career ambitions. By making the regime less ideological and accepting the emerging private shadow economy, the Communist leadership achieved its main task: the depoliticization of the masses. Instead of making collective demands (like the Poles), Hungarians accustomed themselves to following individual strategies to achieve their goals. Informal bargaining and depoliticization characterize the political-cultural heritage of the Kádár regime.

The Immediate Prehistory of the Transition

The failure of the economic reforms of the first half of the 1980s turned the reformers' attention for the first time to the political sphere, which had previously been regarded as taboo. Until 1985 both the reform economists and the soft-liners of the Communist party tried to push through economic reforms without touching the one-party system. In any case no political opposition was effectively able to challenge the political system. By 1985–1987 the paralyzing character of the political constraints on market-oriented reforms (for example, the socialist ideological barrier against private ownership) became clear to the reformist groups. "There is no economic reform without political reform," sounded the leading slogan of the 1985–1988 reformers. The emphasis shifted from economic liberalization to the political sphere.

Soft-liners in the regime, like Imre Pozsgay, gave cautious support to the program of political liberalization. The new electoral law made it possible for nonofficial candidates to contest seats at the 1985 parliamentary elections. The mass media, where censorship was eased, served to shift public attention to the role of the Parliament, the independent candidates, the dissidents, and other actors. Until the end of 1987 no political group—neither the reform-minded members of the MSZMP nor the most radical opposition groups—launched a program of political democratization. Contemporary political reform programs did not go beyond political liberalization.

The Economic Transition, 1987–1992

There is a striking gradualism and continuity in the Hungarian economic transition. Continuity prevails in two senses. First, in the long term, market-oriented reforms began in Hungary in 1968 and continued during the 1980s (see the Appendix). Second, in the short term, the political transition has not produced a radical change in economic policy, if one compares the policy of the last Communist and the first democratically elected government. Therefore this section is structured by policy areas rather than chronologically. The economic policy and reform measures launched by the three consecutive governments between 1987 and 1992 are listed in the Appendix.

The transition to a market economy has been a long process that was started by Communist reformers well before the democratization of the political system. The acceleration of the economic transition, however, was quickly followed by a briefer period of political change. The five-year period of 1987–1992 produced dramatic changes and reshaped the character of both the economic and political systems. In politics, the Communist regime was replaced by multiparty parliamentarism and party rivalry. In the economy, market-oriented reforms, structural changes, and changes in external economic relations were followed by recession, unemployment, and inflation.

The interaction between economic reforms and the political transition will be analyzed later. The focus in this section is on the purely economic factors that motivated the policy of economic adjustment. The transition to a market economy had an economic logic and motivation that could be highlighted or obscured by political factors. These economic problems forced the policy of economic adjustment to occur before the political changes. (The basic economic indicators are given in Table 3.2.)

This section first deals with these economic factors. The dramatic rise of indebtedness, the balance of payments disequilibrium, and the budget deficit played key roles, encouraging not only stabilization measures but also continuation of radical market-oriented reforms, including privatization and bankruptcy law. The structural adjustment policy and the collapse of the traditional export market (CMEA) produced a serious fall in output and the unknown phenomenon of mass unemployment, but by and large the social costs of the transition were moderate. The inherited socialist welfare system, the newly established unemployment schemes, and other sources of livelihood, including the broad shadow economy, contributed to the maintenance of social peace.

The Initial Motives for Change

The economic transition began in 1987, years before the political collapse of the Communist regime. The pressure on the two last Communist governments to continue or accelerate market-oriented reforms had three major sources:

1. the increasing pressure from the reform wing of the ruling party and from public opinion leaders (such as intellectuals and the press)

TABLE 3.2
Basic Economic Indicators for Hungary, 1980–1992

Year	Index of GDP[a] (previous year = 100)	Industrial growth[b] (previous year = 100)	Inflation[c] (previous year = 100)	Unemployment
1980	102.7	97.9	109.1	0.0
1981	102.9	102.8	104.6	0.0
1982	102.8	102.4	106.9	0.0
1983	100.7	100.8	107.3	0.0
1984	102.7	102.7	108.3	0.0
1985	99.7	100.7	107.0	0.0
1986	101.5	101.9	105.3	0.0
1987	104.1	103.8	108.6	0.0
1988	99.9	100.0	115.5	0.1
1989	100.4	99.0	117.0	0.5
1990	96.7	90.8	128.9	1.7
1991	92–93[d]	78.5	135.0	8.5
1992	95[e]	90.2	125.0	11.8

[a]In real terms.
[b]In constant prices.
[c]Consumer price index.
[d]September.
[e]Estimate.
Sources: GDP data are from Central Statistical Office, *Statisztikai Habi Közlemenyek*, nos. 2 and 3 (Budapest, 1992) and *Konjunktúrajelentés* (Kopint-Datorg), no. 3 (1990). Industrial production data are from *Konjunktúrajelentés*, no. 3 (1990), pp. 67–69, and no. 2 (1992), pp. 116–18. Inflation data for 1980–1990 are from Central Statistical Office, *Statisztikai Évkönyv, 1990* (Budapest, 1991); for 1991, G. Obláth, "Külföldi eladósodás és az adósságkezelés makrogazdasági problémái Magyarországon," *Műhelytanulmányok* (Kopint-Datorg), no. 8 (1992), p. 26.

2. the changes in the Soviet Union—that is, the Gorbachev phenomenon, which gave greater scope for maneuver

3. the failure of the 1985–1986 economic policy, the persistent economic stagnation, the debt crisis, and balance of payment problems

The policy of 1985–1986 had aimed to fuel the economy and create economic growth, but it failed, producing a rising budget deficit, a deteriorating trade account, a current account deficit, and a rise in foreign indebtedness. The handling of the debt required regular negotiations about new credits with the International Monetary Fund, and IMF pressure for the implementation of new reform measures in 1987–1988 was the most important external pressure at play.

The general slowdown of economic growth after the end of the 1970s had highlighted the structural problems of the Hungarian economy and also weakened the position of Kádár, who launched the economic policy of acceleration in 1985. After four decades in power, Kádár, the general secretary of the Socialist Workers' party, was gradually losing control. The most powerful challenger in the succession, the political hard-liner Károly Grósz, gained the premiership in the summer of 1987. He tried to portray himself as a liberal and an economic reformer (with significant success in the West) and launched a more restrictive economic policy coupled with economic reforms in the autumn of 1987. The program aimed to improve the external balance again and to stop the increase of foreign debt by 1990–1991 (Kardos and Vértes 1990:30).

Grósz succeeded Kádár as general secretary of the Socialist Workers' party in May 1988, but he had to pass the premiership to the soft-liner Miklós Németh, a young technocrat, in November 1988. Németh, who continued the economic policies and reform measures of Grósz, was politically more acceptable to the emerging opposition, and he remained prime minister during the 1989–1990 political transition. The serious indebtedness, the problems with the external balance of the economy, and the structural crisis of the economy narrowed the room for maneuver in economic policy.

The three major economic factors that increased the pressure for economic reform and stabilization measures were the second wave of indebtedness between 1985 and 1987 (see Table 3.3), the balance of payments deficit between 1985 and 1989, and the record budget deficit in 1985–1986. The accumulated budget deficit was F54 billion in the 1985–1986 period, and it increased further. In 1987 the deficit came to 3.9 percent of gross domestic product (GDP).

After a temporary current account surplus in 1983–1984, the balance of payments was also permanently in the red for the second half of the 1980s. In 1985 the current account deficit was almost US$850 million, and in 1986 it rose to US$1.5 billion (see Table 3.4). The main cause of the current account deficit was the sharp drop in the annual trade account surplus.

The policy of economic growth highlighted the structural backwardness of the Hungarian economy. The rise in exports was lower than the growth in imports that resulted from economic growth. The regular foreign trade surplus and the usually positive balance of the tourism account was not enough to counterbalance the large interest payments on the huge foreign debt. The current account was negative between 1985 and 1989. A stimulating new economic policy in 1985–1986 raised imports and put the trade account into the red in 1986 (see Table 3.4). The serious balance of payments problems were one of the main reasons for the economic reforms at the end of the 1980s.

The failure of the growth-oriented policy provided a further push toward economic reform. The drastic rise of the current account deficit in 1989 (by US$630 million from the previous year) was a direct consequence of a single administrative measure abolishing administrative limits on foreign travel. The monetary authorities softened the hard currency quotas in tourism, and the tourism account went from the regular US$150–350 million surplus to a

TABLE 3.3
Hungarian Indebtedness, 1973–1992

Year	Total external debt (billions of US$)	Total debt/GDP (%)	Total debt service (billions of US$)	Total debt service/exports[a] (%)
1973	2.12	n.a.	n.a.	n.a.
1980	11.45	51.6	n.a.	n.a.
1986	16.91	71	n.a.	75.1
1987	19.58	75	n.a.	55.3
1988	19.60	70	3.35	46.7
1989	20.39	70.6	3.96	38.5
1990	21.27	64.6	3.74	45.5
1991	22.7	73.0	3.72	31.5
1992[b]	23.5	83[c]	3.75	n.a.

n.a. = not available.
[a]Convertible exports, services included.
[b]November.
[c]Author's calculation.
Source: Data for total external debt are from G. Obláth, "Külföldi eladósodás és az adósságkezelés makrogazdasági problémái Magyarországon" *Mühelytanulmányok* (Kopint-Datorg), no. 8 (1992), p. 15; The Economist Intelligence Unit, *Country Profile, 1991–92: Hungary* (London, 1992), p. 37; Central Statistical Office, *Magyarország 1991* (Budapest, 1992), p. 27; and *Konjunktúrajelentés*, no. 3 (1991), p. 75. Data for debt service/exports are from Obláth, p. 27.

TABLE 3.4
Hungary's Balance of Payments, 1970–1992 (millions of US$)

Year	Trade account	Net interest payment	Current account	Capital account	Hard currency reserves
1970–75	−963	−548	−1312	n.a.	n.a.
1976	−176	−109	−363	n.a.	n.a.
1977	−359	−164	−753	n.a.	n.a.
1978	−782	−252	−1242	n.a.	n.a.
1979	−169	−366	−825	n.a.	n.a.
1980	276	−409	−368	n.a.	n.a.
1981	445	−1100	−727	n.a.	n.a.
1982	668	−1118	−299	194	n.a.
1983	772	−758	71	198	n.a.
1984	891	−815	67	1734	2064
1985	127	−833	−847	1603	2793
1986	−482	−963	−1495	1059	3053
1087	36	−987	−876	756	2159
1988	489	−1077	−807	555	1976
1989	537	−1387	−1437	1411	1725
1990	348	−1414	127	204	1166
1991	189	−1331	267	3070	4017
1992	300	−1330	530		4506

n.a. = not available.
Source: Hard currency reserve data for 1984–1987 are from *Konjunktúrajelentés*, no. 3 (1990), p. 67; for 1988–1991, Hungarian Central Bank, *Havi Jelentések*, no. 2 (1992), p. 46. Trade account and current account data for 1970–1981 are from G. Obláth, "Külföldi eladósodás és az adósság-kezelés makrogazdasági problémái Magyarországon," *Mühelytanulmányok*, no. 8 (1992), p. 12. Other figures are from G. Obláth and P. Márer, "A forint konvertibilitása" (Budapest: MTA Kozgazdaság Tudományi Intézet, 1992), p. 48.

US$349 million deficit in 1989. Subsequently, tourist exchange quotas were decreased to keep the tourist account in balance.

The external imbalances increased the indebtedness of the country. Gross foreign debt grew from US$11 to 20 billion (from 54 percent to 75 percent of GDP) between 1984 and 1987 and has not fallen since (see Table 3.3). The level of Hungarian external indebtedness is high even in a comparative perspective. Hungary's ratio of debt service to exports was between 30 and 45 percent in the 1989–1991 period (see Table 3.3). Most seriously indebted countries had similar or slightly lower debt service–export ratios in 1989: Brazil, 40.5 percent; Chile, 29.2 percent; Mexico, 35.1 percent; Nigeria, 27.8 percent; Philippines, 27.3 percent; and Venezuela, 28.3 percent (Obláth 1992:55). The exception was Argentina, at 92.8 percent.

Interest on debt is still a heavy burden on the Hungarian economy, and it usually exceeds the annual budget deficit. On average, the interest payment equals 20 percent of Hungarian exports and 9–11 percent of GDP.

The József Antall government, which was formed after the 1990 demo-cratic parliamentary elections, by and large continued the economic policy of the previous regime. This economic policy called for the following:

- maintenance of the international financial credibility of the country, through servicing the debt and avoiding its rescheduling at any price

- improvement in the balance of payments

- a restrictive monetary policy (high interest rates and decreased total credit)

- an anti-inflationary policy

- appreciation of the real exchange rate, to stimulate capital inflow

- direct benefits for foreign investors (such as tax allowances)

- further liberalization of imports (that is, removing effective protection for domestic producers)

The Antall government gave higher priority to macroeconomic equilibrium than to economic growth and employment. It did not have well-defined industrial and sectoral policies and only occasionally took steps to defend domestic producers and employment. But it presided over an acceleration of the economic transition including macroeconomic stabilization, capital in-flows, privatization, structural changes, and rising unemployment.

From 1990 onward the balance of payments figures have improved significantly, and the current account has shown a positive balance. The main source of the 1990–1992 current account surplus was the high level of unrequited transfers, mainly hard currency savings of the population that were put into banks as hard currency accounts became legal. In 1991 about half of the US$3.07 billion capital account surplus was foreign direct investment, while the other half was financial credit. The US$1.5 billion in foreign direct investment and the unrequited transfers produced the US$4 billion hard currency reserve in 1991. Both the rise of the unrequited transfers and the positive capital account reflected the confidence of the domestic and foreign public.

Liberalization and Deregulation

Economic adjustment policy began with deregulation of prices at the end of the 1970s, continued with liberalization of foreign trade and deregulation of banking at the end of the 1980s, and was completed with the lifting of wage regulations in 1992.

The liberalization of prices began with an early reduction of the massive state subsidies at the end of the 1970s. This process was resumed just a decade later. Government subsidies fell from 13.8 percent of GDP in 1989 to 8.5 percent in 1991 (see Table 3.5). In 1991 the F210.3 billion in total remaining price subsidies was divided among consumer goods (F40.2 billion), medicines (F39.4 billion), housing (F69.9 billion), and producer price supports (F60.8 billion), especially for agrarian prices.

Government control over prices—that is, strict price regulation—was also gradually eased. The Price Office was replaced by the Office of Competition. By 1989, 80 percent of prices were free of central control (Palócz 1992:3); by 1990–1991 90 percent were liberalized. By 1992 state subsidies were scheduled to fall below 5 percent of GDP.

TABLE 3.5
Price Subsidies in Hungary,
1988–1992 (nominal prices)

Year	Billions of F	% of GDP
1988	181.4	12.9
1989	235.4	13.8
1990	213.9	10.3
1991	210.3	8.5
1992	138.8[a]	4.4[a]

[a]Predicted.
Source: Ministry of Finance, *Állami költségvetés 1992*, Vol. 1 (Budapest, 1992), pp. 236, 262; Economist Intelligence Unit, *Hungary: Country Profile* (London, 1992).

Foreign trade (import) liberalization began in 1989. The share of liberalized items in imports was 42 percent by the end of 1989, 72 percent by the end of 1990, and above 90 percent by 1991 (*Konjunktúrajelentés* 1990:87; Palócz 1992:4). No deliberate tariff policy replaced the abolished import-license system.

This drastic import liberalization was possible because the previously powerful industrial lobbies had disintegrated during the political transition. The unlimited liberalization, however, also reflected the lack of a clear industrial policy. The fast and drastic abolition of protection for domestic producers—import competition spread to 90 percent of the market by 1990–1991—worsened the recession and pushed thousands of companies to the edge of bankruptcy (see Table 3.6).

Deregulation, however, did not include wages. Centralized wage control existed until 1988. Partial and indirect wage control was maintained after 1988 to avoid strong wage pressure on inflation. Progressive taxes were imposed on wage increases over the allowed scale, which was one of the important measures of the anti-inflation policy of the Hungarian governments until 1992. Because of these measures and the hardened budget constraints faced by producers, real wages fell by 3.1 percent in 1990 and 5.9 percent in 1991 (see Table 3.7). Since 1992 even indirect wage controls have been lifted, and wage limitations have come under the jurisdiction of voluntary tripartite corporatist wage agreements. Deregulation of the banking system began in 1987 with separation of the functions of the central bank and the commercial banks. The stock exchange was established in 1988. By 1992 commercial banks operated freely on the domestic money market. Trade liberalization and the encouragement of foreign investment in Hungary involved the softening of administrative regulations of the exchange of Hungarian currency. The Hungarian forint achieved partial convertibility: joint ventures can take their profits out of the country without any limit, and since imports have been liberalized, importers

TABLE 3.6
Applications for Liquidation and
Bankruptcy in Hungary, 1988–1992

Year	Liquidations	Bankruptcies
1988	144	0
1989	384	0
1990	630	0
1991	1,268	0
1992[a]	3,880	3,057

[a]January–May.
Source: *Konjunktúrajelentes*, no. 2 (1992), p. 119.

TABLE 3.7
Factors Influencing Inflation in Hungary, 1989–1991
(percentage)

Factor	1989	1990	1991
Supply side			
Subsidies for producers/GDP	5.4	3.9	2.4
Consumer price subsidies/GDP	2.6	1.8	1.7
Growth of gross real wages	2.5	−3.1	−5.9
Real effective exchange rate (1985 = 100)	83.7	85.2	100.4[a]
Demand side			
Net savings of money/total income	3.6	6.8	14.3
Export surplus/GDP	3.3	3.8	−1.0[b]
Investments/GDP	20.1	17.8	17.2[b]
Budget deficit/GDP	1.8	0.0	4.7[b]

[a]January–September.
[b]Preliminary figures.
Source: Å Valentinyi, "Stabilizáció és növekedés" (Budapest: Kopint-Datorg, 1992, unpublished manuscript), p. 8.

can buy foreign currency from the Hungarian central bank without any administrative permit system. For citizens, however, the forint is not convertible at all: each person is permitted to buy only a limited amount of foreign currency annually.

Stabilization

The Hungarian economic transition was not accompanied by hyperinflation. Inflation increased gradually, peaking at 35 percent in 1991. The main causes of inflation were the reduction of state subsidies for the state-owned producer sector and consumer goods, the liberalization of prices in general, the budget deficit, and the structural changes in the economy. In 1992 the rate of inflation began to fall. The macroeconomic balance between aggregate demand and supply was maintained.

What factors kept inflation moderate and brought it down in 1992?[2] On the supply side, the fall of real wages and the real appreciation of the currency decreased producers' costs and the prices of imports (see Table 3.7). Because subsidies had already been reduced to a minimum level, there was no further reduction of state subsidies in 1992 to give a further upward push to prices. Pressure fell on the demand side as well. Besides the general economic recession, other factors also reduced domestic demand: consumer demand fell because of the decline in real wages, the population had an increased propensity to save, investments in the productive sector dropped, and the trade deficit meant that there was an increasing supply of goods on the domestic market.

The growing budget deficit did not put pressure on aggregate demand, since there was a large surplus of resources in the banking sector and in the credit market. The main source of this surplus was the high level of savings of the population, which was inspired by high positive real interest rates.

Balance of payments   Stabilization measures were successful and produced external balance in 1990–1992. The moderate current account surplus of 1990–1991 was a great success during the period when Hungarian exports switched from the collapsed nonconvertible Eastern markets to the Western market. The external balances were further improved by the capital account. A massive capital inflow began in 1991; direct foreign investment rose from US$569 million in 1990 to US$2.1 billion in 1991. Hungary received foreign direct investment inflows of more than US$1.5 billion in 1991, which increased its hard currency reserves. The US$4 billion hard currency reserves were more than one-third of the annual imports (see Table 3.4).

The relatively moderate level of inflation and the rapid improvement in the balance of payments and in hard currency reserves suggest that the Hungarian stabilization problem differs substantially from the Latin American and Polish cases.

Exchange rate policy and the stabilization of the currency   The position of the Hungarian currency was stabilized in the 1987–1992 period. The official and the black market exchange rates grew so close together that by the autumn of 1991 the black market collapsed. The real appreciation policy was applied because the exchange rate was no different from the black market rate and because the capital inflow produced a demand pressure on the Hungarian forint.

The government applied a policy of continuous real appreciation of the currency between 1990 and 1992 to achieve various tasks: the policy helps to keep down inflation, and it increases competition on the domestic market by making imports cheaper. (It appears that in the first half of 1993 the central bank suspended the policy of real appreciation. Recent deterioration in the current account may explain this change in exchange rate policy.)

The contradictory trends of the domestic inflation rate and the real appreciation of the currency ruined the currency black market (the black market rate reached the official rate) and caused a shift in hard currency savings. As hard currency accounts became legal for Hungarian citizens, people began to buy hard currency and put it (and their former savings) into their bank accounts. In mid-1990 about 10 percent of the total savings of the population were in hard currency in spite of the high rate of interest being paid on forint accounts, and this figure rose to 20 percent by mid-1991

(Konjunktúrajelentés 1991:12). More recently, while total savings have continued to increase, the proportion held in hard currency has fallen.

Structural Adjustment

Besides the successful macroeconomic stabilization, the key question of the economic transition was the necessary structural adjustment. The 1987–1992 period witnessed radical structural changes in the Hungarian economy. The following review covers the changes in the enterprise structure, the size of the private sector, the structure of the export market, and the product structure of the economy.

The number of new firms   There was an extraordinary boom in the foundation of new enterprises. The number of firms nearly doubled in 1990 and again in 1991. The number of incorporated firms increased from 10,811 to 63,126 between 1988 and 1992 (see Table 3.8).

The structure of enterprises   The structure of enterprises has changed rapidly. The shifts in the size and number of firms show the radical structural changes in the Hungarian economy (see Table 3.9).

The private sector   There are no reliable sources for the size of the private sector. The Central Statistical Office made comprehensive measurements until 1987. According to its figures for 1984–1987, the share of the private sector in the production of GDP increased from 13.1 percent to 16.1 percent.

TABLE 3.8
Number of Economic Organizations in Hungary,
1988–1992

Year	Incorporated firms[a]	Nonincorporated firms	Self-employed people
1988	10,811	29,657	290,877
1989	15,235	44,062	320,619
1990	29,470	65,400	393,450
1991	52,756	52,136	500,000
1992	63,126[b]	64,471[b]	532,984[c]

[a]Corporations and limited companies.
[b]July.
[c]March.
Source: Central Statistical Office, *Havi Közleményei* (Budapest, January and July 1992); Central Statistical Office, *Gazdaságstatisztikai Évkönyv 1990* (Budapest, 1991), p. 11; *Üzlet*, June 9, 1992, p. 12; and *Figyelő*, September 3, 1992, p. 28.

TABLE 3.9
Size and Number of Corporations in Hungary,
1989–1992

Year	Number of employees (% of total firms)				Total number of firms
	<20	21–50	51–300	>300	
1989	37.6	17.6	25.5	19.3	13,568
1990	59.5	15.0	16.0	9.5	27,662
1991	70.6	12.7	11.4	5.3	45,637
1992	77.0	10.7	9.1	3.2	63,126

Note: Housing and garage cooperatives are excluded. Firms for which there are no data on the number of employees are excluded.
Source: Central Statistical Office, *Statisztikai Havi Közlemények* (Budapest, February–March and August 1992).

(The Central Statistical Office figures for the following years are not comprehensive and not comparable to those for the previous period.) During the unprecedented boom in private economic activity between 1987 and 1992, the private sector at least doubled. I estimate that about 30–35 percent of GDP may have been produced by the private sector in 1991–1992. If shadow economy output and the rapid loss of value of state-owned enterprises are taken into consideration, this level is even higher. Other estimates suggest that 40 percent of 1992 GDP was produced by the private sector ("Survey of Eastern Europe" 1993:10).

Bankruptcies and liquidations   In the socialist economic regime, one of the main barriers to structural change was the lack of effective selection in the economy. The budget constraint was so soft that there was no way to force insolvent and unprofitable firms into bankruptcy.

Unprofitable firms survived on substantial state subsidies in the state-owned sector until the end of the 1980s. There was little change even after the cuts in state subsidies to producers, since commercial banks had an interest in the survival of their main debtors. The collapse of the traditional markets of the large-scale enterprises in 1990–1991 shook the economic positions of these firms. The rapid increase in uncertain credits has forced the commercial banks to implement a more severe credit policy since mid-1991.

Another indicator of the soft budget constraint was the "queuing problem"—that is, an involuntary commercial credit given by the seller firm to the insolvent purchasing firm. The unpaid commercial transactions were estimated at F200 billion, or more than 5 percent of GDP. During 1991–1992 the Antall government implemented a series of tough measures to harden the budget constraint in the economy; firms were pressured to pay their bills to the Revenue Office, the Custom Office, and the Social Security Fund. The new bankruptcy law that has been in effect since the beginning of 1992 brought an unprecedented wave of bankruptcy (and liquidation) and caused more pain for many firms than any other measure (see Table 3.6).

Foreign trade   As early as 1987 the share of hard currency exports already surpassed 50 percent of total exports. The collapse of the CMEA and the Soviet Union forced Hungarian producers to switch more exports to the hard currency markets. Nonconvertible exports fell dramatically to 36.3 percent of total exports in 1989, 25.6 percent in 1990, and 5.0 percent in 1991. In spite of this loss of market, the value of exports in forints grew by 30.4 percent in 1991, a small fall in real terms (*Economic Trends in Eastern Europe* 1992:61). The surplus of the trade account, however, fell.

The Fiscal Trap: Budget Problems

The new Hungarian regime inherited a redistributive state from the Communist period. More than 60 percent of GDP was redistributed by the public sector, and there has been no change in this respect since the parliamentary government was formed in 1990 (see Table 3.10).

A reduction of this comparatively high redistribution is not likely in the

TABLE 3.10
General Government Operations in Hungary,
1981–1992 (percentage of GDP)

Year	Revenues	Expenditures	Deficit/surplus
1981	61.0	63.9	−3.2
1982	59.1	61.2	−2.1
1983	60.9	62.0	−1.1
1984	60.8	59.4	+1.4
1985	60.0	61.2	−1.1
1986	63.2	66.0	−2.9
1987	60.3	64.1	−3.9
1988	63.7	63.6	0.0
1989	61.3	63.7	−2.5
1990	61.5	61.5	0.0
1991	62.2	66.4	−4.2
1992[a]	60.1	62.3	−2.2
1992[b]	62–64	68–70	−7–8.0

[a]Figures originally expected by the government.
[b]Central Bank estimates.
Source: J. Kornai, "A posztszocialista átmenet és az állam. Gondolatok a fiskális problémáról," *Közgazdasági Szemle* (June 1992), p. 495.

short or medium term.[3] The 1991 and 1992 data show a sharp increase in the budget deficit, which was expected to exceed 8 percent of GDP in 1992. The government faces a fiscal trap because of the inflexible expenditures and shrinking revenues of the public sector.

The reduction of the effective economic intervention of the state—that is, public sector expenditures—has been a political slogan since the mid-1980s. The main goal of the reform economists was to reduce government financing of loss-making firms and industries. The more technocratic economic administrations reduced state subsidies for enterprises from 21 to 16 percent of GDP between 1985 and 1989 (Kornai 1992:497). The policy of severely reducing subsidies involved the government subsidies for production, housing, and consumer prices (see Table 3.5). This policy was continued by the Antall government in 1990–1991. By 1991 subsidies for producers fell to 4.0 percent, while the consumer price subvention fell to 2.3 percent of GDP (Gyulavári 1992). Further reduction was scheduled in the 1992 budget, which aimed to reduce all subsidies below 4.4 percent of GDP.

The reduction of price subsidies could not counterbalance the rising welfare expenditures. The largest item of public sector spending comes in the form of social security transfers. The extension of social rights (such as pensions and maternity benefits) in the late 1960s and the 1970s by the Kádár regime produced an explosion in welfare expenditures in the 1980s. Pensions, for example, grew from 3.8 percent to 10.1 percent of GDP between 1970 and 1990 (Tóth 1992:22).

According to analyses of Hungary's 1991 public finances, the general government social security transfers came to 57 percent of total public sector expenditures and 37 percent of GDP. The latter figure makes Hungary look like a well-developed welfare state. International comparison shows that Hungary has a higher proportion of welfare expenditure as a share of GDP than low-income countries of the Organization for Economic Cooperation and Development (OECD) like Spain or Greece. Figures for OECD countries show social service expenditures rising from 16.2 to 19.9 percent of GDP between 1985 and 1990 (Kornai 1992:507). Welfare rights were much greater than the development of the Hungarian economy could sustain.

The Communist welfare state—that is, a state budget with a high proportion of welfare services—has become the norm for the public. In periods of stagnation and recession, while personal wages and consumption decreased in real terms, public consumption was constant or increased. Financing this inherited welfare state is one of the major policy difficulties of the economic transition.

Revenues have not been able to keep up with rising spending. The tax base of the state is shrinking, owing to privatization and the long-lasting recession. The heavy tax burden keeps alive a massive shadow economy, which is estimated to produce 15–30 percent of GDP, since high taxes discourage the legalization of shadow economy businesses. In 1990 direct taxes (based on income and wages) and social security contributions came to 36.9 percent of GDP, which is the second highest proportion when compared with nineteen OECD countries.[4] The tax-raising capacity of the state is not strong enough to keep this high level of taxation, and the emerging private sector (as well as the surviving state-owned enterprises) resists paying this heavy burden. From 1990 to 1991 the government could raise its tax revenue by only 12 percent (in nominal terms), instead of the scheduled 20 percent, far below the price index (Mizsei 1993). In addition, the outstanding debt of the Social Security Fund was over F60 billion at the beginning of 1992. The widening gap between public sector expenditures and revenues has caused a rising budget deficit and a fiscal crisis in the Social Security Fund.

While economic stabilization and market reforms have been successful, and privatization is also in progress, the extremely high level of public expenditures seems to be frozen. The political costs of diminishing the public sector appear to be higher than politicians in the opposition or in the government are willing to pay. The contracting economy and growing unemployment increased the burden on the budget and enforced the maintenance of resource centralization. The economic consequence was overtaxation, which extended the recession and was the most serious constraint on domestic capital accumulation, at least in the formal sector of the economy.

As noted earlier, however, the budget deficit itself has not produced immediate problems. Since the financial market was relatively well developed and there was a resource surplus on the capital market, the increasing budget deficit was financed easily in 1991 and 1992 by borrowing from the public. Because of the high consumer savings and low investments, the increasing public borrowing has not so far crowded out investments in the private sector directly. Public debt, however, is piling up rapidly and crowding out may occur.

Privatization

Hungary's socialist regime ran an almost completely state-owned economy. Some 85–90 percent of the economy belonged to the state-owned or to the quasi-state-owned cooperative sector. In 1989 there were two thousand state-owned enterprises. In 1989–1990 there was a consensus on the necessity for privatization, but views diverged on its methods and speed and on what other preferences should be taken into consideration during the process. Private ownership, which was until then merely tolerated, became desirable and a basis for expansion. In the final years of the old regime a series of economic policy measures were passed that encouraged the development of private firms. The breakthrough was the 1989 Company Act, which ended the ideological and administrative differentiation among economic organizations under various types of ownership, permitting their equal treatment and setting free channels of capital collection (Gem 1993:6). Limitations on private entrepreneurship were lifted.

"Spontaneous" privatization began in 1988, under the technocratic Németh government. The managers of a state-owned enterprise could sell parts of the firm as if they were the owners, because the 1985 decentralization of the public sector had cut direct links between the central economic administration and the enterprises in the state-owned sector, shifting the formal property rights to the Enterprise Councils, which were falling under the control of the managers. The 1987 Corporation Act made it possible for state-owned enterprises to transform themselves into corporations or public limited companies, which was a precondition of the transactions. In 1990 the Antall government established the State Property Agency (SPA) to control the spontaneous privatization and to start central privatization programs.

In 1990–1991 the SPA had F30 billion in income from the sales, and in 1992 it expected F50 billion (Urbán 1992b). By spring 1992 about 20 percent of the state assets (based on book value) had been transformed into private companies. State-owned enterprises were transformed into corporations, and about 10 percent of state-owned property was privatized (that is, was under majority private control). Although savings were high, intermediaries, which could transform savings into capital investment, were lacking. Therefore, about 85 percent of the property privatized by the SPA was sold to foreign investors.

The notion of privatization itself is widely debated in Hungary. The lack of a consensus over the meaning of the expression is probably one of the reasons why there is no big-bang plan, no single model. A variety of methods and channels are used in the Hungarian privatization process. The sale of state assets is, however, far from being the most important channel for the "destruction" of the massive state-owned enterprise sector.

In the following review I will try to estimate the current and future distribution of the wealth of the state sector and its two thousand enterprises according to channels of transformation into different types of private and public ownership.[5] The distribution described below and summarized in Table 3.11 is more or less determined by the 1990–1991 legislation of the Hungarian Parliament and by economic trends, and it is based on book value.

First, four hundred insolvent and bankrupt state-owned enterprises with a book value of F350 billion were liquidated. The liquidation of bankrupt state-owned firms is a form of denationalization: it means a destruction of a significant part of the state-owned sector, which decreases the proportion of the public sector in the economy.

Second, the size of the future state sector was estimated to be about one hundred enterprises (worth F500 billion), which would be preserved in the long run as state-owned firms by the contemporary government. (In the meantime the government published a list of 219 companies in which it

TABLE 3.11
Predicted Distribution of the State-owned Sector in
Hungary

Channel of distribution	Number of firms	Book value (billions of forints)
Liquidation	400	350
Preserved state sector	100	500
Local government I	400	250
Local government II		30
Social Security Fund		300
Employees Program	1,100	90
Compensation acts		70
Invisible privatization		n.a.
For sale		410
Total	2,000	2,000
Costs and guarantees of the privatization		90
Net income from sales		320

n.a. = not available.
Source: L. Urbán, "A tulajdonviszonyok alakitása, a privatizáció makro-és mikro-tényezöi" (Eötvös University of Budapest, 1992, unpublished manuscript).

expected to maintain partial state ownership, in most cases between 25 and 50 percent of the shares of the given firms.)

Third, the local government property program "decentralized" about four hundred state-owned enterprises (10 percent of the total value) without compensation. Any future privatization of this property depends on the local governments.

Fourth, local governments also own a share in the state-owned enterprises. Their share is estimated to be 5 percent of the value of these enterprises, that is, an additional F30 billion, which should be added to the estimate of public property controlled by the local governments.

Fifth, property worth F300 billion is to be given to the Social Security Fund without compensation, to stabilize its finances.

Sixth, the employee shareholder program provides for sale of an average 10–15 percent of shares in the state-owned enterprises, with a maximum 50 percent price reduction, to the enterprises' own employees.

Seventh, as a consequence of the Compensation Act, about F70 billion of state property will be distributed freely to the victims of property confiscation and other violations of law committed by former political regimes between 1939 and 1987.

Eighth, invisible privatization occurs through the passing of property from state-owned enterprises to new private or "mixed" companies by various financial manipulations. This is one of the main channels of the birth of the domestic bourgeoisie from the group of managers of state enterprises. The value of the invisible privatizations is estimated by some experts to be as high as the value of property officially sold under the auspices of the State Property Agency.

Ninth, the sale of firms (or shares) to domestic or foreign investors accounts for about 15 percent of the book value of the former state-owned corporate sector.

Privatization in the narrow sense of sale to private investors, therefore, forms only a minor part of the overall process of denationalization. Other channels, like the decentralization of state property to local governments or passing property to public bodies like the Social Security Fund, are privatization only in the legal, not the sociological or economic, sense. The firms are then controlled neither by the government nor by private investors; they belong to the "grey zone" of the mixed economy, where the concerns of owners or controllers can be very different from the attempt to maximize profits.

In addition to the privatization of the state sector, there is a parallel, and in some areas of the economy an even more important, process: the emergence of new private firms, which increases the share of the private sector in the economy. Sometimes, through mixed companies, this process is connected with the privatization of the state sector. The invisible privatizations also speeded up the enrichment of the new private sector.

The Recession

The changes in economic policy and the collapse of the traditional export markets forced the Hungarian economy into a painful adjustment process. While Hungarian firms have to compete with liberalized imports on the domestic market, Hungarian exports to the European Community (EC) have to face not only high competition but import quotas and administrative barriers as well.

The years 1991–1992 witnessed a deep recession. While in 1990 GDP fell by 3.3 percent, in 1991 it fell by 7–8 percent. The contraction of industrial production was even more serious. In 1990 it declined by 9.2 percent, in 1991 by 21.5 percent, and in 1992 by 9.8 percent (see Table 3.2). The contraction of the economy, however, is not a simple recession, but also involves structural changes.

The Social Costs of the Transition

Besides the recession, the social costs of the economic transition were high in the following spheres: moderate inflation appeared, real wages fell, factory closures increased, unemployment reached 13 percent, and the budget deficit increased.

Economic success in other spheres, however, averted social tension: inflation was halted, real incomes did not fall in 1989–1991, the gap in income differentials widened but not dramatically (see Table 3.12), and finally the substantial shadow economy ensured additional nontaxed income (Kolosi and Róbert 1991:23). The relatively mild overall social costs of the economic transition are an important factor in explaining the social peace and political stability that characterized the 1990–1992 period.

The Main Economic Dilemmas

The major dilemmas of economic policy have been gradually changing. In 1989–1990 the main challenge of the economic transition was to decide between gradualism and shock therapy. The victory of the moderate right at the 1990 elections produced the maintenance of a gradualist version of transition in most spheres of the economy (such as privatization, budget reform, social security, and convertibility of the currency), but rapid changes were implemented in some spheres (such as employment policy and price and trade liberalization). In other areas, like the collapse of Eastern Bloc trade or the emergence of previously unknown unemployment, spontaneous economic processes shocked the economy and forced an adjustment.

In 1990–1991 the method of privatization became one of the key issues. By 1992 the disputes concerning economic policy took on a new dimension: Should Hungary continue a restrictive economic policy or should it stimulate economic growth? Policy makers feared that economic growth would lead to increased imports, which might fuel inflation and produce a current account deficit.

At the same time, they feared a long-lasting recession, which would

TABLE 3.12
Income Differentials in Hungary, 1982–1991

Year	Difference between top and bottom deciles	Difference between second and ninth deciles
1982	5.1	2.7
1982[a]	4.2	2.2
1987[a]	4.7	2.4
1989	5.03	2.53
1991	6.01	3.04

[a]Central Statistical Office figures (others are TÁRKI figures).
Source: T. Kolosi and P. Róbert, "A rendszerváltás társadalmi hatásai" *Gyorsjelentesek* 5 (Budapest: TÁRKI, 1991), p. 24.

deepen the budget deficit, increase unemployment to an unbearable level, and ruin domestic industry. In particular, the continuous overvaluation of the forint through the exchange rate policy, the lack of tariff protection for domestic producers, and the high interest rates have attracted increasing criticism. Economists and politicians are much more concerned about the rate of unemployment than before.

Evaluation

The Antall government gave priority to macroeconomic balance and the reduction of inflation over economic growth and employment. In some instances the government had specific preferences (like the method and principles of privatization), while in most other areas a libertarian attitude of noninterference has prevailed. The government did not adopt, for example, effective antimonopoly measures or an industrial policy.

The Antall government followed an economic policy designed to further the economic transition. It continued liberalization and privatization, increased the independence of the Hungarian central bank,[6] began an antiinflationary monetary and exchange rate policy, and created competition on the domestic market through its exchange rate policy (real appreciation of the forint). In various areas, such as import liberalization and exchange rate and tariff policies, the government strategy seems to be contributing to the deepening recession of the economy.

In an evaluation of Hungary's economic transition and economic system, the main question is whether after the 1987–1992 transition period Hungary has yet become a market economy. In fact, the main features of the market system of contemporary mixed economies did arise during the 1987–1992 period. In general the following conditions exist in Hungary:

- There is a liberalized market (import liberalization).

- Prices are determined by the market and not by the state.

- The government does not subsidize producers (subsidies were reduced to 4–6 percent of GDP).

- By 1991–1992 budget constraints were hardened for economic units (commercial banks introduced tough credit conditions, and a wave of bankruptcies and liquidation began).

- The prices of resources orient and motivate the business decisions of economic actors.

- The establishment of market institutions is in progress (including corporations, commercial banks, a stock exchange, a security market, a tax system, and bankruptcy laws). In some areas, however, such as business law, conditions are still seriously backward.

- Formally, Hungary still has a nonconvertible currency, though significant progress has been achieved in this respect, and the monetary regulations have achieved the functions of convertibility for trade and investment (Obláth and Márer 1992).

There are two major areas in which Hungary appears to be far from achieving the condition of the Western mixed economies. First, although the share of the private sector is increasing fast, the state-owned sector is still dominant and much higher than in the Western countries. The experiences of the Western countries and the postsocialist Eastern European countries show that privatization is not a short-term process. The economic activity of state-owned enterprises, however, is not under the direct control of any government agency (except the State Property Agency, which has a role in privatization). Second, government spending and public transfers have a massive role in the economy (about 65 percent of GDP), imposing a large burden on the competitive sector and keeping an enormous shadow economy alive. The slow pace of change in these two areas creates serious structural barriers to the government's economic objectives.

The State of Political Transition, 1988–1992

The Character of the Transition

The Hungarian political transition can be characterized by three main traits. First, the transition was the gradual result of an ongoing development, not a single dramatic event, a "revolution," or a political crisis. The political transition began in 1987, when the first opposition movement was established, and multiparty elections were held in March 1990.

Second, the political transition had an elite character. Democratization was the consequence not of a revolution or street riots, but of a long and delicate political struggle among small groups of politicians. Both the Communist party leadership and the opposition were divided. The four main actors were the hard-liners and the reformers of the Communist party on one side and the moderate and radical opposition on the other (Körösényi 1992a). Since Hungarian society had no bourgeoisie under the Communist regime and only a weakly organized working class, various groups of value-oriented intellectuals became the major actors in the changes. The reform Communist intelligentsia backed Imre Pozsgay and Rezsö Nyers's soft-line wing within the Communist party. The populist intelligentsia of cultural life organized the

Hungarian Democratic Forum (MDF), the moderate opposition movement, in 1987–1988 and remained its core group later on. The urban intellectuals dominated the radical opposition dissident movement and the Alliance of Free Democrats (SZDSZ) from its 1988 foundation. Professionals and other middle-class groups joined the battle later, during the winter of 1989–1990, when democratization already seemed irreversible. Workers and peasants, however, were not involved.

Third, the lack of mass participation characterized the transition process not only at the pressure group level, but also at the electoral level. The turnout at the first free elections was lower than expected and lower than in most established Western European democracies (see Table 3.13).

The low turnout was the political-psychological consequence of the lack of mass participation and popular involvement in the transition process. The political mobilization of the newly enfranchised millions was less successful in Hungary than in countries where the transition was engineered by mass movements and popular participation. In those countries the electoral turnout was also much higher: Czechoslovakia, 95 percent; Bulgaria, 91 percent (74 percent in the second round); and East Germany, 90 percent (Körösényi 1993).

These three factors—the gradualism of the transition, its elite character, and the lack of mass mobilization—became political factors in the stability of the new regime.

TABLE 3.13
Electoral Turnout in Hungary, 1989–1990
(percentage)

Date	Type of election	Turnout
Hungary		
November 1989	Referendum I	58
March 1990	Parliamentary elections	65
April 1990	Parliamentary elections runoff	45
July 1990	Referendum II	14
September 1990	Local elections	40
October 1990	Local elections runoff	29
1989–1990	Average	42
Western Europe 1985–1989	Average	79

Source: Western European figures are from J. E. Lane and O. S. Ersson, *Politics and Society in Western Europe* (London: Sage, 1991), p. 182; Eastern European figures are from A. Böhm and G. Szoboszlai, eds., *Önkormányzati választások 1990* (Budapest: MTA Politikai Tudományok Intézete, 1992), p. 272; S. Kurtán, P. Sándor, and L. Vass, eds., *Magyarország politikai évkönyve* (Budapest: Ökonómia Alapítvány-Economix Rt., 1992), p. 80; G. Vajda, "Választók és választottak," *Valóság* 3 (1991), pp. 12–14.

The Constitutional Setting of the New Regime

The political struggle over the Constitution and the form of democratic government began well before the 1990 parliamentary elections.

Two series of amendments to the Constitution (in October 1989 and in May–July 1990) created the Constitution of the new democratic regime (Bozóki 1992). The result was a parliamentary form of government with a chancellor system, in which executive power is centralized in the hands of the prime minister. The position of the prime minister is strengthened in relation to both his cabinet and the Parliament by the following rules. First, the members of the cabinet are responsible not to the Parliament, but to the prime minister.[7] Second, the position of the prime minister is stabilized by the constructive vote of nonconfidence; in other words, it is not possible to dismiss him without electing his successor by the same vote.[8]

On the other hand, strong constitutional constraints were established to curtail the power of the legislative majority. These constraints included the establishment of the Constitutional Court with extraordinary powers and the minority veto on constitutional amendments. Other legislation called the "two-thirds laws" limited the power of the government and its parliamentary coalition and gave unusual power to the parliamentary opposition in order to motivate the parties to reach a consensus in specific legislative areas. Under these laws, the approval of two-thirds of the members of Parliament is required to pass any bill in about thirty-five legislative areas, such as electoral laws, laws on the military and national security, and laws on local self-government.

In accordance with the chancellor system, the president of the republic was given little more than symbolic power, which was further curtailed by the decisions of the Constitutional Court in 1991–1992. However, President Árpád Göncz, a member of the Alliance of Free Democrats (SZDSZ) emerged as a political figure who challenged the executive power of the government in some areas.

By and large, the constitutional engineering was successful, and the new arrangement was a major factor in political stability in 1990–1991. Some weaknesses of the constitutional setting, however, have become clear in the meantime. According to Arend Lijphart's typology, Hungarian democracy has been much closer to a "consensus" than to a "majoritarian" democracy. Political power has been widely distributed among various political actors and not given to a single (majority) party, as in, for example, the Westminster model. The features of the Hungarian power structure in this respect are the following:

- There is a written constitution and a Constitutional Court with wide jurisdiction and strong power over the legislature.

- The legislature has extraordinary powers in relation to the government or the ruling majority through the system of two-thirds laws, which is un-known in Western European parliamentary systems.

• Executive power is also shared. First, there is a coalition government; that is, three parties share executive power. Second, in some areas, the president emerged as a power to counterbalance the prime minister or the government.

• Although Hungary is not a federal or decentralized state, local governments have substantial autonomy. Most are controlled by parties that are in the opposition in Parliament (the liberals and the socialists).

The two-thirds laws have often produced legislative deadlock instead of the intended consensus. For example, a political conflict between the prime minister and the president led to a minor constitutional crisis in 1992. The unusual features of the constitutional system may prove to be a handicap and a source of political polarization in the medium term. The consensus model of democracy may turn out to be ineffective.

Political Parties and the Party System

The political parties have been major actors in the democratic transition. It is widely held, with some justification, that the character of the party system may have as important an effect on the mechanism of the political system as the constitutional and legal-institutional setting.

The pluralization of the party scene began in 1987, when the first opposition movement appeared. By the 1989 round-table negotiations a dozen political parties were sitting on the opposition side. In 1990 fifty-four parties put up candidates, but only six parties gained seats in the first multiparty Parliament. The sharp reduction in the number of parties was due to deliberate constitutional engineering—that is, to the new electoral system. Out of 386 mandates, 176 were contested in single-member constituencies. The other 210 seats were distributed among political parties by proportional representation. The rules of the nomination process excluded from the proportional representation contest parties that could not put up candidates in most regions of the country by collecting the required number of signatures for each constituency. Twelve parties were able to qualify for the proportional representation contest, but only half of these beat the 4 percent threshold in the elections (Körösényi 1992b).

In this way the election produced a moderately fragmented Parliament with six parliamentary parties. Three form the coalition government (the Hungarian Democratic Forum, or MDF; the Smallholder party, or FKGP; and the Christian Democratic People's party, or KDNP), and the other three are in

TABLE 3.14
Distribution of Seats in the Hungarian Parliament,
May 1990

Party	Seats	Percentage
Hungarian Democratic Forum (MDF)	164	42.49
Alliance of Free Democrats (SZDSZ)	92	23.83
Smallholder party (FKGP)	44	11.40
Hungarian Socialist party (MSZP)	33	8.55
Federation of Young Democrats (FIDESZ)	22	5.70
Christian Democratic People's party (KDNP)	21	5.44
Others	8	2.57
Total	386	100.00

Source: A. Körösényi, "The Hungarian Parlimentary Elections, 1990," in A. Bozóki, A. Körösényi, and G. Schöpflin, eds., *Post-Communist Transition: Emerging Pluralism in Hungary* (London: Pinter and New York: St Martin's, 1992), p. 79.

opposition (the Alliance of Free Democrats, or SZDSZ; the Federation of Young Democrats, or FIDESZ; and the Hungarian Socialist party, or MSZP). The composition of the Parliament is given in Table 3.14.

The composition of the Parliament has changed little in the first three years after the elections. As of mid-1993, five out of the six parliamentary parties were able to maintain their unity: the number of defections from parliamentary groups was below 10 percent of the total number of members of Parliament (MPs).[9] Parliamentary groups have shown a high level of party discipline in their voting behavior. The government is backed almost by the same legislative coalition and, in spite of the defection of some MPs, has proved stable. In 1992 the national political scene was dominated by the same six parliamentary parties that reached the Parliament in 1990. No new challengers have emerged outside of the Parliament.[10]

The government is an oversized coalition formed by a group of parties to the right of center.[11] The solid majority (230–156 in May 1990) and the high level of voting discipline in the coalition parties, together with constitutional factors like the constructive vote of no-confidence and the lack of parliamentary responsibility of the cabinet, produced a strong government position in relation to the opposition (and allowed the executive to dominate the legislature), except in the legislative areas of the two-thirds laws, where the opposition has the power of veto. However, the coalition character of the government, as well as the existence of factions within the parties, sometimes made action difficult for the government and produced a behind-the-scenes bargaining process to push through some bills, especially the annual budget.

The first two years after parliamentary elections produced a relatively stable party system in Hungary, which in turn contributed to the stabilization of the democratic regime. In 1992 the centrifugal elements of party rivalry became stronger and political polarization among parties increased, but so far without significant mass mobilization. Polarization in Hungarian party politics does not necessarily mean polarization at the electoral level, because of the following factors: (1) Hungarian society is relatively homogeneous and (2) the voters are moderates, and their political preferences are close to the center of the political spectrum. These factors may decrease the effect of the centrifugal party competition.

Government Policy

The aim of the 1988–1990 Németh government, the last government in the one-party system, was to differentiate itself from the Communist party and to portray itself as reformist. In fact, it introduced firm measures to create a market economy through both its economic policy and its institutional reforms.

Comparing the post-Communist Antall government to the last Communist Németh government, analysts often conclude that the Németh regime was more efficient and more committed to market reforms. Although by and large the Antall government has continued the economic policy of its predecessors, in fact it has often been slower and more hesitant, owing to its lack of experience in office, the partial disintegration of the central state administration, and the high turnover in the civil service in 1990 (the peak year of the change in regime). As a democratic government, it also has political account-ability, unlike its predecessors, and therefore it does not have a purely technocratic character. Moreover, as a coalition government, it is not a unified actor in the political sense. The logic of political compromise among the parties of the coalition often triumphs over a technocratic attitude, as in the case of the Restitution Law. (The Restitution Law aimed to give compensation to those whose property was nationalized by the Communist regime. Restitu-tion also became a channel of privatization.)

The government has had a broad program and a general commitment to market reforms and stabilization policy, but it has not had a clear guiding concept. Its activity can be characterized as the ad hoc handling, or administer-ing, of problems that have arisen, rather than the taking of actions determined by a prewritten scenario. This approach has been due partly to the gradualist attitude of the Democratic Forum and Christian Democrat politicians and partly to the professional background of the prime minister. Antall is a historian, with more interest and skill in parliamentary government and foreign policy than in economics. There was no single outstanding figure, no "man of vision," among the economists of the coalition who might have designed and carried out a clear strategy.[12]

Government policy, therefore, is mostly the consequence of the political composition of the ruling coalition. The coalition of the Democratic Forum, the Smallholder party, and the Christian Democratic People's party is a broad group of centrist, conservative, Christian democratic, and populist forces, predominantly moderate but with radical elements as well. Prime Minister Antall stabilized the position of his government by establishing an oversized coalition, adding the Christian Democrats as a third party to the Democratic Forum–Smallholder party coalition, which was the minimum needed to win.

Government policy is independent from the direct influence of the parliamentary parties and the constituency rank and file to a great extent, because of the constitutional setting of the chancellor system and party discipline in parliamentary voting. The coalition character of the government, however, has strongly influenced government policy in the distribution and redistribution games, as I will discuss later.

Interest Groups and Organizations

Under the Communist regime interest groups were under the political control of the Communist party. By 1990–1992, however, the former system of economic interest organizations had declined or disintegrated. The 1987–1990 political transition undermined the special position and the organizational monopoly of the Communist trade union association, the National Council of Unions (SZOT). It had to face (1) falling membership, (2) a leadership and organizational crisis, (3) a serious legitimacy crisis, and (4) the challenge of new independent unions. The first independent union, the Democratic Union of Research Workers (TDDSZ), was founded during the winter of 1987–1988, and others followed its example.

One consequence of the disintegration of the Communist regime and the political transition was the continuous fall in union membership. The old unions lost more than 40 percent of their members between 1986 and 1992, and the new unions were not able to absorb such numbers (Thoma 1992:7). While in 1986 90 percent of all workers were union members, by 1990 this proportion had dropped to 85 percent and by 1991 to 78 percent (see Table 3.15), according to union sources. Other sources estimate a dramatic fall of union membership from the previous 76 percent to 37 percent of the adult population by September 1991.[13]

In terms of origin, three categories of unions are now active. First, there is the revitalized association of seventy-three ex-Communist unions, the National Association of Hungarian Unions (MSZOSZ). Between 1990 and 1991 its membership fell from 67 to 55 percent of total union membership, but it still had a majority of the unionized work force in 1991. Although formal links were cut, the MSZOSZ remained a close ally of the Hungarian Socialist party. Second, there are the old unions that did not join the MSZOSZ. These unions organized three new associations, the Association of Unions of Professionals (ÉSZT), the Cooperative Forum of Unions (SZEF), and the Autonómok. One-third of total union membership belongs to these associations. The third group consists of the new unions that have been established since 1987. They formed three

TABLE 3.15

Membership in Unions in Hungary, 1986–1991 (thousands of members)

Union	1986	End of 1990	September 1991
Democratic League of Independent Unions	—	130	250
Workers Councils	—	106	45[a]
Solidarity Workers Association	—	75	150
Autonomous unions	—	374	350[b]
Association of Unions of Professionals (ÉSZT)	—	63	90
Cooperative Forum of Unions (SZEF)	—	557	750
National Association of Hungarian Unions (MSZOSZ)[c]	4,400	2,682	2,000
Total	4,400	3,988	3,635
Union members as a % of the active work force	90	85	78

Dash indicates not applicable.
[a]Number of members who pay membership fees.
[b]Beginning of 1991.
[c]Out of the 2 million MSZOSZ members in September 1991, 1.1 million declared that their membership fee can be regularly or automatically deducted from their wages.
Sources: Union membership figures reported by the unions (*HVG*, September 14, 1991, p. 6); the number in the active work force on January 1, 1992, was 4,668,700; Central Statistical Office, *Magyarország 1991* (Budapest, 1992), p. 7.

associations: the Democratic League of Independent Unions (or the League), the Workers Councils, and Solidarity Workers Association (or Solidarity). The League was formed by white-collar unions, some of which were originally founded by Budapest intellectuals who did not or could not make a political career in one of the new parties. Through strong personal overlaps and connections, the League has become a close ally of the left-liberal Alliance of Free Democrats. The establishment of some of the Workers Councils was a spontaneous movement, while others came into being with the support of the Hungarian Democratic Forum. Veterans of the 1956 revolution and socialist intellectuals also held some influence and positions in 1989–1990 within the movement, but the Democratic Forum retained the strongest influence over the National Association of Workers Councils. The Workers Councils have built up their organizations first of all in industries in recession, and most of its members have been unskilled or semiskilled workers. Solidarity was built up by a grass-roots blue-collar union movement and has remained independent from party political influence. Solidarity has since declined and become the weakest association within the third category.

The challenge from the new unions turned out to be less serious than expected. The old unions that make up the MSZOSZ were able to keep 50–75 percent of their former membership.[14] How were old unions able to maintain this proportion of their members? Three factors may explain this unexpected phenomenon. First, the workers have been generally nonparticipatory and passive. Second, the unions own and distribute selective (inherited) incentives, like access to holiday, recreation, and other welfare facilities.[15] Third, the new need for the defense of workers' interests during the privatizations and dismissals of the economic transition may have increased the legitimacy of the old unions.

Trade union power   Trade union power can be evaluated by membership, popular appeal (legitimacy), and bargaining power in industrial conflicts. In terms of membership, the Hungarian unions are powerful. Hungary's trade union organizational density is about as high as that of most Western European countries, though the membership ratio has been rapidly declining (see Table 3.16).

Even though the ex-Communist MSZOSZ is the strongest in terms of membership, it has a serious legitimacy deficit. Public opinion surveys show that of the major public institutions, trade unions rank low. On a scale of 1 to 100, unions were given an average of 39 points, compared with 79 for the president, 73 for the courts, 68 for the Constitutional Court, 67 for the press (including television and radio), 66 for the army, 64 for the police, 61 for both local government and the churches, and 57 for both the Parliament and the

TABLE 3.16
Union Membership around
the World, 1975 (% of the
active work force)

Austria	59
Belgium	66
Denmark	67
Finland	75
France	25
Germany	33
Italy	47
Netherlands	40
Norway	61
Sweden	82
United Kingdom	51
Hungary	
1986	90
1990	85
1991	37–78[a]

[a]Estimates.
Source: Data for Western Europe are from J. E. Lane and O. S. Ersson, *Politics and Society in Western Europe* (London: Sage, 1991), p. 347. Data for Hungary are from Table 3.16 and a Mareco Kft. Survey.

government. Political parties, however, were rated below the unions, with 37 points on the scale (Lázár et al. 1992:597). In addition, the relatively low figures for the unions are not a specifically Hungarian phenomenon. Comparative surveys found similar results for the unions during the 1980s elsewhere.

Open and organized industrial conflicts were unknown under the Communist regime. The first strike, the August 1988 coal miners' strike, happened as the old one-party regime began to disintegrate. The illegal character of strikes was abolished when the Parliament passed the Strike Law in 1989. The number of strikes, however, remained low. The *HVG*, a Hungarian economic weekly, listed eighteen strikes in the ten-month period between January and October 1991, most of them local conflicts at the workshop or enterprise level. The Central Statistical Office, however, did not register any strike action at all.

The most serious conflict, which paralyzed the whole country for four days in autumn 1990, was not a union action. It was a spontaneous and illegal action of the well-organized taxi and transport workers (most of whom are self-employed), who were infuriated by a drastic rise in the price of gasoline. The paralyzing effects and the efficiency of the transporters' action was a sharp contrast with the weakness of the trade union actions; it also highlighted the weakness of the state.

No clear conclusion could be drawn from the mixed result of these industrial conflicts. Some local or sectional union actions were successful, but most of the actions of the trade union associations proved much less effective. The bargaining power of the unions seems to be much weaker than its organizational strength and membership figures would suggest. They were not able to halt the fall in the real wages. Real wages fell by 5.1 percent in 1990 and by a further 5.8 percent in 1991 (Mizsei 1993).

The second half of 1992 witnessed changes in union and interest representation. The hostility between old ex-Communist and new independent or democratic unions was eased by a pact in August. They agreed on the distribution of the inherited property of the ex-Communist union association. The MSZOSZ and the other old unions sacrificed about half of their property in exchange for winning legitimacy in the view of the new democratic unions and an alliance with them against the government. After two years of success, the government strategy of divide and conquer finally failed. The success of the Hungarian Socialist party at a series of by-elections also strengthened the legitimacy of the MSZOSZ, whose alliance with the socialists has become open. The Railway Unions organized a successful warning strike and unions in other industries threatened strikes during their negotiations at the Interest Conciliation Council (ÉT), which is the bargaining forum for the unions, the employers, and the government. In November the government had to submit to the united union demands on various issues, which increased further the deficit in the planned 1993 budget. By the end of 1992 the unions had become an important factor in the distribution game.

Employers' associations   Producers also had centralized interest organizations under the Communist regime. State-owned enterprises, cooperatives, and artisans had their own single-interest associations, which often had compulsory membership and an organizational monopoly.

The Hungarian Economic Chamber (MGK) was the official organization of the state-owned enterprises under the Communist regime. It is still the biggest business interest organization in Hungary, representing 7,500 mainly state-owned enterprises. The emerging private sector produced two rival interest organizations. The National Association of Entrepreneurs (VOSZ) was founded in 1988 and represents small- and medium-scale private enterprises. The 6,000 member firms of the VOSZ have about 500,000 employees. According to VOSZ reports it represents 70 percent of the Hungarian private sector, which is obviously an overestimate. The National Association of Hungarian Industrialists (MGYOSZ) was founded in 1990. It has 100 members, mainly the largest Hungarian private firms such as Müszertechnika Rt., Controll Rt., and Mikrosystem Rt., but state-owned firms that began privatization are also members of the MGYOSZ (Kurtán, Sándor, and Vass 1992:711–12).

By and large these interest associations are in the initial stages of organizing and are still weak. They have no direct or institutional influence on the economic policy of the government.

Interest organizations and parties   At the time of the 1990 parliamentary elections and afterward, another main characteristic of Hungarian politics was the lack of organized economic interest groups behind the political parties. The year 1991, however, witnessed some new developments. Links have developed between parties and organized interest groups. Business and employers' associations have become more powerful and influential than they were at the time of the 1990 election. They are represented in the Hungarian Democratic Forum (even in the party leadership and the parliamentary faction), so that the Democratic Forum has the best chance to become the party of business interests.

Despite being the target of the antiunion legislation of all the nonsocialist parties, the ex-Communist unions (MSZOSZ) strengthened their legitimacy and began to rebuild their links with the Hungarian Socialist party.[16] This process may increase the potential for the revival of the Socialist party as a social democratic party. If the Socialist party can escape from its current marginal position and become a major party on the left, its moves may restructure the political landscape and push the left-liberal Alliance of Free Democrats and Federation of Young Democrats into center positions. The left-liberal Alliance of Free Democrats has built up close relations with the new largely white-collar unions' association, the Democratic League of Independent Unions. The Smallholder party, as the party of the farmers and rural Hungary, has built up a strong relationship with the Farmers Association.

There are wide overlaps between party and interest organizations at both the leadership and membership level.

The Politics of Transition

In the previous sections I examined the state of the economic and political transition. In this section I would like to consider and characterize the main strategies of the institutional and social actors in the process (Nelson et al. 1989). I will also try to explain why the previously all-powerful social-political group, the nomenklatura, accepted—and even took part in—the transition process.

The Analytical Framework

Two types of actors will be differentiated in the following analyses. The first set comprises institutional actors: political parties, the government, the opposition, unions, associations of businesspeople and the self-employed, and foreign and international institutions. In the previous section I concluded that the first years of the Hungarian transition were characterized by the weakness of the organized interests (such as unions and business associations). Therefore the main institutional actors of the game were the political parties and the government.

The second group of actors is made up of the major social groups: the old nomenklatura elite, the intelligentsia, the middle class, the civil service, managers, peasants, blue-collar workers, and the growing underclass.

Both the attitudes and the strategies of the major institutional and social actors have an influence on the process. Specific interactions and alliances among these actors may support or undermine economic and political stabilization.

In the following analysis of the political-economic transition two different types of games are considered. I will call the first one the distribution game, referring to the distribution of property formerly owned by the state. Since there is a broad consensus about one of the major tasks of the economic transition, the denationalization of the large public sector, the disputes are mainly about the methods of the process. These disputes concern how to distribute the state property of the economy, who may have a share, and who is to be excluded. Denationalization is a short- or medium-term process and therefore belongs especially to the period of economic transition. There is a single pie, the public sector of the economy, which can be distributed only once and then disappears. Those who would like to take their share must do so soon. This distribution game is peculiar to the economic transition from a socialist to a capitalist economy.

The second game is the redistribution game. A feature of all modern economies, this game is the long-term process of redistributing income and other resources through state measures such as taxation, social transfers, and economic policy. While the distribution game is a temporary game specific to the transition, the redistribution game is a permanent game. In the following sections I will focus on the strategies of the main institutional and social actors in these games.

The Social Actors of the Game: Winners and Losers

The economic and political transition involved not only legal and institutional reforms, but also changes in relations between key interest groups, parties, and the state. It might be expected that the transition to a capitalist market economy and a democratic regime would produce high social mobility and reshape the social structure and power relations among the various social groups. In fact, some groups declined, others advanced, and still others kept or transferred their position, but the overall changes have not been dramatic so far.

The outright winners in the transition were the new political class and the new business elite. The new political class was recruited first of all from the intelligentsia, but also from professional groups and the non-Communist middle class. Academics from the social sciences and the humanities, writers, lawyers, journalists, and economists composed the key groups of the new political class, especially at the beginning of the transition. Intellectuals in the dissident movement or critical public opinion leaders moved their "cultural capital" across into politics successfully. Because of their exposure in the mass media, they are more influential than their positions in the Parliament or in the political parties might indicate. Culture and politics, especially mass media and politics, are closely knitted together.

The new business elite was recruited from the more flexible managers of state-owned firms, from self-made men in the private sector (or in the shadow economy), and from the proliferating financial sector. The privatization of the large state-owned sector made political links and political patronage an important economic resource as well.

The losers of the transition were the employees of the public sector, like the low- and medium-level civil servants, teachers, blue-collar workers of industries in recession, employees of the noncompetitive part of the public sector, pensioners, and the underclass (unskilled workers and gypsies). As income differences among Hungarians increase, these people are sliding down the economic ladder. The growing number of unemployed have also come from these groups.

Some key groups of the former regime totally disintegrated, while others lost influence and power. Most of the former elite groups, however, were able to preserve their positions or transform them in some way. The creation of a new middle class is a medium- or long-term process, and it is still unclear how successful that process will be. The contemporary social elite has its origin in the elite groups of the former political-economic regime. The old economic and cultural elite groups (and the top and medium level of the political nomenklatura) were able to transform their previous positions into business or political positions (Urbán 1991:303–9). The former economic and political nomenklatura elite, who had "convertible" professional skills, turned toward emerging opportunities in business. The administrative elite within the civil service also kept their positions (or slipped into the more prosperous business sector). There were no radical changes even on the highest ministerial levels. When the first Antall government was appointed, there were no changes in half of the eighty to ninety state secretary positions. At the local level much of the old political, administrative, and economic elites saved their positions. For example, 50–70 percent of village mayors—the local political bosses—who stood as candidates were reelected in October 1990. Most of the directors of state-owned companies, formally run by enterprise councils, were also reelected in the autumn of 1990.

The ability of the nomenklatura elite to convert their status during the political-economic transition was due to the fact that they had a technocratic rather than an ideological outlook. They made up a professional stratum, much more educated than the first generation of Communist activists recruited from badly educated peasants and blue-collar workers. By the 1980s the nomenklatura elite had become a well-educated, open-minded, Western-oriented technocratic elite, with convertible professional skills (see Table 3.17). Membership in the Communist party no longer represented an ideological alignment, but an entrance ticket into a political or professional career.

TABLE 3.17
Qualifications and Skills of the Socialist Workers' Party Elite and Top State Bureaucracy, 1981 and 1989 (percentage)

| | Party cadres | | State bureaucrats | |
Qualification or skills	1981	1989	1981	1989
University or college degree	44.2	57.1 (79.3)	77.5	92.8
Doctorate/Ph.D.	8.1	12.5 (26.7)	33.7	45.4
Knowledge of foreign language	15.4	19.2 (50.6)	53.7	69.4
Professional experience	22.3	27.8 (44.3)	39.4	55.5
"Convertible" skills	17.6	28.5 (48.9)	49.6	71.4

Note: Figures for the central party apparatus are in parentheses.
Source: L. R. Tőkés, "Hungary's New Political Elites: Adaptation and Change, 1989–1990," in G. Szoboszlai, *Democracy and Political Transformation: Theories and East-Central European Realities* (Budapest: Hungarian Political Science Association, 1991), p. 278–80.

The new nomenklatura elite has had some interest particularly in the marketization of the economy, if not the democratization of the political regime. They had two kind of resources—professional skills and a wide social and administrative network—that they could transform into business positions.

The Government's Strategy

The methods for carrying out the economic transition are influenced by the general political attitudes and interests of the center-right coalition. Economic policy is always social policy as well and therefore has distributional consequences (Przeworski 1991). These may strengthen or weaken the electoral chances of a given political coalition in office (or in opposition). Besides the permanent income redistribution involved in economic policy, large-scale privatization involves property redistribution as well. Therefore privatization became one of the most sensitive political issues.

The government's strategy was to a great extent determined by the fact that it was a coalition government. A coalition game always requires a wider distribution of political and other resources among the parties of the government. Its coalition character explains the government strategy especially in the distribution game (for example, compensation for churches), but to some extent in the redistribution game as well (for example, high tax relief for peasants and self-employed agrarian producers).

Government strategy in the distribution game   The extension of the political base of the coalition at the constituency level was one of the political aims of the government. The government had a double social and political task: to create a new middle and entrepreneurial class and to make a tacit pact with the old nomenklatura elite (with the technocrats, managers, and civil servants, but not with the former political elite).[17]

One of the ways in which government policy could establish a new middle class and widen the constituency base of the coalition parties was in its compensation policy. That is, it could compensate citizens whose property had been confiscated; victims (or their heirs) of breaches of law (for example, deportation, internment, and execution by the Communists or Nazis); and the established churches, which had suffered heavily from the nationalization of private property. The aim of the Property Compensation Act of 1991 was to give compensation to the historical middle class and peasantry of the pre-Communist period for property that had been confiscated by the Communist regime. About 1 million people reported claims under the act. Hundreds of thousands of Hungarians may benefit from the three kinds of compensation laws, which might help to stabilize and widen the constituency of the coalition parties.

Compensation is also connected to privatization. In its privatization policy the government again aimed to benefit not a single social group but a wider circle of potential winners. The various channels of privatization spread the benefits as widely as possible:

- Compensation was designed to contribute to the foundation of a domestic bourgeoisie (but there was no exclusive preference for the historic middle class, as shown by the low scale of compensation).

- Decentralized privatization and invisible privatization aimed at letting the old managerial-technocratic elite transform their positions in state-owned enterprises into business positions in the emerging capitalist economy.

- Sales were made to foreign investors.

- Sales were made to domestic investors, offering special credit schemes that may multiply the assets of the emerging domestic bourgeoisie.

- Employee shareholder programs included the medium and lower managers and blue-collar workers among the beneficiaries.

- The recentralization of the public sector and the centralized version of privatization offer channels for the parties in office to create their own clientele in the economy. The role of the government or government agencies in privatization may give room for building political linkage and patronage for the coalition parties. The opposition parties, which control most local governments, have similar opportunities at the local level, since local governments have substantial property even in the productive sector. Each party has begun to create its own patronage system.

Regarding the short-term interaction between economic and political transition, my conclusion is that the spread of the benefits in the distribution game can increase political stability. Ineffective execution, however, may cause a boomerang effect and frustrate people who are entitled to the distributed benefits.

Government strategy in the redistribution game   During the transition organized interests have been weak. The weakness of the unions, in particular, made possible a liberal economic policy. No wage-push inflation occurred, and the stabilization (or anti-inflationary policy) was therefore successful. The government attempted to deepen the division between old and new unions using political and legislative measures. It was successful for two years. Beginning in August 1992, however, old and new unions formed an alliance and together became a stronger actor in the bargaining process.

The weakness of business associations is clear from the following facts: there was a heavy and increasing overall tax burden (and social security contribution) on business,[18] the forint continued to appreciate in real terms, and import liberalization and tariff policies did not offer any effective protection to domestic producers. By and large the government was not under strong pressure from organized economic interest groups, which made it easier to follow a restrictive economic policy.

This economic policy, however, has not affected the high level of state income redistribution. The cause of the huge redistribution (two-thirds of GDP) is not the pressure from organized interests, but rather the inheritance of the high welfare expenditures. (Some minor institutional reforms were taken to make possible future reductions.[19]) With the economic recession and the fall of GDP, the share of public expenditures in GDP increased even further. While revenues declined, expenditures have remained "stickier." In addition, new demands have appeared and placed a heavy burden on the welfare system. The new Unemployment Benefit Fund was expected to redistribute about F100 billion in 1992. The inherited welfare system produced the paradox that since the end of the 1970s, while real wages declined, "social incomes" and consumption increased until 1989 (Central Statistical Office 1991:14). Adopting the label of "social market economy," the Antall government continued this policy of high expenditures, which helped to prevent the rapid increase of income differences (see Table 3.12) during a period when the market forces spread through the whole economy and society.

In the redistribution game the government had two goals. First, it wished to keep free from the demands of organized pressure groups. Second, it aimed to adapt the welfare system to the new situation to keep social peace. It was successful at achieving its first goal for two years, until the autumn of 1992. Its success at the second goal, the maintenance of the high welfare expenditures, however, presents a major structural barrier to the reform of the public sector and the reduction of the high level of redistribution.

The Opposition's Strategy

The government faced opposition from four groups: the Alliance of Free Democrats, the socialists, the radical nationalists (both inside and outside the coalition), and the unions.

The largest opposition party, the Free Democrats, wished to pass the state-owned sector to foreign investors and to the incumbent manager-nomenklatura stratum, which it saw as the most appropriate potential property owners. This proposal had an economic rationale, but it also aimed to maintain the position of two old elite groups: the nomenklatura and the intelligentsia, for the fastest version of property transformation would defend the old technocrat nomenklatura manager strata and create career opportunities for the "comprador intelligentsia," the domestic representatives (staff, agents, and experts) of foreign investors.

The position of the socialists was similar to that of the Free Democrats, with two qualifications. First, they placed much less emphasis on foreign investors. Second, their left-wingers maintained a vague idea of "true" workers' ownership (or workers' self-management), while the more pragmatic socialists proposed the wider introduction of workers' shareholder schemes. The position of the Hungarian Socialist party was a consequence of the fact that the two major social groups behind the party were the "Communist" middle class nomenklakura elite and left-wing intellectuals but not blue-collar workers.

The radical right has become an opponent of the government strategy from within the coalition itself. Their program called for radical elite change— in other words, a purge of the "Communist" nomenklatura elite and the creation of a new (or a recreation of the old) national middle class. They represent former pre-Communist property owners and other frustrated for- mer middle-class groups. With their strong national appeal, their influence increased but remained limited.

Threats to Democratic Consolidation

The key issue of the transition is the compatibility of the economic and political aspects: whether market reforms are compatible with the democra- tization of the political regime. The dissatisfaction of the masses with the high costs of the transition may be one threat to democratic stability or the marketization and liberalization of the economy. The threat of mass move- ments against the regime has not yet appeared in Hungary.

There are, however, already political ideologies that have the potential to destabilize Hungarian politics. Elements of them existed before, but they grew stronger and more influential in the period between autumn 1992 and spring 1993. Each challenges the legitimacy of other actors in the political game or the parliamentary system as a whole. Each regards the transition as if it were not finished and aims to establish a "real" or "true" democracy. Each offers a mobilization strategy to achieve its aims.

The four ideologies are (1) ultranationalism, or the radical right; (2) left liberalism, or the antifascist "people's front"; (3) trade unionist left-wing economic populism; and (4) the new plebeian radicalism of the ex- Communists.

Ultranationalism   The ultranationalists regard the 1989–1990 transition as an unfinished revolution. The MDF program for a moderate elite change was only partly achieved. The radical ultranationalist wing of the Democratic Forum, represented by Istrán Csurka's paper, the weekly *Magyar Fórum*, has become frustrated and demands a radical change in the current elite—for example, purges in the state administration, the state-owned economic sector, and the state-owned and -controlled television and radio. They condemn the mass media and accuse them of being hostile to national values and to the coalition in office. Their scapegoats are the Communist nomenklatura, the new liberals, and the Jewish members of the cultural, business, and political elite. They condemn the "cosmopolitan" liberal-Bolshevik alliance which preserved key positions in the mass media and the state administration. The radical right rejects the tacit pact between the nomenklatura and the pragmatic-conservative Democratic Forum–led coalition government.

The smoothness and peacefulness of the transition—that is, the preservation of the social and economic positions of the old elite—radicalized the ultranationalists. When the coalition in office accused the public television and radio of being sympathetic to the opposition parties and tried to make changes in the leadership of these public institutions, the president vetoed the move, infuriating the radical right and increasing political polarization. The ultra-nationalists have become an intraparty opposition, an opposition of the government from the right. Their first mass mobilization was a demonstration in September 1992 of ten to twenty thousand people in which they demanded the resignations of the presidents of state-owned television and radio.

The economic views of the populist right also differ from the government policy. They support a "third-road" populism, which rejects international capitalism and the market. They demand a more "national" administration and the defense of the national interest in the economy. They criticize the role of the international financial organizations (the International Monetary Fund and the World Bank) in Hungarian economic policy and the sale of Hungarian enterprises to foreign investors. A group of Democratic Forum MPs formed the Monopoly Group, which scrutinizes the privatization process and calls attention to controversial cases in which they believe the national interest is violated.

The social base of the radical right has been the ideology-oriented intellectuals of the party, local Democratic Forum militants, and those who suffered under the Communist regime; some are from the Christian middle class and the landed peasants of the pre-1948 period. Veterans of World War II and the 1956 revolution also support some of their demands.

Another, more agrarian, radical right that exists within the Smallholder party withdrew from the coalition at the beginning of 1992.

Left liberalism   The left liberals began a mass mobilization against the radical right under an umbrella organization called Democratic Charter. Their scapegoats are not only the extreme right, but the whole conservative, Christian democratic right and the entire coalition in office. The focus of their criticism falls on issues like anti-Semitism, church schools, national identity, value conservatism, and centralism in the state administration.

The left liberals support a radical democratic concept of the state in which the executive would not have any significant authority or autonomous role. The legislature, the president, the Constitutional Council, and local governments would dominate the national executive.

Given their ex-Marxist ideological background and their political interest as members of the opposition, their aim is to discredit the conservative government as antidemocratic and anti-Semitic.

Their strongholds are the Alliance of Free Democrats, the Hungarian Socialist party, the left-liberal press, influential members of the Budapest intelligentsia, former reformist Communist intellectuals and former dissidents, professional journalists and other public opinion leaders, members of the Jewish intelligentsia, and the middle class.

Unionist populism As mentioned earlier, unions have become more active since the second half of 1992. The new union strategy has increased the pressure on the government through united actions and the threat of mobilization.

Ex-Communist radicalism The ex-Communist politicians, political analysts, and intellectuals concentrate their critique on the elite character of the transition and on the alleged unrepresentative character of the parliamentary regime. According to their analysis, the parliamentary parties (especially the new parties) are "divorced from the masses," especially from the working class, and do not represent major social groups. Therefore these parties are not legitimate. The ex-Communists' emphasis is on the weakness of the civil society and organized interests, and they regard the ex-Communist trade unions and the alliance between the Hungarian Socialist party and the National Association of Hungarian Unions (MSZOSZ) as the "true" representatives of the workers.

For them, as for some of the liberal radicals, civil society is not made up of voluntary associations between individuals and the state but is an organized movement in relation to the state. Pure representative democracy is not legitimate without the elements of corporatism and direct participation. This kind of argument justified the action of the Association of People Living under the Poverty Line (LAÉT), which called for the dissolution of the current Parliament by a referendum. According to their view, the members of Parliament work only for their parties and not for the people's interest. The LAÉT action followed the hunger strike of dozens of their members against the government's scheduled reform of the value-added tax (VAT). The petition for the referendum was signed by more than one hundred thousand people, most of them unemployed, poor, and on pensions—in other words, the main losers of the economic transition. All parliamentary parties criticized their action, except the Hungarian Socialist party. But the Constitutional Court declared the dissolution of the Parliament by referendum unconstitutional.

Conclusions

One of the preconditions of successful liberal economic reforms is either the neutralization of trade unions or a pact with them. Since the Hungarian interest organizations were weak, suffering from internal problems and a lack of either power or legitimacy, the Hungarian government chose the former strategy. This policy was successful until August 1992. The government combined the division of the interest organizations with the methods of channeling demands (through the Interest Conciliation Council). Since the formation of the union alliance in August 1992, the government now emphasizes the latter policy.

Government and opposition strategies were rather different. The government strategy in the distribution game was to create a wider domestic middle class beside the inherited nomenklatura elite. In the redistribution game it aimed to weaken trade unions and other economic pressure groups but at the same time to maintain welfare redistribution as a means of creating a paternalistic state in a "social market economy." The strategy of the parliamentary opposition was to preserve the benefits of the distribution game for the nomenklatura elite (the incumbent managers), while in the redistribution game it aimed to preserve the welfare state through a strong corporatist-union structure.

The government strategy aimed to create a stronger state and a wider middle class but weaker institutional actors against the state. The opposition strategy aimed to weaken the state and strengthen the institutional actors against it. The government philosophy searched for the social base of a stable democracy (and for the authority of the state); the opposition searched for institutional safeguards (on the constitutional and corporative levels) against the state. Some radical groups of the opposition went even further. They challenged the legitimacy of the political system and with their polarization/ mobilization strategy threatened the consolidation of democracy.

Links between Economic Transformation and Democratic Consolidation: Summary and Some Hypotheses

In general, Hungary's economic and political situation was relatively stable during the transition, especially during the first two years after the 1990 parliamentary elections. The political transition has been successful, while the economic transition is still in progress. The economic reforms of the former regime made it easier for the new government to handle the transition.

The Links between Economic and Political Transition

There was no direct relationship between the economic and political transitions. First, in 1987–1988 the economic transition began without any political change. The political liberalization of 1989–1990 was motivated mainly by political goals but was also perceived as necessary to effect further economic reforms. The 1990 systemic change in politics, however, stabilized the economic reform measures taken before and deepened the changes. The character of economic transition under the new democratic regime (methods, speed, and preferences) was shaped very much by political factors, such as the political composition of the government and the influence of the former nomenklatura.

The Inherited Economic Background of Democratic Stabilization

It is usually assumed that in the long run (1) a market economy is necessary for a stable democracy and (2) economic efficiency is necessary for regime stability. The short- and medium-term compatibility of democratization of the political regime and marketization of the economic system as simultaneous processes was the focus of this chapter. Market reforms made by the pre-1989 Communist regime produced favorable conditions for the 1989–1992 simultaneous transition process. In addition, the relative competitiveness of the Hungarian economy makes it possible to increase exports to the West (convertible currency market) and to survive the recession resulting from the collapse of the CMEA/Eastern Bloc market. Inflation was successfully kept under control. The balance of payments has improved rapidly. The inflow of foreign capital was relatively high (US$2 billion in 1991 and again in 1992). Foreign currency reserves have been raised from US$0.8 billion to over US$4.0 billion in the last two years. The social security system and other social services, which were built up during the 1960s and 1970s, softened the deterioration of the living standard of the masses of unemployed people during the economic transition.

The Character of the Transition

One of the main reasons for the gradualist character of the economic and political transition was the fact that the nomenklatura—the elite groups of the old regime—were able to save their positions and power or transform them within the new economic and political establishment. Another reason for the gradualist transition was the elite character of the changes, that is, the low level of participation of the masses and the demobilization policy of the main political actors (Bruszt 1992). There was a tacit consensus over the nonpoliticization of the society among the main political actors. Radical political groups that openly challenge this consensus, however, have been gaining more influence since the autumn of 1992. The depoliticizing tradition of the Kádár regime also had an effect on the character of the transition. The demobilization of the masses might be an essential factor for the stability of the democratic regime, since the unemployment rate increased from 1 percent to 12 percent between 1989 and 1992. Low mass participation means an elitist rather than popular democracy, but it decreases the direct pressure on the new government and contributes to political stability.

The Initial Stability of the Constitutional and Political Setting

The gradualist, "negotiated" character of the political transition in 1989–1990, and especially the political stability of the 1990–1992 period, improved Hungary's image abroad. International political recognition made it possible for Hungary to become an affiliated member of the European Community. Coupled with relatively well-developed market institutions, political stability produced enough business confidence in Hungary to encourage significant capital inflow into the country. Without this capital inflow, it might have been hard to preserve the external balances.

Political stability, however, cannot be taken for granted. Party rivalry and political polarization have created some centrifugal forces, leading to minor political and constitutional crises (note the conflict between the president and the prime minister). In spite of the appearance of some political efforts at mass mobilization, however, these conflicts have been limited to the level of elite and party politics.

The Weakness of Interest Organizations

One characteristic of post-Communist politics in Hungary is that social groups have not been well organized. While the party system seems to be stable, since there has been no serious extraparliamentary challenger so far, unions and other interest organizations have low organizational capacity. The potential for social protest has also been relatively low. Business interests have had no direct influence on government policy either. Ex-Communist trade unions, struggling for legitimacy, have attempted to organize industrial action against liberalization and closures, but the number of industrial conflicts has been low. The slow process of institutionalization of interest groups might be enough to channel social unrest.

Informal economic lobbies, like formal interest organizations, were not strong actors in the 1989–1992 period. Because of the political transition, the managers of the state sector have lost their former political influence. Three new, informal interest groups, however, may take on this role in the long run, although their effect is still occasional. They are the following: (1) foreign investors, especially multinational firms, which sometimes gain special state protection in return for their investment in Hungary (for example, General Motors and Suzuki), creating an exception to overall trade liberalization; (2) beneficiaries of the emerging patronage system in the public sector, which push to slow privatization, since political patronage of the central and local governments depends on the preservation of the public sector; and (3) a coalition of private businesspeople and politicians at both the national and the local level.

Initially during the democratic transition there was a broad consensus among political parties on the necessary economic measures, and there was no populist political force on the party level. Therefore party rivalry did not involve strong economic demands from political parties. In 1992 the liberal and the socialist opposition still showed considerable responsibility in this respect, although economic populism, fused with political radicalism, appeared on both the left and right.

The Role of Popular Expectations

The population's general expectations concerning democracy and capitalism were positive. The existing value system and public attitudes favor market reforms because of cultural traditions and the earlier economic reforms of the socialist regime, which had produced a wide semimarket system in several sectors of the economy (partly in the shadow economy). The majority of the population took part in the semimarket or shadow economy. In spite of right- and left-wing radicalism, neither antimarket nor anti-Western attitudes appeared as a mass phenomenon, and the privatization of firms was not challenged by hostility from employees.

The notion of democracy was associated with economic progress and welfare for the people on the street (the model is Western Europe), thereby increasing material expectations. These high expectations make it difficult to cut the "overdeveloped" welfare state and deepen the problem of the budget deficit.

In the long run material progress can stabilize democracy. In the short run, however, the pressure on the new democratic government—which faces expectations that are hardly possible to meet—may weaken its legitimacy and destabilize the democratic regime. The lack of high popular participation lowered the level of direct and immediate demands on and expectations of the new democratic regime and government. Nevertheless it suffers from a deficit in legitimacy. Although there were no challenges to the Parliament for two years, trust in the new Parliament and other institutions of the democratic regime, especially the political parties, has been declining. The more than one hundred thousand signatures for the dissolution of the current Parliament and for a new election, collected by the Association of People Living under the Poverty Line, reflect this feeling.

Government Strategy

The main channel of political integration in the government strategy was to spread benefits in the distributive game. Initially the government prevented the establishment of a corporatist structure in income redistribution and reduced real wages, but to keep social peace it maintained the inherited welfare system. The demobilizational strategy proved to be successful for two years, but it was challenged by political groups from both sides of the political fence after the autumn of 1992. The interest bargaining process was given legal status (through the Interest Conciliation Council), which was activated when social tension or union demands were intensified.

The Welfare State and the Budget Deficit

The most serious handicap facing the transition is the inherited role of the public sector. The high level of redistribution is a structural barrier to further changes in the relationship between the public and private sectors. However, reducing the absolute level of public redistribution does not seem to be feasible for political reasons. The budget deficit may be a long-lasting structural problem during the recession period, until economic growth widens the tax base and decreases the relative share of redistribution.

Nonetheless there was a boom in the private sector, since three other channels were open for its development: (1) the shadow economy; (2) the inflow of foreign capital; and (3) the purchase of public firms much below their value by domestic entrepreneurs through the privatization process.

The Capacity of the State

For my purposes I will consider the capacity of the state in three respects: (1) to maintain public order if social or political tension threatens it; (2) to ensure the resources for public finances, that is, to collect taxes; and (3) to set up and enforce reasonable rules for economic activity (including business laws and jurisdictions and administrative and legal procedures).

Without making a comprehensive review of these fields, my assumption is that by and large the Hungarian state administration and civil service did not disintegrate during the political transition. It worked continuously, but there were and are serious constraints on the capacity of the state in all the three areas. Some signs of disintegration and weakness of loyalty appeared in the state administration and the police in the initial period of the democratic government, which was clear in the case of the autumn 1990 taxi strike. The weakness of the state is also reflected in its insufficient capacity to collect taxes. The capacity of the state administration seems to be limited to preserving and developing competition in the market, as the ineffective nonintervention activity of the Competition Office showed.

There is a general antistate attitude and a lack of confidence in the authorities, which can be partly explained by the traditionally weak political integration of the masses under most twentieth-century (democratic or parliamentary) regimes in Eastern Europe, and partly by the fall in legitimacy of the state during the Communist regime. These traditions and the low level of popular participation in the 1989–1990 democratic transition may represent a handicap for the democratic government in the medium run. However, since social groups were not well organized and the direct pressure on the government was weak, it gave room even for the relatively weak government and weak state to push forward the economic and political transition.

Economic Constraints and Transitional Costs

High external debt diminishes the available internal resources in a period when transitional costs and the economic recession might also threaten political stability. The shadow economy has been further expanding. It has stabilizing effects as an additional revenue source for the people, but it does not produce revenue for the overburdened government budget. The broad shadow economy therefore raises taxation problems and highlights the limited capacity of the state in imposing and collecting taxes.

The social costs of the economic transition have been the following: (1) a slightly increased gap between the higher and lower income groups and spreading impoverishment at the bottom of the income redistribution, owing to structural changes; (2) inflation; (3) growing unemployment; and (4) recession and falling living standards. The costs have weakened the legitimacy of the democratic regime and may produce social conflicts among social groups and between interest groups and the state in the future. So far, however, disappointment has mainly increased political apathy and has not yet produced social unrest.

The social costs of economic transition render difficult, but not impossible, the stabilization of the democratic political system. (Fragmented signs of dissatisfaction are likely, but not riots.) How can Hungary overcome or survive the difficulties? How can it survive the high transition costs?

- It can improve the relative competitiveness of the economy.

- It can allow for individual strategies to overcome material difficulties (for example, the role of the shadow economy can help in this regard).

- It can aim for a less dramatic gap in income differentials (see Table 3.12).
- It can maintain the demobilization strategy.
- It can institutionalize interest bargaining to the extent necessary to avoid mobilization.

Political Constraints

The increasing costs of the transition may deepen the gap between the record of the new government and the expectations of the public. High transitional costs affect political parties as well and may increase political polarization in the future. The political cycle (the approach of elections) may motivate the government to bring the recession to an end. Increasing public expenditures, protectionism, and the devaluation of the Hungarian currency might be used by the government as measures to stimulate the economy in the short and medium run.

The ideological map within the political elite is rather colorful, running from extreme nationalism to economic populism (an anti-Western "third-road" ideology), even within the parties of the coalition government. (Economic populism does not seem to be very influential, since 85 percent of the property privatized through the SPA has been bought by foreign investors.) Etatism and paternalism, as general attitudes, are more influential among the political elite and among the people on the street as well. Orthodox liberalism, on the other hand, also characterizes government policy; for example, the government has pursued trade liberalization without an adequate tariff policy and industrial policy, perhaps causing potentially viable firms to collapse. The liberal opposition, which represents the mainstream approach of the reform economists of the 1980s, is more ideological than pragmatic in its economic views and is inclined to favor restrictive monetary policy, a reduced role for the economic state, and socialist redistributive aims simultaneously.

Prospects for Consolidation of the Economic and Political Transition in Hungary: Two Scenarios

A stability scenario   One possible scenario, based on events of the 1989–1992 period, is that the transition will lead to greater economic and political stability. Under this scenario the demobilization strategy succeeds. The prevailing traditions make it possible even for a relatively weak state to resist social pressure and make simultaneous economic and political transitions compatible.

The social costs of the transition and criticism by the mass media may lower the popularity of the government and the coalition in office. The loss of popularity by the government, however, does not threaten the new democratic regime, since, with the party system and the pattern of coalition making, there is an alternative coalition competing to get into office.

The opposition can win what the government loses. A liberal-socialist coalition or a shifting coalition may implement an alternative policy. The room for changes in policy, however, is rather limited.

A polarization scenario There is also the possibility that the weakness of the state and the low legitimacy of the new democratic regime may encourage existing tendencies toward polarization and mobilization. The trade unions, for example, in their struggle to gain legitimacy, are beginning to declare political aims and organize political actions. The other source of potential political polarization and instability—the centrifugal tendencies in party politics and the constitutional debate—may threaten economic and political stabilization if the major political actors give up the nonmobilization principle, which has worked successfully so far. Some events of the second half of 1992 suggest that this change in the pattern of transition cannot be excluded. Both the ultranationalist radical right and an emerging liberal-socialist-union alliance are ready for mass mobilization. The ultranationalists demand a radical and comprehensive change in the elites, while the liberal alliance defends the status quo.

The third potential source of mobilization is a spontaneous antiparliamentary and antielitist mass movement of marginalized social groups, the "losers" of the transition (like the petition movement of the Association of People Living under the Poverty Line).

I see a much higher chance that the stability scenario will occur in the short and medium term, but there are arguments and evidence for the polarization scenario as well.

Appendix to Chapter 3
Basic Indicators and Chronology for Hungary

TABLE A3.1

Basic Economic and Social Data for Hungary

Area	93,000 square kilometers
Population (end of 1991)	10,335,000
Population density	111.1 people/square kilometer
Urban population	62 percent
Currency	Forint
Exchange rate (May 1, 1992)	F80.13/US$
Life expectancy at birth	71
Adult female illiteracy	<5 percent
GDP per capita (1991)	US$2,974
Average annual growth rate of GDP	
1980–1989	1.6 percent
1985–1990	0.5 percent
GDP from manufacturing (1991)	36.8 percent
GDP from agriculture (1991)	14.6 percent
Inflation rate	
1991 (peak year)	35 percent
1992	25 percent
Total external debt/GDP (1991)	73 percent
Total debt service percent/exports	
1990	48 percent
1991	35 percent
Unemployment (end of 1992)	12 percent and rising

Source: Central Statistical Office, *Statisztikai Évkönyv 1992* (Budapest, 1992), pp. 5, 11, 49–51; *Magyarország 1991* (Budapest, 1992), pp. 7, 19, 85.

TABLE A3.2
Chronology of Events in Hungary, 1956–present

The long-term transition

After 1956	Agriculture is collectivized, but a household farming system is maintained.
1968	The New Economic Mechanism is introduced. The system of compulsory economic directives is abolished.
1980–1982	Private partnerships are legalized (for example, small cooperatives and small entrepreneurs within public enterprises). Limitations on the self-employed sector are lifted. The domestic price system begins to simulate international market prices.
1984	Self-management is established in state enterprises. Price regulations are further liberalized.
1987	Commercial banks are established. A restrictive economic policy is initiated (the government tightens control on domestic demand by restricting credit and investment and by increasing the tax burden).
1988	First privatizations take place through exceptional permissions.
1989	The Company Act is passed, allowing for limited liability and joint stock companies. Administrative import controls are lifted, and liberalization of imports is expected to be completed in three years.

The short-term transition

June 1987–November 1988	Grósz government: A restrictive economic policy is adopted (using credit and investment restrictions and increased taxes). A personal income tax is initiated. Foreign investors are offered incentives. The first Banktrupcy Act is passed.
November 1988–May 1990	Németh government: The Company Act is passed. Imports are liberalized. Spontaneous privatizations take place. Consumer price subsidies are reduced. The government stimulates small private enterprises with preferential credits and tax relief.
May 1990–present	Antall government: Price regulation is abolished. Subsidies for state-owned enterprises and consumer prices are abolished. A restrictive monetary policy is adopted. The tax burden is increased. The Compensation Act is passed. The State Property Agency is established, launching government privatization programs. The Central Bank Act lifts government control of the central bank. The Competition Act and Concession Act are passed. Import liberalization is completed. Wage regulations are lifted. The second Banktrupcy Act is passed. Regulation of foreign exchange is softened. Indirect wage regulations are abolished.

Source: Author.

CHAPTER 4

The Bulgarian Transition: A Difficult Beginning

Ekaterina Nikova

Most Western theories on the Eastern European transition to a market economy and democracy are based on the experiences of Poland and Hungary. The reasons are obvious—these two countries, together with the Czech Republic, share many of the Western cultural and political traditions. Their problems are more comprehensible. They have a longer history of dissent and reforms under the former model. And last but not least, they possess a substantial amount of self-analysis and empirical information, as well as a number of Western-trained, foreign language–speaking economists and political scientists who are able to present the cases of their countries to a Western audience.

From a theoretical point of view, the rest of Eastern Europe—the countries of the Balkans and the former Soviet republics—probably look too messy to be analyzed by the established tools of Western science: its neat paradigms can hardly be used to organize and understand such a complicated, disorderly, and unclear reality. The selective and self-limited evidence on the transition process in the region, however, seriously distorts the theory of transition because it simplifies and stylizes the problems. The examples of the countries outside of the "civilized troika" of Hungary, Poland, and the Czech Republic contradict the common rationality of behavioral patterns of the West. Developments there are often illogical, dramatic, and tragic, and the outcome is far from certain. These countries have a different level of development, a different political culture. Communist regimes there differed substantially from those in Central Europe.[1] If we accept G. Schöpflin's (1990) definition of Eastern Europe as a transitional zone between the Western tradition of division of power and the Eastern tradition of concentration of power, then the farther east a country is, the better soil communism found and the deeper roots it put down. Consequently, its end and its heritage are different.

The theoretical argument about the character of events in Eastern Europe—a revolt, a revolution, or a "refolution"—loses sense when the region is seen not as a single entity but as the sum of different countries. Despite the universality of the gradual decay of the totalitarian economic and political model, there were considerable differences in the speed of the process throughout the region. The countries of central Eastern Europe have undergone an evolution of long-ripening social, economic, and political changes. In the countries of southern Eastern Europe, despite the inevitable decay of the old regime, basic structures changed little. Thus, the revolutions there came suddenly, with all the destructive force of an explosion. They brought these states to the brink of collapse, causing in addition an upsurge of ethnonationalism and violence. The communist parties (no matter what they call themselves) remain strong, and the ongoing political struggle is far from over. The transition to a new social and economic order, therefore, is being postponed or prevented.

Ralf Dahrendorf's *Reflections on the Revolution in Europe* (1990) came late to southern Eastern Europe. Translated in 1992, this otherwise exquisite book sounded too rational, vague, and paternalistically general to those who were not "gentlemen in Warsaw" in 1990. Edmund Burke, who inspired Dahrendorf, wrote his famous *Reflections on the Revolution in France* in 1790, that is, when the revolution was only a year old. Thus, he could not know of the coming terror, the Thermidor, the Napoleonic Wars, or the Restoration. Likewise, there were many things Lord Dahrendorf did not know in 1990. He could not foresee the disintegration of the Soviet Union, the civil war in Yugoslavia, or the unprecedented scale of the economic and social depression.

As the year 1989 recedes, it becomes clearer that Eastern Europe as a whole is only at the beginning of a long and painful era of transformation. It also becomes obvious that how long and how painful it will be will vary substantially from country to country.

In this connection the case study of the Bulgarian transition deserves attention. Bulgaria is definitely an example of a country accomplishing a simultaneous transition to the market and democracy. At the same time it is a typical representative of a broad spectrum of countries of southern Eastern Europe and the former Soviet Union, countries differing from the troika model by the suddenness of the changes and by the continued presence of strong former communist parties and few if any of the prerequisites for transition called for by that model. But Bulgaria represents an understandable example; it is a sort of intermediate case between the troika and the rest. Experiencing most of the economic and political difficulties of the group, it was spared ethnic and civil unrest, violence, and anarchy. There is a clear distinction between the opposition and the former Communists, and the transition is taking place in a generally orderly and peaceful manner. As the country searches for its own path to the market and democracy within the general pattern of the transition, its case study can be valuable as a test of the universality of the overall Eastern European transitional model and of the role of national peculiarities.

The greatest methodological difficulty in analyzing the Bulgarian transition stems from the fact that it is a continuing phenomenon going on before our eyes. Any interim evaluation of such large-scale, long-term changes, occurring at lightning speed, is risky. The time span of the changes in the country is so short (three years) and the situation so volatile that it is almost impossible to maintain a historical perspective. In addition, most of the statistical data and observations are unreliable. Thus, conclusions are often hasty, and generalizations can easily be misleading. For latecomers like Bulgaria (compared with front-running Poland and Hungary) timing is different, and the researcher should be aware of the demonstration effect—there exists the danger of wishful thinking and a mechanical transplantation of preconceived hypotheses from different contexts. The period analyzed is too short to reveal objective laws; rather, the role of accidental developments, aberrations, or human errors is great.

The Starting Position

Socially and economically, Bulgaria was little prepared for the abrupt changes that began in the autumn of 1989. In 1987 Richard Crampton predicted a long and happy life for Bulgarian communism in his "Short History of Modern Bulgaria." In an interview given on November 9, 1989, the day of the fall of the Berlin Wall and one day before the resignation of Todor Zhivkov, Bulgaria's head of party and state, the Bulgarian-born French philosopher Tzvetan Todorov declared flatly that nothing could be expected to happen in the country for the next ten years (Krastev 1991).

Before World War II, Bulgaria was considered the most homogeneous society of eastern Central Europe in terms of both property distribution and status flexibility: a country of small and middle peasants, it had no nobility or landlords, but a good and accessible educational system, a social security system, and, together with Denmark and Slovenia, one of the best-developed cooperative movements (see Rothschild 1974). Like the rest of the region, Bulgaria suffered the agony of the interwar period, with political violence, international isolation, and a shaky economy. At the end of World War II, although less damaged than its neighbors, the country found itself again on the losers' side, as it had after the Second Balkan War (1913) and World War I (1918).

Communism offered the promise of easy solutions to most of its national, political, economic, and social problems. Russia was looked upon as a traditional friend and liberator, so the radical left solution seemed acceptable to much of the population.

Bulgarian (and Balkan) communism differed substantially from communism in Central Europe not in theory and practice but in the way it was assimilated by society. Not only did it promise an outlet from the helplessness of the interwar years and an end to the economic backwardness even greater than that of Central Europe, but it was also planted in different soil—an egalitarian society with a preserved patriarchal spirit and traditionally strong communist and leftist parties. The bulk of the intelligentsia and the analogue of a middle class in these countries were created during the postwar period, so they were closely connected and loyal to the communist parties. In a special way communism also blended with the historical Eastern Orthodox tradition of subjection to a central power and with the psychology of the people— survivors, living at one of the world's crossroads. Communism was perceived as the latest in a historic chain of evils—an alien force, like the Ottomans or the Hapsburgs—with which they had to put up. After a short initial period of people's courts, mass purges, and labor camps, most of the real and potential enemies of the regime were annihilated or intimidated—peasants, "bourgeois elements," and the very thin layer of the country's intellectuals and professionals. After 1956 Bulgarian communism took a form that was more paternalistic and corruptive than openly repressive.

Socialist Bulgaria was considered an economic success story (see Table 4.1). In the course of three decades, the country was believed to have achieved one of the highest rates of growth in Europe, profound structural transformation from a backward agrarian economy into an industrialized one, and a

TABLE 4.1

Macroeconomic Indicators for the Bulgarian Economy, 1981–1990 (average annual percentage growth rates)

Indicator	1981–1985	1986–1990
Gross ouput	3.90	0.40
National income	3.70	0.10
Per capita national income	3.50	−0.10
Gross industrial output	4.30	−0.45
Gross agricultural output	−0.60	−0.50
Capital investment	3.83	9.81
Foreign trade	6.60	−5.30

Source: Central Statistical Office, *Statistical Yearbook of Bulgaria 1991* (Sofia, 1992).

considerable rise in the living standards of the population. The editor's introduction to the monograph *The Bulgarian Economy in the Twentieth Century* claims that "it has been one of the great success stories of the twentieth century, with the highest rate of growth in Europe and a degree of structural change second to none" (Lampe 1986). The stable and dynamic economic development legitimated and consolidated the communist regime and was one reason for the country's high level of internal political stability, rare in the Soviet Bloc. The feeling of making progress, of surpassing their Balkan neighbors and the countries of the Council for Mutual Economic Assistance (CMEA) was very strong among the great majority of the Bulgarians, and it was kept alive as late as the beginning of the 1980s.

Bulgaria has followed the general model of the socialist transformation of Eastern Europe: nationalization of industry, collectivization of land, crash industrialization with a strong emphasis on heavy industry, and foreign trade oriented chiefly to the CMEA. Bulgarian socialism presented, however, a number of peculiarities, which will have a direct impact on the country's further development. First, the nationalization of industry and services and the collectivization of land went further than in any other socialist country. Second, the country appears to have been conquered by two manias: growth and gigantomania (Feiwel 1977). Even by Eastern European standards, the Bulgarian case represented an extreme exception: intense economic development, made possible by huge inputs of labor, capital, and imports and a superconcentration of production. Similar trends in the rest of the region were less extreme, particularly if one considers the small size and limited resources of the country. In 1980 the average number of workers employed in a Bulgarian state industrial enterprise was 660 (575 in 1965 and 625 in 1987), which was very close to the number employed in an average large international corporation. In terms of size, Bulgarian farms probably had no equal in the world: in 1975 the average farm operated on 30,800 hectares and employed 5,855 workers (in 1980 the numbers were 17,100 hectares and 2,823 workers, and in 1987, 2,360 hectares and 367 workers) (Nikova 1991).

This type of development was made possible by the excessive CMEA orientation. The secret behind Bulgaria's rapid export-led economic development was a simple barter: imported cheap Soviet raw materials were manufactured into not-very-high-quality goods and exported back to the Soviet Union. The country's share of CMEA trade remained high throughout the socialist period, and no serious attempts were made to reorient it to the West. Bulgaria had the highest export-to-gross national product (GNP) ratio among the Eastern European states. Opened to the closed market of the CMEA, Bulgaria was virtually insulated from the world economy.

Limited economic reforms started in the early 1960s, and they continued in subsequent waves of concentration and deconcentration of economic authority for twenty years (1963–1965, 1968, 1970–1972, 1981, 1985–1987, and finally 1989). These reforms looked, however, like badly conceived and often confusing administrative changes and in fact attempted to preserve the status quo. Limited, hesitant, and superficial, they did not affect the extreme centralization of decision making, in contrast to Hungary, for example. They were mainly organizational, and market instruments were never seriously discussed. Western observers usually described Bulgaria as a rationalized, administratively planned economy in the group of the so-called conservative pragmatists (see Vögel 1975, Crampton 1988, Jackson 1988).

Because of its orientation toward the CMEA, Bulgaria did not feel the external disturbances of the mid-1970s immediately. Since the effects of the oil shocks and the recessions came late, the economy's reaction to the new economic environment was slow and inadequate. In the mid-1980s the Bulgarian economy, instead of adjusting, took a wrong macroeconomic course, deviating further from its natural advantages. A group of party elites decided to channel Bulgaria's foreign loans and scarce resources into several high-tech sectors (mainly electronics) that were supposed to pull the whole economy forward. The results were growing external and internal imbalances, the accumulation of a huge debt and inflationary pressures (see Table 4.2).

The last attempt to rationalize the organizational structure of the Bulgarian economy occurred as late as 1989, when, following a special, much-publicized decree on economic activity (Decree No. 56), a one-level company-based economic structure was established. This first serious attempt to break from the vertical hierarchy of central planning degenerated into a new round of concentration and monopolization. In the absence of real market conditions, the socialist state managed to keep its grip upon the economy.

With few exceptions Bulgarian economists and social scientists were conformist: most of the country's scholars and institutions were closely connected with the government and remained loyal to the party line. Isolated from the world more than in any other socialist country except Albania, social

TABLE 4.2
Bulgarian Foreign Debt, 1981–1990
(millions of U.S. dollars)

Year	Debt	Year	Debt
1981	4,080.9	1986	5,511.6
1982	3,500.1	1987	7,404.0
1983	3,068.5	1988	9,125.7
1984	2,922.9	1989	10,656.9
1985	4,119.7	1990	11,049.6

Source: Bulgarian National Bank.

scientists tried to reconcile their own views with state doctrine. Important data like the external debt, the level of inflation, and some sociological surveys were classified. As a result, by the time the democratic changes began, the state of economics and statistics was dismal. Since there were few independent analyses, the public was unaware of the real situation. Thus, there were months of scholarly discussions on whether the country was in a crisis or a catastrophe.

The first real debates about the present and the future of Bulgarian society and economy started in the autumn of 1989, when a group of young economists and sociologists opposed the communist government's cosmetic perestroika-type reforms and stated explicitly the need for market-oriented reforms. The debates opened the eyes of Bulgarians to the problems of the economy and to the basic notions and principles of the market economy. The same group, undefined politically from the beginning, later formulated the economic program of the opposition Union of Democratic Forces (Pishev 1992).

As already mentioned, Bulgaria had almost no opposition to the communist regime. The majority of the population was satisfied with the constantly rising living standards and the cunning system of small privileges and social safety valves. The intelligentsia, the majority of whom were first-generation intellectuals who owed their social positions to the socialist revolution, was also kept silent by a combination of flattery, privileges, and subtle intimidation. Even the victims of the immediate postrevolutionary terror (such as political prisoners and the former bourgeoisie) kept a low profile.[2] Two events destroyed this almost idyllic relationship with the party: Mikhail Gorbachev's perestroika and the campaign to assimilate the Turks in 1984–1989. The revelations of widely read Soviet magazines and literature and the new winds in Moscow had a striking effect on Russophile Bulgaria. The forcible renaming of nearly 1 million Bulgarian Muslims, which led to a major ethnic crisis and complete international isolation of the country, opened the eyes of even the most loyal to the true nature of the regime. Dissent was further stimulated by the worsening of the economic situation after 1985 and especially by growing awareness of the country's grave environmental problems. The groups that would form the basis for a future civil society in Bulgaria did not arise until 1988. The first organizations of intellectuals, human rights activists, and environmentalists, as well as the independent trade union Podkrepa, appeared in 1988–1989, two years before the fall of the regime.

The Transition to a Democratic Political System

Democratic changes in Bulgaria have some similarities in essence and direction to those occurring in the rest of Eastern Europe.[3] However, the process has been far more polarized.

The Political Process

The democratic transition in Bulgaria (1989–1992) had five distinct stages.

November 1989–June 1990   Political changes began as a typical palace coup when a supposedly reformist wing of the Politburo of the ruling Communist party forced the aging Todor Zhivkov to resign after thirty-five years in office. Reformers intended to make a fresh start based on Gorbachev-style perestroika. In the stormy autumn of 1989, however, this revolution from above soon collided with such powerful pressure from below that it turned into a real revolution (in the broadest sense of that notion). In mass rallies and demonstrations the Bulgarians, like most Eastern Europeans, declared categorically their wish to abolish the system, not to correct it.

In December 1989 the intellectual, environmental, and human rights groups united in the Union of Democratic Forces (UDF). They were joined by several restored parties (the Social Democratic party, the Democratic party, and the Radical Democratic party) that had been crushed after the Communist takeover and a wing of the influential Bulgarian Agrarian National Union (BANU). Thus, rather unexpectedly, the weak Bulgarian opposition managed to unite itself in an impressive bloc confronting the Communists still in power. As a whole, however, the UDF had no clear theoretical ideas and no practical experience or stratification along ideological lines. Its aim was to abolish the communist system, challenging the perestroika-type corrections launched by the Bulgarian Socialist party (BSP). (The Communist party was renamed the Bulgarian Socialist party after a hasty referendum in April 1990.) Backed by considerable popular support, the UDF was guided by the universal principles of democracy and the market. Lacking well-known leaders, practical experience, and vision, the Bulgarian opposition relied mostly on the enthusiasm of its supporters and the overall atmosphere in Eastern Europe. It managed to impose round-table negotiations, which legitimized and popularized it as a political force and set the rules for further democratization.[4] But the negotiations revealed the weakness of the bloc, although its adversary—the Communist party—also showed a surprising lack of confidence.

June 1990–November 1990   In contrast to the developments in Central Europe, the Bulgarian democratic opposition (the UDF) did not win the first free elections. By winning 47 percent of the votes, the Socialist party ensured itself a majority of 211 in the four-hundred-member Grand National Assembly, which was to adopt the new constitution of the country. The popular vote created a strange situation, later repeated in other southern Eastern European countries and former Soviet republics,[5] in which radical changes had to be accomplished by the parliamentary majority and a government of the former Communists. The Communist party was not marginalized: it remained on the political scene, and no matter how reformist it tried to portray itself, it was actually acting in the direction of preserving of the status quo.

In a Balkan context, however, the Bulgarian opposition did rather well. Young and inexperienced, it managed in the course of only six months to organize itself into a mass movement, to form an impressive parliamentary faction, and to stay united despite the serious ideological and tactical disagreements among its sixteen constituent member organizations and groups.

Soon after the election it became clear that the game had ended in a draw. Elected with the votes of the elderly and less-educated people, deprived of the support of the youth, the intellectuals, and the urban populations, the BSP was not able to rule the country. A combination of strong pressure in the Parliament and continuing mass discontent with the passivity of the two successive socialist governments neutralized to a great extent the electoral victory of the BSP. The opposition gradually worked its way into the structures of power, gaining experience and self-confidence. First came the election of the leader of the UDF, Zhelyu Zhelev, as president of the republic in August 1990. Then the UDF began to share responsibility within the local authorities, when people's councils were replaced by provisional executive committees in which all political forces were represented proportionally. Finally it achieved a depoliticization (that is, a decommunization) of the army, the police, the judiciary, and the diplomatic corps.

In November 1990, six months after the elections, growing mass indignation with the government's passivity forced the Socialist prime minister to resign.

December 1990–October 1991   In December 1990 a coalition cabinet was formed under an independent prime minister. The ministries were divided among the BSP, the UDF, and the Agrarian Union. All the economic posts were given to the UDF team. In February 1991 the economic reform started at last. The coalition government remained in office until the autumn of 1991. On July 12 the Grand National Assembly adopted the country's new constitution and voted its own dissolution; it then continued to function as an ordinary legislature.

October 1991–December 1992   The UDF won the October 1991 elections by a small margin, despite an earlier split of the bloc into the UDF Movement, the UDF Center, and the UDF Liberals. The proportional electoral system required that a party win 4 percent of the popular vote to be represented in Parliament, producing an unusual configuration in Parliament. Only three parties could pass the 4 percent threshold: the UDF, the BSP, and the ethnic Turks' Movement for Rights and Freedoms (MRF). Backed by the MRF, the UDF formed a minority cabinet and declared its intention to speed up the radical change of the system. The first half of the year was marked by vigorous activity; in the second half tension started to grow between the government and the trade unions, the press, the Parliament, the president, and finally its MRF partners.

December 1992–the present   The UDF government was toppled by a no-confidence vote in December 1992 and replaced by a cabinet of experts appointed on the mandate of the Turkish MRF and backed by a mixed parliamentary majority of supporters drawn from the MRF, the BSP, and the UDF.

The Character of the Transition

Institutions and elections   The character of the Bulgarian transition to democracy is a mixture of gradualism and radicalism, of compromise and sharp confrontation, of constitutionalism and "revolutionary impatience." In the period 1989–1992 Bulgaria had two parliaments, three rounds of elections, and four governments.

The Grand National Assembly (July 1990–September 1991), following the historical tradition of the nineteenth century, was to turn a new page in the country's history by developing the new constitution. Although preoccupied with the constitution, it was working at the same time as an ordinary parliament, adopting a number of urgent laws, including a few economic ones. The assembly was the main arena for political discussions and confrontation and for the legislative change of the system. The second (ordinary) National Assembly (October 1991 to the present) undertook a more ambitious legislative program, despite continuing sharp political confrontation.

In July 1991 Bulgaria became the second Eastern European nation to adopt a new constitution. It showed the general difficulties of constitutionalism in Eastern Europe at that stage of political development. Controversial in content and in its method of adoption,[6] the constitution nevertheless created the legal framework of the transition and was later seen as a pillar of democracy even by its former opponents.

In the course of two years, the Bulgarians went to the polls three times— twice for parliamentary elections (the second parliamentary election was combined with local elections) and once for a direct presidential election. The first elections, in June 1990, were monitored by international observers, who noted minor violations as well as more serious intimidation practices on the part of the former Communists. The conclusion of the international delegation to the second elections in October 1991 was that democracy in Bulgaria had gained strong roots (National Democratic Institute for International Affairs and International Republican Institute 1992). Bulgarians demonstrated a high degree of motivation and political involvement: electoral turnout was high by any standard (see Table 4.3).

TABLE 4.3
Election Results and Voter Turnout in Bulgaria, 1990 and 1991

Election	Percentage of the vote won by each party				Turnout (percentage)
	UDF	BSP	MRF	BANU	
June 1990	36	47	7	8	93
October 1991	34[a]	33	7	—[b]	84

[a]UDF Liberals won 2.8 percent, and UDF Center won 3.2 percent; BANU "N. Petkov" won 3.4 percent, and BANU United won 3.9 percent.
[b]Less than 4 percent.
Source: *Darzhaven Vestnik.*

In January 1992 the UDF presidential candidate, Zhelyu Zhelev, won 45 percent of the vote, the BSP candidate received 31 percent, and Georges Gantchev (a comic Bulgarian Tyminski) won a surprising 16 percent—a clear sign of the growing political fatigue and negativism of the electorate.

Parties and party structures   Strictly speaking, from 1989 to 1992 no party in Bulgaria had a clear identity or program; that is, there was not even one real party. Most of the existing one hundred parties were post-totalitarian formations typical for a transitional period. This was true both for the traditional parties with their long history and for the new parties with their attractive labels of "Christian" or "liberal." Three years after the beginning of the democratic changes, the political space of Bulgaria was still occupied by two giants, the UDF and the BSP, linked together like Siamese twins, each torn apart by internal contradictions but finding their raison d'être in their mutual antagonism.

The Union of Democratic Forces was created as a broad electoral coalition and mass anticommunist movement. It had a surprisingly good start for the Balkans—it managed to unite the weak unknown opposition groups and the restored old parties; it stayed together for quite a long time and gradually worked its way into power by a combination of pressure and compromise. In 1991 when the former Communist party was voted out, the UDF formed a minority government. The UDF was the symbol and driving force of the democratic changes in Bulgaria. In contrast to Solidarity in Poland, the Civic Forum in Czechoslovakia, or the Front for National Liberation in Romania, however, the UDF did not split apart soon after the old system collapsed. It preserved its basic structure and its dual character as both a coalition and a mass movement under three different sets of circumstances: it was a street opposition, a parliamentary opposition, and then a ruling party. As it faced a strong and united adversary—the Socialist party—the UDF artificially froze itself into its initial prepolitical state. In the name of discipline, internal ideological differences were suppressed, and the normal and natural development of parties was hindered. The mavericks were expelled or frozen out, and the biggest and strongest parties (the Social Democratic party and the Agrarian Union) were forced to leave. Once the euphoria of the anticommunist movement was exhausted, the UDF lost its rainbow character and failed to evolve into a genuine coalition of real parties. Decision making was concentrated in a handful of people on the Coordinating Council. Consequently, after a year in office, the UDF found its support shrinking; it broke with its founders, including the president; it lost the intelligentsia and the youth; and it quarreled with the trade unions, the press, the extraparliamentary forces, and all its actual (MRF) and potential allies. The rapid rise and decline of the UDF were predictable and typical for a movement and coalition based only upon anticommunism and drawing from a broad and undefined social base. The crisis of the UDF was the crisis of young Bulgarian democracy, for as a rule a stable democracy relies upon independent consolidated parties representing specific interests.

The Bulgarian Socialist party remained the country's biggest and single most organized political force. Its inability to break with its communist past (including with the leaders who personify this past), to admit its historical responsibility, and to reform itself made it a very strange political mutant. The party was caught in a identity trap; transformed overnight from communist to socialist by a new name, it had to stay united in order to survive, suppressing the differences among the nine different internal factions, the two most important of which were the factions favoring social democratization and recommunization. Unity became the magic word, and it hid the profound differences between the social democratic ideas of the ambitious and pragmatic younger leaders and the old apparatchiks, skilled in power struggles. This unity was necessary to keep the support of the "pig-iron" electorate of elderly and less-educated people. In the name of this unity, all attempts to reform the party into a modern social democratic party of the left failed: power remained in the hands of a few apparatchiks, supported by the traditional electorate. Despite the leftist rhetoric, the BSP could hardly be seen as a leftist party. Judging from its behavior (both in Parliament and out of it), the party had been busier preserving a certain role in the political life than defending the interests of its members and supporters, of its own nomenklatura, or of the socially weak and impoverished.

The bipolar model and confrontation   The victory of the BSP in the first elections and its strong presence on the political scene had a distorting effect on the Bulgarian transition. This effect was both direct, through the BSP's concrete activities as one of the two major rivals for political control, and indirect, through its role in the opposition and political life in general. The electoral victory of the BSP in the first elections and its small margin of loss in the second created a stalemate. Neither side was strong enough to topple or neutralize the other. Each of them felt threatened and forced to stay united. During the first communist-led government, the transition was delayed. The communist majority in the Parliament fought to preserve the status quo, postponing vital economic legislation and insisting on the adoption of a new constitution and other laws. The delay of the reforms gave rise to a "revolutionary impatience." It brought to the fore the most radical wing of the UDF, which won the October 1991 elections, and marginalized the centrist forces within the UDF.

Consequently, Bulgaria was caught in a situation of political confrontation, in which extreme politicization and polarization characterized every issue. The few moderates on both sides were pushed aside and lost real influence over events. The political atmosphere was tense: mutual accusations replaced discussion. Power was concentrated in the hands of a limited number of people, and politics became personalized. "Whoever is not with us is against us"—the old Bolshevik saying used by both sides—showed that the communist political mentality was strong in all the parties. The pursuit of internal enemies was extremely active. By the summer of 1992, not one of the initial creators of the UDF was still in a position of leadership. Some left; others were expelled, including President Zhelev. Similarly, a number of intellectuals left the BSP. The funny term "fish scales" became the word for all those who left the main bodies of the two giants and were doomed to political oblivion or secondary positions. The stalemate between the BSP and the UDF trapped the country in a three-year political brawl. Huge amounts of societal energy were wasted arguing on ideological, often symbolic issues, connected mostly with the past, at the expense of the country's urgent current problems. A dividing line went through families, work places, and newspapers; it also affected the church—the symbol of tradition—for both the Christian Holy Synod and the Islam Mufti split into two.

As time went on, anticommunism, normal and explicable initially, did not fade away but intensified instead. Contrary to what one might expect, the confrontational bipolar model was preserved and cemented. It impeded the normal process of party differentiation within each of the blocs. Thus, during the whole period of 1989–1992, Bulgarian politics remained in a phase of prepolitics or antipolitics. Revolutionary rhetoric was kept alive, together with an anachronistic paranoic preoccupation with the past, the KGB, Moscow, and various conspiracies. The configuration of political forces has remained simplified—black and white, red (BSP) and blue (UDF). The real political process was interrupted. The ideas of moderation and reconciliation (supported and embodied by President Zhelev) were rejected on grounds of the need for mobilization and acceleration of reforms. As a result, the ruling elite of the UDF has narrowed its own basis drastically, while the Socialists pre-served their nucleus of loyal followers.

The overpoliticization of the Bulgarian transition was partly an inevitable outcome but partly artificially intensified. It was kept alive deliberately be-cause it suited the two big parties' elites and their tacit unholy alliance. The proportional electoral system also favored the prolongation of the dictatorship of the party apparatuses. Even the few strong and large parties (Agrarians, Social Democrats, and Greens), instead of consolidating themselves, split. In both the UDF and the BSP there was hardly any party hierarchy, and this characteristic facilitated the crucial role of elites and the individualization of politics. Because of the strong personalization of political life, in the paranoic atmosphere of postcommunist Eastern Europe, personal alliances and hatreds acquired utmost importance.

To make matters more complicated, there was no real alternative to the UDF as the main engine for change. The one-hundred-year-old Bulgarian Socialist party, as one of its leaders, Alexander Lilov, said, was too tired to govern. New political formations were difficult to imagine, and outsiders (nonparliamentary forces) had little practical importance. The alternative—the centrists and the liberals—ruined their own chances in the October 1991 elections by misjudging the political situation: they underestimated the strength of the radical anticommunist feelings in society and the referendum character of the vote—for or against the system. Their second mistake was that they could not unite in order to pass the 4 percent threshold and were left out of active political life. In the period after the elections, the centrists and the liberals continued their internal arguments and were not capable of formulat-ing clear centrist programs, strategies, and tactics; they could not mobilize and organize the existing centrist and liberal tendencies in the society, which obviously was growing tired of permanent revolution.

Thus, after the three initial years of transition, Bulgaria's political system was legitimately formed and all the institutions were available and formally stable. Questions remained, however, about how viable this democracy was, whether it was working, and whether it was capable of solving the country's problems and fulfilling mass expectations. Even in the short period of three years, Bulgarians have seen the pitfalls of young democracies. Faced with a theatrical, talkative Parliament, inefficient government, and shaken institu-tions, they realize that democracy not only is a structure and system of ruling but also involves a certain mentality, political culture, and tolerance and that one of the strongest legacies of communism consists of behavioral stereotypes.

The pendulum returns to the center?   The sharp political crisis of the end of 1992 was in fact a crisis of the entire political model of the Bulgarian transition in 1989–1992. The failure of the two biggest political forces, the UDF and the BSP, to rule and their virtual abdication of power revealed their conceptual and practical weaknesses. The formation of a nonparty govern-ment with the mandate of the small ethnic Turks' Movement, backed by a dynamic majority of members from the three parliamentary parties, can be seen as an end of the confrontational bipolar system and probably as the beginning of a new division—not along party lines, but between ideologues and pragmatists. The appearance of significant moderate trends and factions in both the BSP and the UDF is a sign of the country's fatigue with endless and fruitless ideological confrontation and its openness to dialogue and compro-mise. By the end of 1992 half of the electorate did not associate itself with either of the political giants: the real political center ultimately seems to be associated with moderation, tolerance, and professionalism (Ivanova 1992).

Yet real political differentiation in Bulgaria is still forthcoming. This differentiation will be predetermined by the ongoing changes in society, as a normal political spectrum develops to represent various interests.

Stabilization Policies and Market-oriented Reforms

Economic reforms in Bulgaria began in February 1991—more than a year later than those in Poland and Hungary and under much worse initial conditions. According to the World Bank, the breadth and scope of the reforms were enormous and unprecedented: the fact that stabilization and market reforms were both needed more or less at the same time meant that everything became urgent (World Bank 1991). As for the pace of reforms, Bulgaria had no choice; in the winter of 1990/1991 the deliberate delay of reforms had brought the country to the brink of total collapse and famine. Compared with the rest of Eastern Europe, Bulgaria had two big disadvantages: no foreign sources of finance and the greatest economic disequilibria.

There was hardly another Eastern European country more heavily hit by unfavorable external factors. The loss of the Soviet and the CMEA markets alone, which accounted for 84 percent of Bulgarian exports and 74 percent of imports in 1989, was enough to cause a catastrophic decline in production.[7] According to rough evaluations, half of the drop in Bulgarian gross domestic product (GDP) was caused by the loss of the Eastern markets, the sharpest decline being registered in the export industrial sectors. The situation was further aggravated by the Gulf crisis of 1990 and the accompanying loss of the Iraqi and other Middle East markets. Then came the embargo against Yugoslavia, which upset most of the country's trade routes. Thus the beginning of the reform coincided with the loss of 90 percent of Bulgaria's traditional outlets. Internationally, the country, which joined the IMF in September 1990, had a poor financial reputation. Bulgaria's March 1990 moratorium on foreign payments made the US$13 billion debt negotiations difficult and closed the doors to direct investment.

Stabilization Measures

On February 1, 1991, Bulgaria undertook the classical stabilization program of shock therapy, coordinated with the approval of a stand-by agreement with the IMF. As elsewhere in Eastern Europe, the program aimed to eliminate the accumulated macroeconomic imbalances.

The reform package included orthodox elements that had already been tested in Poland:

* elimination of the accumulated excess money through a price shock effect; depression of domestic demand and inflationary expectations
* cuts in incomes; devaluation of the lev; forcing of exports
* liberalization of prices and the foreign trade and exchange rate regimes
* curtailment of the deficit in the balance of payments, financed by the international agencies

Short term and anti-inflationary in character, the program did not stress the systemic institutional changes of the economy; they were somehow taken for granted (Agency for Economic Coordination and Development 1992c).

As elsewhere in the region, stabilization in Bulgaria relied upon two anchors: tight credit and income policies. The third habitual anchor—the exchange rate—was not implemented in the Bulgarian case because of the absence of a stabilization fund. Credit control was achieved through direct limitations (credit ceilings) and high nominal interest rates (45 percent in February 1991, 54 percent in August 1991, 49 percent in July 1992, and 41 percent in September 1992). The generally positive effect of the credit policy was offset, however, by active interim credits. Wage decline was sharpest at the beginning of the reform; wages fell by 68 percent in the first quarter of 1991. The decline of real wages was greater than expected. A system of wage negotiation was introduced to regulate the mechanism and to compensate for a part of the first price shock effect on real incomes.

As a result the 550 percent inflation of 1991 was reduced to 79 percent in 1992, and residual inflation after the price shock was limited to 3–5 percent monthly. According to the AECD, this was mainly cost-push inflation. Later it was not clear to what extent the restrictive policy became a pro-inflationary factor, for the sharp drop in production certainly caused a rise in prices too.

The first price shock brought a substantial absorption of money; private housing credits were prepaid; and the volume of credits remained low. The targeted budget deficit, initially planned to be cut to 3.5 percent of GDP in 1991 (from 13 percent in 1990), indicated an ambitious fiscal adjustment. Yet higher-than-planned expenditures were made for social purposes and energy. In general, fiscal restrictions assumed greater proportions than elsewhere in Eastern Europe and were considered successful. But equilibrium has remained unstable, and budget revenues uncertain (see Table 4.4).

Liberalization Measures

Liberalization measures included price and foreign trade liberalization, together with a limited convertibility of the sharply depreciated lev. Ninety percent of the retail and producers' prices were liberalized: an exception was made for thirteen essential foods and public transportation, which remained under government control; energy prices were the only ones to remain fixed centrally. (Liberalization of housing was never a major issue, since the vast majority of Bulgarians owned their houses.) Consumer subsidies were cut drastically to 12 percent in 1991 and 3 percent in the 1992 budget. The actual price shock turned out to be more severe than expected; prices skyrocketed, and the inflation pressure was eased only by the very restrictive monetary and wage policies.

By any standard the social price of the Bulgarian reform turned out to be high: real incomes dropped by 46 percent in 1991 and by another 25 percent in

TABLE 4.4

Economic Indicators for Bulgaria, 1989–1992 (percentage change unless otherwise noted)

Indicator	1989	1990	1991	1992
GDP				
% change	−2.4	−9.1	−16.7	−12.5
Total (billions of US$)	19.6	6.9	8.0	9.3
Per capita (US$)	2,180	768	891	1,066
Gross industrial production	−2.6	−12.5	−21.7	−23.0
Gross agricultural production	−4.8	−3.7	−12.5	−12.9
Inflation	6.4	26.3	480.0	79.4
Average real wage	1.0	5.3	−55.9	−9.0
Unemployment				
%	0.0	2.1	11.5	15.3
Thousands of people	0.0	65	420	550
Budget deficit (% of GDP)	1.4	8.5	3.6	4.8
Exports (billions of US$)	3.1	2.6	3.7	5.1
Imports (billions of US$)	4.3	3.4	3.8	4.6
Trade balance	−1.2	−0.8	−0.1	0.5
Gross foreign debt (billions of US$)	10.7	11.0	11.4	12.9
Reserves (billions of US$)	1.0	0.2	0.3	0.9
Exchange rate (lev/US$)	0.9	2.2	19.0	26.6

Source: National Statistical Institute, Bulgarian National Bank, OECD, Economist Intelligence Unit.

1992; consumption of basic foods diminished sharply. In two years two-thirds of the households fell below or close to the social minimum.

The rise of unemployment from virtually zero in 1989 to 550,000 (15.3 percent of the labor force) at the end of 1992 was dramatic, especially in view of the fact that restructuring of the state sector had not yet begun. A system of unemployment benefits was introduced in 1990; the unemployed are entitled to six to twelve months of compensation. The labor market is only at the beginning of its transformation.

In foreign trade, export control measures (minimum prices) were imposed only on agricultural goods and were gradually cut later. The reform abolished state monopoly and ensured the free access of numerous new exporters and importers to foreign markets (30 percent of them private). It also included a new import tariff and liberalized import licensing. But in Bulgaria, unlike Poland, foreign trade could not play the role of an engine for export-led growth. The primary reasons were two: the high import-intensiveness of exports and the loss of nearly 90 percent of the country's traditional markets (the former Soviet Union and the CMEA, the Near East, and the Balkans). In 1990–1992 foreign trade declined sharply in volume but underwent a substantial reorientation: the share of former CMEA countries decreased by half and that of OECD countries rose more than threefold.

The Bulgarian foreign debt has been one of the strongest constraints to reform and recovery. With a debt of US$13 billion and US$1,300 per capita in 1992, Bulgaria ranked second after Hungary among the Eastern European debtors. To make matters worse, a sudden unilateral moratorium on debt payments by the last Communist government in March 1990 spoiled the country's financial reputation for years ahead and doomed it to financial isolation. Bulgaria was admitted to the IMF and the World Bank in September 1990. In April 1991 the Paris Club agreed to reschedule US$2 billion (15 percent of the debt). The rest of the sum is owed to the commercial banks of the London Club—US$8.5 billion, plus US$1 billion in interest. The renegotiating of this sum turned out to be very difficult, further aggravating Bulgaria's international position. Partial debt-service payments were resumed in 1992 in an attempt to appease creditors. Foreign financial requirements (US$3.1 billion in 1991) were covered by international institutions (the IMF and the World Bank) and rescheduling.

Foreign capital has historically played a minor role in Bulgarian economic development compared with the other countries of the region. The unsettled debt problem, together with the general impression of instability, changing legislation (the Law on Foreign Investment, adopted in 1991, had to be corrected by the new Parliament in 1992), unclear property rights, and banking regulations, has closed the way to new credit lines for the Bulgarian economy. The amount of foreign investment—less than US$100 million in 1991–1992—could hardly act as a catalyst for development.

Institutional Reform

Institutional system transformation was the second important aspect of Bulgarian economic reforms. Like other countries in Eastern Europe, Bulgaria had to create a market framework, with its specific structures, instruments, and rules of the game. This aspect of the Bulgarian reform, however, proceeded at a different speed and with different levels of success. The legal basis had to be transformed completely—in a short time the Parliament adopted a number of important laws, like the Accountancy Bill; the Land Act; bills on statistics, foreign investment, and competition; the Trade Act; the National Bank Act; and the Cooperative Bill. At the same time, many of the old administrative acts and laws remained in effect (Decree 56 of 1989), making the legal situation inconsistent—a mixture of old and new laws. In general, however, institutional reforms lagged because of political indecisiveness. Preoccupation with the constitution and disputable and ineffective laws characterized the activity of the Grand National Assembly. The next Parliament worked more vigorously in this direction—sixty-five laws were adopted in the first nine months of its mandate. But many of them corrected the ones already adopted by the previous assembly (such as laws on foreign investment and land reform). Three years after the beginning of reforms, important pieces of economic legislation like laws on taxation and social security, the second part of the commercial code, and laws on labor relations and bankruptcy were still lacking.

The institutionalization of private property—the most symbolic element of the reform—also proved to be very difficult in Bulgaria. Bulgaria was the last Eastern European country to adopt a law on privatization of state-owned enterprises. It was passed hastily in April 1992, obviously under the pressure of international agencies. Based on market principles, it involved predominantly selling shares, 20 percent of which were to go to special funds and 20 percent to be sold to companies' employees. According to initial intentions, privatization in Bulgaria was to be carried out under the strong control of the executive—the Agency for Privatization, the council of ministers, and the ministries. By the end of 1992, not a single enterprise had been privatized: 96 percent of the assets remained in the hands of the state. The delay of privatization led to the spontaneous hidden privatization and mass decapitalization of state property that was typical of the whole region. Opinion polls show a stable egalitarian mood—very few Bulgarians intend to participate in privatization. At the same time there are strong negative feelings toward dirty money (of the old and new nomenklatura). Paradoxically (at first glance), the percentage of people opposing the mass privatization (30 percent) is equal among the supporters of the two ideological adversaries, the UDF and the BSP.

The restructuring of the state sector in the direction of decentralization and commercialization has been hesitant. The beginning of the transformation of the enterprises into corporations was stopped by the democratic opposition because it feared that the nomenklatura would dominate the process. In June 1991, following the recommendations of the World Bank, Parliament passed an act on the transformation of state-owned companies into single-person commercial partnerships. Demonopolization consisted of disbanding the huge associations and transforming their constituent departments into independent enterprises. But in the absence of real market criteria, it is unclear how economically viable the new units are. Despite the fact that most of the enterprises are heavily indebted (bad credits reached almost 100 billion leva at the end of 1992), there has been not a single bankruptcy. The postponement of a bankruptcy law can be explained by politicians' fear of a domino effect.

The unconditional restitution of ownership of urban real estate to former owners seems to be one of the unusual features of the Bulgarian reform, compared with the rest of the region. Because of the strong parliamentary lobby of people directly profiting from restitution, the package of laws regulating it was given priority at the expense of the laws on privatization. The restoration of small shops, hotels, and restaurants changed the image of Bulgarian cities almost overnight. It created one of the few groups of real economic agents and stimulated retail trade and services—notoriously weak sectors of a socialist economy. On the other hand, however, preoccupation with restitution, which affected no more than 3–5 percent of population, put the wrong emphasis on the reform process. Because it was not accompanied by similar progress in other spheres (for example, stimuli for the nascent private enterprises), restitution created the perception that reforms were profitable for a limited number of people, who were mostly elderly, less active economically, and connected with the social structures of 1939.

Agricultural reforms had two major aims: dismantling the system of cooperative farms and restoring the land to previous owners. The adoption of the Land Reform Act in February 1991 by the Grand National Assembly was celebrated as a major event in this traditionally peasant country. In a short time, 1.7 million applications for restitution of land were registered, claiming ownership of 5.8 million hectares of collectivized land. The celebration, however, turned out to be premature. The law was unable to cope with all the political, administrative, legal, and technical difficulties of the process. In February 1992 the new Parliament made substantial revisions in the previous law, proclaiming that the land would be returned to its original boundaries and that cooperative farms would be compulsorily liquidated. The idea was to accelerate and simplify the procedures. The new legislation brought new complications; both political and technical. The restoration of land made slow progress: by the beginning of 1993 only one-third of the land had been restored.

Banking reform has only begun. Its aim is to change the system of small regional, undercapitalized banks burdened with bad loans by consolidating the seventy existing banks into nine or ten. The first consolidated bank—the Unified Bulgarian Bank—was formed by merging twenty-two small banks. The basic framework for banking reform also includes establishing the appropriate regulatory and supervisory mechanism for the banking sector, clearing the portfolios of these state banks of the inherited bad (nonperforming, noncollectible) loans, strengthening their capital base, and encouraging competition and privatization. Ten private banks were registered during the past two years. A special Bank Bill made the Bulgarian National Bank noncommercial and, what is more important, independent of government. An important factor in the reform, this bank has been one of the few indisputably successful institutions. It managed to maintain the currency's internal and external stability, to supervise the commercial banks, and to strengthen its autonomy in relation to the government.

The share of the private sector in the national economy has remained modest, although it has risen rapidly (see Table 4.5). By mid-1992 the Center for the Study of Democracy noted that 200,000 small private businesses were registered, representing 5 percent of national assets, 2.5 to 3 percent of industrial production, and 4.3 percent of employment. Most of the companies were single-person firms, and the average number of employees was 3.4. Their main spheres were transport and services, and industrial activity was almost an exception. There are some signs, however, that the real weight of the sector has become much greater than the official statistics show. According to the Agency for Economic Coordination and Development, by the end of the period the private sector contributed about 10 percent of GNP, 50 percent of retail trade, 25 percent of exports, and 20 percent of personal income (AECD 1992a). Any evaluation of the real scope of the emerging private sector should also consider the vast "twilight zone" between the state and the private sector, including areas like foreign trade and the leasing of state property; its importance can only be estimated.

TABLE 4.5
Share of the Private Sector in GDP in Bulgaria, 1989–1992 (percentage)

	1989	1990	1991	1992[a]
Private sector in total GDP	7.2	9.5	11.9	15.6
Agriculture	4.6	6.7	5.5	4.5
Industry	1.8	1.7	3.9	6.1
Services	0.8	1.1	2.5	5.0

[a]Preliminary data.
Source: National Statistical Institute.

Yet, comparisons with other postcommunist countries show that however dynamic it is, the private sector of the Bulgarian economy still has little impact on overall economic change. Despite the government's declared intentions, the conditions for the development of a private sector are not favorable. The restrictive financial and fiscal policy—the high interest rates, credit limitations, and inconsistent but tight tax policy—have been its greatest obstacles. Private entrepreneurs feel like Cinderellas: legislation is confused and incomplete and often does not protect them from corrupt administration, frequent changes in state policies, and the disloyal competition of the state sector. Promised privileges, including tax relief, were not given. A special Fund for Encouragement of Small Business was never activated, and an analogous law never reached the National Assembly. The general business climate remains unfavorable, and the opportunities for long-term capital-intensive investment are minimal. In addition, there is some mistrust of private economic activities; suspicions of money laundering and profiteering are strong among the public and the authorities. Still, according to polls, the majority of the population (55 percent) approves rapid development of the private sector, and this percentage is especially high among young people.

In general, in 1989–1992 the private sector in Bulgaria had very little importance in the economy or in politics. This is one of the typical features of the Bulgarian transition and an important constraint on the pace of reforms. The greatest challenge to the old system, ownership reform, was not accomplished during this first stage of the transition.

Despite the severe external constraints and internal imbalances of the Bulgarian case, the short-term objectives of the radical macroeconomic stabilization were reached. Bulgaria avoided hyperinflation, eliminated monetary overhang, and achieved a relative financial stabilization in a short period of time (about eighteen months). Reserves amounted to US$1 billion in 1992, and confidence in the national currency grew owing to the remarkably stable lev/dollar rate of exchange. The reform was less successful in creating the basic institutions of a market economy. The old system turned out to be much more resistant than supposed: basic economic agents did not change their behavior, and the inertia of the old structures worked in direction of preserving the status quo. The Agency for Economic Coordination and Development concluded that most parts of the national economy were merely simulating market behavior. There were special relationships among some private enterprises, state firms, banks, and the national budget, which resulted in the accumulation of 100 billion leva of bad loans at the end of 1992 and presented the danger of a generalized chain of insolvency (AECD 1992b). Macroeconomic policy carried out within the old structures provoked the financial destabilization of the state sector. Thus a new type of financial crisis appeared, reflecting the structural one.

As the Organization for Economic Cooperation and Development's 1992 assessment of Bulgaria states, much has been achieved in extremely difficult circumstances, but the most difficult part of the road may still lie ahead. The high ratio of spontaneous to organizing factors, of destruction to creation in general, sharply diminished the degree of manageability of the economy and brought a new, different form of instability. Like the other Eastern European countries, Bulgaria could not develop even a short-term strategy and select the future strong sectors; the link between stabilization and structural reform seems uncertain. The recession of 1991–1992 was so deep that the real economy might be close to the critical point. Important sectors like machine building, electronics, chemicals, and food industries are being destroyed. By several indicators—a 55 percent drop in production in three years, 15 percent unemployment—Bulgaria is the champion of Eastern Europe.

Two years after the successful start, reform in Bulgaria stumbled and virtually stopped. The transition to the next structural phase looks impossible under the existing semimarket conditions. In addition, the broad public consensus of the beginning of the reform can hardly be preserved with a rapidly rising unemployment rate, mass impoverishment, and general reform fatigue.

Society under Stress: Actors and Proxies

Like other postcommunist countries, Bulgaria inherited an amorphous social structure with a peculiar relationship between state and society and between interests and politics—a relationship so different from the Western model that one might doubt its very relevance. In the Bulgarian case the observer should also take into consideration the abruptness and the suddenness of the changes, which were not prepared for or even anticipated in the previous period. Almost overnight, a country that had enjoyed at least two decades of political stability, rapid economic growth, and relative prosperity was thrown into a profound crisis. Like the other Eastern Europeans, Bulgarians experienced a sudden and drastic drop in living standards, a rapidly changing social climate, a shattered value system, redistribution of social roles (the intellectuals, for example, lost social prestige), and the marginalization of certain groups (such as minorities). Living standards of more than half of the population fell to the subsistence level, and food accounted for 50 percent of total household expenditures. The prevailing perception is that people are fighting for their survival. The results of the December 1992 census, especially the unprecedented rise in emigration and mortality rates, created the impression of a demographic catastrophe. Since the previous census in 1985 the country had lost half a million out of its population of 9 million. One out of four is retired. The changes also brought a wave of unfamiliar social phenomena like crime, political tension, aggressiveness, and insecurity. It is no wonder that the country shows all the signs of a social depression, slow adaptability, and unpredictable reactions. For this reason all sociological analyses and their conclusions should be taken with reservations.

The present undefined social and economic structure of Bulgaria is a serious constraint to the reforms: real economic and political agents with typical and predictable behavior are few. In the usual Eastern European interregnum the labels do not correspond to the content. "Theater of the absurd," one of the most frequently used metaphors to describe the postcommunist reality of Eastern Europe, is appropriate for the Bulgarian case too. The observer is lost amid proxies, actors playing someone else's role, illogical motivations, fictions, and labels.

In view of the continuing absence of widespread private property and social stratification, political representation does not exist; political elites are not rooted in economic life. There is a confusion and misappropriation of classical concepts: almost identical party programs, a fake party of the left (BSP), a rightist coalition (UDF) whose core is a leftist trade union (Podkrepa), trade unions that behave like leftist parties, peasants who boycott the Agrarian Union. The failure of the promising Greens is typical: once in Parliament, "Ecoglasnost" completely forgot about the environmental problems and became preoccupied with politicking. The once-powerful Agrarian Union was mired in internal political quarrels and had little influence on issues vital for its electorate, like land reform. Even the Turks' Movement for Rights and Freedoms—one of the few parties with a clearly defined electorate— neglected its constituents' specific needs, busy playing high politics.

One of the paradoxes of the political process in Bulgaria is that the existence of a strong Socialist party not only did not prevent the right-wing character of the new legislation, the shock therapy, the unconditional restitution of former property, and the Thatcherite hostility toward trade unions, but in fact probably stimulated these conditions. At the same time, populism (perhaps inevitably in an egalitarian country like Bulgaria) is gaining ground.

Interest group formation is under way in Bulgaria too, but it demonstrates a number of peculiarities. Many pages have been written on the weakness of the liberal tradition in Bulgaria and on the basic contradiction that a collectivist revolution is bound to introduce an individualistic ideology in a traditionally egalitarian and collectivist society, very far from the coveted but nonexistent bourgeois middle class.

An AECD report finds that typical entrepreneurial behavior characterized a relatively small but quickly expanding number of authentic agents: real estate owners, private businessmen, and people whose property was restored. Neither large enterprise managers (subjected to various pressures) nor workers at large had market-based incentives (AECD 1992b).

The contours of a new social structure are becoming visible, although rather hypothetically:

- The delay in the reforms created a new caste of former and present rulers that includes the ex-party and economic nomenklatura. Unified by common economic interests, they operate in the twilight zone between the private and the state sectors. Their connections and access to information and power levers make up the priceless capital they share. The slow pace of the reforms and the general chaos are favorable for this small elite.

- The former owners of nationalized property whose property was restored to them were strongly represented in the Parliament and the UDF government. Their future economic role, however, is dubious; in most cases they are elderly people who intend to lease their property. Polls show that they intend to use mainly the rents.

- The young entrepreneurial class is the most dynamic group. Although the reforms are being pursued in their name, they are not feeling any benefits; the legislative and administrative chaos and the unclear rules of the game are seriously hindering them. But their interests are ambiguous. The creation of a strong legal framework, tax reform, tax enforcement, and order in general works against them. They favor the continuation of both the inefficient state sector and weak executive power. The twilight zone of the transition is their best chance. There have been several attempts to organize and politically represent the interests of the nascent private sector in Bulgaria, but most of them have remained insignificant. The first organization, the Union for Private Economic Enterprise, influences public opinion through a powerful press group (1 million circulation). The Bulgarian Business Party and the Bulgarian Business Bloc took part in the 1991 elections, but they received only 3 percent of the vote.

- It is unclear whether the 2.5 million retired people in Bulgaria are capable of effectively defending their interests. The decline in their real incomes, the worsening medical care, and the general insecurity define them as one of the greatest losers.

Public attitudes are difficult to assess. The reliability of public opinion research is under question for methodological weakness and for suspicions of political partiality. The picture these studies reveal is mixed; opinions change quickly, strongly influenced by current events and the media.

In general, Bulgarians, while still very politicized (as shown by the high election turnout), share the common Eastern European fatigue with politics. In the course of one year, 1992, the two main parties lost a considerable part of their electoral support. Among the institutions, the presidency (with 60–70 percent support) and the army enjoy a high degree of confidence; the government and Parliament command lower confidence. Two-thirds of the population believed in May 1992 that they were living poorly and in a state of deepening permanent crisis. Apathy, cynicism, and fear of the future are signs of growing social isolation.

Most Bulgarians want to have the best of both worlds—they are in favor of both the market economy and the welfare state. Historically, the country has been and remains egalitarian. Egalitarian moods seem to be fortified by the indecisive course of the economic reform. A survey of March 1992 shows that half of the Bulgarians believed that the reform had stopped, 62 percent that the maximum wage should not exceed the minimum one by more than threefold, and 41 percent that privatization should be stopped because for the time being it will benefit only the rich. Still, in the course of two years the percentage of people who will not accept the country's being divided into rich and poor dropped from 70 percent (January 1990) to 47 percent (March 1992). So three years after the abolishment of socialism, socialist morale and reflexes were alive. The legacy of the past blended with a reaction to the emerging wealth.

Attitudes toward private business and privatization are also mixed. In the eyes of many Bulgarians, business is connected with illegal profiteering. This attitude is partly due to the real situation of active money laundering and law evasion, but it is certainly aggravated by the media and the political debates. Half of the respondents in the March 1992 survey approved of private economic initiatives, but 63 percent would not undertake one. Two-thirds of the population had no intention of participating in the forthcoming privatization. Another 15 percent intended to participate with symbolic sums of money. This response is a signal that privatization will not have broad support, for both psychological and financial reasons.

Much to the disappointment of opinion pollsters and electoral results analysts, it is obvious that people do not have a clear sense of their own interest. Their political consciousness is almost religious, based on good and bad, "us" and "them." The electoral behavior of the Bulgarians is difficult to explain in rational terms. The peasants, who were considered to be the greatest victims of the socialist transformation of the village, voted in favor of the BSP in June 1990, while city dwellers voted for the Agrarian Union. Most of the electoral results still can be explained by the referendum character of the vote—for or against the system—so they do not correlate with political power. The modest electoral results of the private business parties, as well as the failure of the Agrarian Union in the 1991 elections, can be attributed to the ongoing political confrontation between the UDF and the BSP. Voters neglected their specific interests, instinctively feeling that those interests would be better defended at a higher political level.

Interest groups favoring or opposing economic reform are difficult to define. A perspective focusing on winners and losers does not help explain Bulgarian society. The perception is that with the exception of the 3–10 percent (according to various estimates) of owners to whom property was restored and the thin layer of well-paid high administrative and political elites, the bulk of the population has lost ground. Nevertheless, in the initial stages of the reforms, people were convinced that sacrifices were necessary. The electoral victory of the UDF came after seven months of a severe austerity program carried out mainly by the UDF economic ministers in the coalition government. Even Ivan Kostov, who played much the same role in Bulgaria that Leszek Balcerowicz did in Poland, was reelected a member of Parliament with a great majority in the city of Plovdiv—proof that radical marketization was widely accepted. Still, the picture is not quite clear. Do workers, peasants, and intellectuals really back this policy, which inevitably brings them hardship?

New political elites are arising in the current feverish atmosphere, and there can be no doubt that further development of the economic transition will differentiate the actors in Bulgarian society and make them more influential. Which tendencies will take the upper hand—the neoliberal, the populist, or the social democratic—it is too early to say. And why not a hybrid combination of all of them?

Trade Unions, Tripartism, or Social Partnership

For better or for worse, the Bulgarian transition to the market and democracy is marked with the presence of strong independent trade unions and trade union pluralism. Two large union organizations (besides several smaller ones) unite a considerable share of labor and seek to play a key role in the reform process and in the nation's life as well. The number of union members is subject to highly contradictory estimates (just like the numbers of participants in strikes), but the most likely figures indicate that at the end of 1991 Podkrepa had about 600,000 members and the Confederation of the Independent Trade Unions of Bulgaria (CITUB), 2 million. In any case, the degree of unionization is high (70–80 percent), close to that of the Scandinavian countries. Bulgaria has a tradition of active syndicalism dating from the 1930s and 1940s. Democracy and the management of the economic reform gave the unions new life and a strong position to reestablish themselves after fifty years of being "the transmission belt of the party."

The CITUB emerged from out of the former official Bulgarian trade unions. Although many people were initially suspicious of the new union, its ambitious new leaders (such as Krustyu Petkov) broke with the Communist party and launched a program in defense of social democratic principles and a regulated social market economy. The CITUB claims to be the first reformed trade union of Eastern Europe and is closest to the centrists in Bulgarian politics.

Podkrepa, the first nonformal independent trade union, was created in 1989 as a dissident organization by seven intellectuals after the model of Solidarity. It later became one of the founders of the UDF, its backbone and most militant detachment. Within the UDF, Podkrepa had an observer's status. After the October 1991 electoral victory it left the bloc, although it had its own lobby in the parliamentary group of the UDF. Podkrepa's platform is rather contradictory: it favors rapid free market reform and decommunization but is also in favor of social compensation. It supports a strong right-wing government that is kind to the socially weak.

In the short history of the beginning of the Bulgarian transition (1989–1992), there were several distinct phases in the relationship between the trade unions and the government. In late 1990 Bulgarian trade unions became aware of their political strength. The general strike initiated by Podkrepa and supported by the CITUB dealt the final blow to the last Communist government of Andrei Lukanov and forced his resignation.

The height of the unions' influence was the period of Dimitar Popov's coalition government, which relied heavily on union support. A special agreement, signed in January 1991, between the two unions, the government, and the Association of Employers (which is rather undefined under conditions of prevailing state ownership), confirmed the unions' important role in preserving the social peace and, more broadly, in regulating the country's economic and social life. This Tripartite Commission was created as a mechanism for coordinating every step of the initial stage of the reform. In retrospect, it is clear that most of the success of this initial stage of the reform was largely due to that coordination.

In November 1991 the new government of Philip Dimitrov (UDF) took a different stand. It felt politically stronger than the former coalition government and was reluctant to continue the policy of dependence on the unions. The prime minister himself and his two advisers explained in the press that "a syndicalist dictatorship is emerging in Bulgaria" and that "strong unions mean a weak state." The government canceled the Tripartite Commission and launched a campaign against the unions, accusing them of mafialike activities.

The attacks of the government made possible what had earlier seemed incredible: the reconciliation between the two unions in the second half of 1992. The tension between the government and the unions soon turned into a political war. The Tripartite Commission was renewed in July but canceled again shortly afterward. In May the two unions made a joint declaration, accusing the government of deliberately excluding them from talks on the new round of liberalization of prices. In a joint memorandum to the National Assembly just before the votes of no confidence (May and November 1992), the two confederations expressed their dissatisfaction with the course of the economic reform: the emphasis on monetary solutions at the expense of social ones, the lack of a comprehensive program, the neglect of the military and petrochemical industries, the delay of the structural reform, the antagonism toward private business, and the deepening of the recession. The government accused them of direct interference in politics. The conflict reflected two concepts of the transition: the neoliberal monetary approach of the government and the social market economy favored by the unions.

In December 1992 the nonparty government of Luben Berov restored the national system for social partnership, institutionalized in the National Council, adding representatives of private business. In a short time a series of agreements was signed to deal with long-standing social problems of income policy: unemployment benefits, compensatory payments, and wage levels.

Several factors predetermined the unions' important role during the initial phase of the Bulgarian transition. In a country where political representation of interests is not quite clear, the unions are one of the few exceptions—they have a large motivated membership, a nationwide network of structures, ambitious leaders, qualified experts, and an influential press (the newspapers *Trud* and *Podkrepa*). The absence of a real left-wing party and the lack of social legislation mean that additional tasks fall to them. The two big confederations, in contrast to many organizations, did not split and even managed to overcome their mutual hostility and act together, especially when attacked by the government. Strong internationally, both unions established direct contacts with the IMF. Bulgaria's association agreement with the European Community includes provisions on union participation in power sharing.

The Bulgarian case offers an interesting perspective on the role of trade unions in a period of transition. Podkrepa was created as a militant union fighting against the totalitarian system. The reformist forces in society relied on it for overthrowing the last communist government and for keeping social peace during the painful economic reforms and during the firing of a great number of middle-level economic nomenklatura. Later, when the reformist forces, through the UDF, came to power (again with the assistance of the unions), relations became more difficult. The eternal problem of the limits of the unions' interference in politics arose dramatically. The two Bulgarian unions made no secret of their wish to influence events in their country directly. Their vision was that in times of profound systemic change pure syndicalism offers a utopia. Unlike politicians, the unions and their ambitious leaders (who personify the unions to a great extent) wield enormous real power. In an impoverished country, manipulating or using social discontent is not difficult, particularly through several crucial, well-organized detachments of union members like miners, doctors, bus drivers, and teachers. Although in most cases the unions have denied acting on political motivations, most of their actions have had political aims. In January 1992 the CITUB declared a general strike seemingly based on economic demands, only days before the presidential election. In April and May 1992 Podkrepa's miners went on strike, protesting against the closure of mines and unpaid salaries and calling for individual accountability—the resignation of two of the economic ministers (of finance and industry and trade). The government refused to consider any demand of that character, but later one of the ministers was replaced. New attacks directly against the government were undertaken in July with a strike of city transport workers in Sofia. The UDF passed a special declaration condemning Podkrepa—its founder and former chief ally—of "anarcho-syndicalism." In retrospect, it looks as if the break between Podkrepa and UDF was inevitable and even desirable; Podkrepa could not become a formal state trade union, for it was too strong to become a puppet controlled by any political force. But the break was a symbol of the nondialogue policy of the government and finally became one of the main reasons for its fall at the end of 1992.

As the reforms stumbled, the unions acquired a stronger voice: they rejected the monetarist approach of the UDF government and declared themselves in favor of gradual, coordinated, step-by-step changes. For this reason they insisted on an overall program for the reform process and accused the executives of inertia, lack of vision, and incompetence.

It is difficult to assess the unions' role in the Bulgarian transition. Are they shadow powers, able to support or overthrow governments, or responsible first-rate actors in the nation's life? Despite the polarization of opinion, society as a whole lays hopes on their activity—polls at the end of 1992 showed a 44–49 percent approval rating, far higher than many other institutions.

Initially pluralistic, the political system turned out to be not very democratic. After the elections of autumn 1991, the UDF had no effective adversaries in the government. The extraparliamentary opposition was negligible, and the BSP was only the shadow of a left-wing party. The trade unions therefore were one of the few real opponents to the ruling team of the UDF, who demonstrated surprisingly authoritarian reflexes. Thus the unions acted as a second center of real power; they offered a dialogue and a balance between the power structures so that neither could get the upper hand.

Even during the short period discussed here, Bulgarian trade unionism evolved. As time passed, membership in large unions melted and smaller branch trade unions replaced them. During the initial stage of the transition, the unions were preoccupied with political issues rather than with pursuing the interests of unions as large-scale institutions, but that trend is gradually reversing. The unions have been connected with some private banks and foundations, and they control their own banklike fund and their own huge property. They have expressed their intent to take part in privatization, too, and want to play a major role in the forthcoming transformation. "I am afraid that we have come very close to the limit, beyond which the syndicates acquire the role of a parallel structure or super structure," wrote the CITUB's leader Krustyu Petkov in May 1993.

The Bulgarian example demonstrates that in times of sweeping and socially painful change, when a country has set records in inflation and unemployment, the trade unions can serve as important regulators of the socially acceptable price of the transition and also as corrective and coordinating organs, sharing responsibility for social peace.

The Primacy of Politics over Economics

The balance sheet of the first three years of the Bulgarian transition to market and democracy is mixed. On the positive side, Bulgaria has achieved a multiparty representative democratic political system; three rounds of free elections; four peaceful transfers of power; two parliaments; the adoption of a new constitution; new legislation; independent trade unions; free press, radio, and television; a politically active population; and, last but not least, the successful management of an ethnic crisis. These great changes have taken place within the framework of a peaceful scenario: in contrast to its immediate Balkan neighbors, Bulgaria has avoided violence and bloodshed and could play a stabilizing role in the region.

But the Bulgarian case has its negative side too: the stalemate between two main political forces, the UDF and the BSP, has trapped the nation in what is falsely characterized as a confrontation between left and right. This stalemate has impeded the normal process of differentiation and party building and has caused the sharp polarization and politicization of every issue, including the economy.

The economic reform remains the weakest point of the Bulgarian transition. By the end of 1992, three years after the changes, not a single enterprise has been privatized; the share of private business is modest; important pieces of basic system-changing economic legislation, like laws on taxation, bankruptcy, budget, and social security, are still missing. In sum, to quote President Zhelyu Zhelev, with 95 percent state ownership, Bulgaria still looks very much like a communist country.

In the Bulgarian case the assumed connection between market-oriented reforms and the consolidation of representative democracy is valid only to a point. The interaction between politics and economics and the sequencing of the economic and political changes are not quite clear and definitely not linear. There can be no doubt that the processes of market-oriented reform and democratic change are simultaneous and interlinked. In contrast to the superficial reforms of the pre-1989 period, real economic reforms were made possible only with the political collapse of the Communist regime. These reforms are a precondition for and a means to reinforce democracy. But the short span of time since the reforms began and the speed of the processes to date do not give enough evidence to confirm the general proposition of this volume on the interdependence of economic and political reforms. Nonetheless, it is clear that economic and political changes proceed at unequal speed and that there is a definite predominance of political over economic motivations. A rough comparison of the time, societal energy, and attention spent on both major issues would reveal a surprising neglect of the urgent economic problems. The ability of the newly created political system to initiate and support economic reforms depends on political stability. The old planned economy had to be destroyed as a condition of starting to build a new one. It was not a question of transformation, of gradual step-by-step changes in the degree of state participation, because state socialism was more than a matter of different mixtures of market and command (Kaminski 1991). Democratic politics was, moreover, viewed as a means of solving economic problems (Murrell 1991). In Bulgaria, where little if any change had occurred within the economic system, the transition was bound to create new institutions, new rules of the game, and even a new mentality. All of these were achievable only through political means, for in the absence of real economic agents, the political sphere acquired the utmost importance. Furthermore, in the Bulgarian case the role of politics became even greater because of the political confrontation, or unresolved power game. Economic issues were subordinated to narrow party and even personal interests.

Economic reforms in Bulgaria in 1989–1992 were carried out under four different configurations of power and four respective correlations of the economy and politics: each of the four governments adopted a name reflecting its goals.

- *The Government of Spoluka (Success)*. The BSP won the 1990 elections with the slogan, or promise, of a smooth transition. Unable and unwilling to undertake painful measures, the former Communists tried to preserve the status quo and delayed radical reform at the expense of the country's last reserves.[8]

- *The Government of Reform*. Also called the kamikaze coalition (November 1990–November 1991), this regime began the big bang stabilization program backed by an agreement on social peace and a Tripartite Commission for coordination of interests. While the economic ministries in the cabinet were given to the opposition, the Socialist party preserved a majority in Parliament and could influence the character and the speed of adoption of the economic laws. Meanwhile, on the local level, the socialist middle nomenklatura was also blocking the reform. Thanks mostly to the high motivation of the population and the role of the trade unions, social peace was preserved during the most painful stage of the reform.

- *The Government of Radical Change*. This government came to power in 1991 with a sufficient majority to speed up the process of economic change. The government later received another name, however—"the government of restitution." Because of the strong lobby of people interested in having their property restored, this government gave priority to the three restitution laws, leaving aside the privatization laws. In addition, the new Parliament felt obliged to revise a number of economic laws adopted under the Socialist majority, like the Land Reform Act and the Law on Foreign Investment. The reform process lost momentum.

• *The Government of Privatization.* The experts' nonparty government elected at the end of 1992 ambitiously and hastily gave itself this name, emphasizing its basic aim.

As this chronology shows, all the governments during this first stage of transition have had short lives and shaky support. The ongoing acute political struggle in the country led to an ideologization and politicization of the economic reform. Economic rationality came second after political considerations. In the Bulgarian case, because of the absence of private sector and authentic economic agents in general, political decisions acquired utmost importance and the economy could not become autonomous. Concerned about their survival, governments rejected the very idea of political pragmatism toward the economic transformation. The Parliament could not play its supposedly primary role in changing the system. Economic issues were systematically pushed aside by political scandals.[9] Parliament was more an arena for political struggles than a legislative framework for change; and this situation was, in the words of one of the authors of the UDF economic program, Roumen Avramov, one of the biggest initial disappointments.

Two examples clearly show how politics dominates economic concerns. First is the reform of agriculture. Reforms in this basic sector of the Bulgarian economy were primarily shaped by political considerations. In the course of three years, two different land reform acts were adopted. In February 1991 the Grand National Assembly, with a majority of socialists, passed a law restoring the equivalent value and quantity of land to original owners. Besides its numerous faults (no free market of land, many restrictions), this law authorized the former party bosses of the villages to carry out the changes. The next Parliament, dominated by the UDF, adopted a new version providing for the liquidation of the 2,500 collective farms and the restoration of land to former owners within their actual original boundaries. The new law aimed at accelerating the change in the villages by destroying the old structures and eliminating the control of the old nomenklatura. Thus it had a decidedly political focus; it was called the law of the decommunization of the Bulgarian village, since it was meant to hit the basic supporters of BSP. The socialists actively opposed the law. Not only did they vote against it, but, following time-tested conspiratorial tactics, they organized mass protests in the villages. Following from the law, special liquidation councils (what a name!) were appointed by the district governors: in most cases their members were chosen for their political loyalty and were often incompetent outsiders. In view of the slow reform of the sector and the sabotage of the old nomenklatura, this political, administrative approach was indispensable from the point of view of the ruling UDF. It did, however, provoke tension in the villages and in some cases strikes, violent rallies, and police intervention. Some of these protests were the result of BSP-organized resistance, but there was also wide discontent with the administrative-bureaucratic approach to the problems, which was again imposed from above with little if any participation by the peasants themselves.

Thus, the Bulgarian village was turned into a battlefield in the political confrontation between the BSP and the UDF. Questions of rural productivity and efficiency, the true problems of the agrarian reform, had little place in the heated political debates. As a result, the restoration of property (a difficult process from technical, practical, and legal points of view) was delayed and mismanaged. Huge waste and pillage and the destruction of basic infrastructure and resources (such as irrigation systems, farm machinery, and herds) were reported. The process looked very much like an antipode of the collectivization of the 1950s.

The liquidation councils were accused of liquidating agriculture: 1992 collective agricultural production was reported to have dropped 27 percent, offset partly by the 14 percent rise in private sector production. Retail prices of milk and meat skyrocketed. Without a doubt, Bulgarian society is paying a high price for this type of reform. If the return to small-scale family farming is the final aim, how long will it take to create it, and can it be effective in the face of present and future competition from the European Community? The average size of a farm will vary from about 1.6–20 hectares—that is, five times smaller than that in the EC. As opinion polls show, because of the lack of machines and capital, most owners prefer the cooperative form; only 4 percent are ready for private farming. But proposals for new cooperative farms were met with hostility, because the owners feared a return to the previous collective farms and former party secretaries were suspected of being behind their restoration. Thus, owing to the political confrontation, in contrast to the piecemeal rural transformation in the rest of Eastern Europe, land reform in Bulgaria took a sweeping form. Aiming to correct a historical injustice, it turned more to the past than to the present or future development of the sector.

The second example concerns the delay of privatization of sizable state enterprises. Despite the general consensus about the importance of privatization as the core of effective change of the system, by the end of 1992, after three years of political and two years of economic reforms, not a single large state enterprise had been privatized in Bulgaria. The Privatization Law was adopted in April 1992 under international pressure; the long, administrative procedures of the Agency for Privatization complicated matters further. The privatization of small firms, shops, and restaurants was blocked by an opposition-sponsored moratorium preventing the old nomenklatura from profiting.

The number of legal, technical, and administrative difficulties connected with such a massive transfer of property should not be underestimated. True for all of Eastern Europe, they will be even greater for the extremely centralized and monopolized Bulgarian economy. Still, the most serious obstacles seem to be political ones. A political process as much as an economic one, privatization in Bulgaria fell prey to political polarization. In other words, privatization is universally considered to be the panacea for the economy; no political force openly opposes it. In practice, however, it looks as if nobody is seriously interested in it. In contrast to the restitution laws, where real owners were directly represented in Parliament and were capable of imposing the laws and directly profiting from them, the political dividends from privatization are not that clear. In principle, since privatization will create real owners and economic agents, it will put an end to the absurd postcommunist structure of Bulgarian politics in which it is not clear who represents whom. But do the parties really want this issue clarified? The answer is probably no, for it might be easier to manipulate undefined social groups with slogans and keep the level of excitement and politicization high. Instinctively or deliberately, politicians in office and in opposition have neglected this basic instrument of social transformation and democratic order. The 96 percent share of state ownership is the basis for the ongoing superconcentration of economic power and consequently for authoritarian trends in politics. From this point of view, political crises seem inevitable: the basis of Bulgarian society—ownership relations, legislation, etc.—has not changed very much during these first years of the transition.

Since real life does not allow a vacuum, the delay of legal privatization has caused a wave of spontaneous and hidden privatizations, leading to massive degradation and pillaging of state property. In contrast to the paralysis in official reforms, real changes are occurring in the shadow economy. Their scope and economic consequences are difficult to assess. Thus the Bulgarian case demonstrates how time lost to political indecisiveness and lack of general vision can jeopardize the outcome of reform.

The Controversial Role of the State

The short history of the Bulgarian transition to the market and democracy shows the ambiguous and paradoxical role that Bulgarians expect the state to play. In an Eastern Orthodox country with a strong tradition of centralism and a weak civil society, the state was supposed to be the major engine of change. Even more than in the rest of Eastern Europe, the state was expected to organize the structural reform and privatization, to ensure that there was a social safety net, and to develop infrastructure and an industrial policy. In these specifically Balkan circumstances, the paradoxical role of the state—in organizing its own withdrawal from the economy—took a peculiar form. The young Bulgarian democracy demonstrated an inclination to concentrate economic power and to continue to use authoritarian and administrative patterns of governing. Market rhetoric did not screen the actual recentralization and intensification of state control over the economy during the first years of the transition. The conduct of macroeconomic, financial, and fiscal policy gave unprecedented power to the economic team of the government. State budgets were still developed according to the old law of the socialist budget of 1965. A prerogative mainly of the executive branch (the Ministry of Finance), the budget did not assume a new role, and parliamentary debates were almost formalities. Curiously enough, the new democratic rule not only did not put an end to the practice of direct state intervention in the economy, but in fact resorted to it extensively. Thus, the much-publicized decommunization of economic management and state administration—when the former communist nomenklatura was replaced by politically suitable cadres—left the system of political control intact. The conflict between the UDF government and the trade unions and the appointment of liquidation councils in the villages can also be explained by the executive's strong effort to hold all levers of economic power. All forms of direct democracy in the economy were abandoned; directors and managers were appointed by the political parties and trade unions. The merging of political and economic authorities has further bureaucratized the economy and the reforms; indeed, bureaucrats seem to be among the few beneficiaries of the changes.

At the same time, however, the state did withdraw from one of its most important functions—that of the owner of more than 90 percent of the country's wealth. The massive illegal transformation of state property into private property has been taking place in different ways. The delay and discrediting of privatization and other real reforms have created a twilight zone between the state and private sector where there are no clear rules of the game. As in other countries, economic changes in Bulgaria profited those already in good positions—political or economic—who had access to information, scarce resources, credit, and international connections. The lack of rules, reform legislation, and financial inspection (its structures were virtually dissolved), created an interregnum that suits many. These circles do not want normalcy, which would bring control and order. Are they influential enough to affect the policy-making process? In the minds of many paranoic Eastern Europeans, the answer is positive. Bulgarians have seen many examples of the corruption of the new elite and the rapid shifts between the old and the new elites—the red and the blue. The unpardonable delay of privatization and tax legislation and the postponed creation of an Audit Office offer grounds for speculation. Premeditation might have existed in some cases, but the most probable explanations are neglect, incompetence, and the low priority of economic matters.

The Crisis of the End of 1992

Two years after the beginning of economic reforms and three years after the political change, the Bulgarian transition reached a crossroad. The economic reforms stumbled and virtually stopped. The fall of the UDF government revealed a crisis of the whole model of transition. The political crisis deepened the economic one. But the dismal state of the economy had little if any place in the political debates. This tendency is a true sign of overpoliticization: the main arguments against the government came from non-economic spheres. They concerned the war of the institutions and the secret service and its authoritarian style, against which influential forces had united. But the most probable, mostly unspoken reason for the fall of the UDF government seems to be the general feeling that reforms had lost direction and were not going well. The demands for a left turn and more socially oriented reforms should be understood as demands for a change in both politics and economic policy.

Concluding Remarks

The Bulgarian transition confirms some truisms. Both theory and simple rationality suggest that politics has immense importance for young democracies. Preoccupied with a political confrontation, the country has unpardonably delayed, neglected, and politicized the economic reforms. And yet, outside of the central troika of Hungary, Poland, and the Czech Republic, in a broader Eastern European context Bulgaria suffers from one of the mildest crises, compared with other countries from the region in which military hostilities are literally destroying the economy.

Bulgarian developments also show that there is a gap between willingness to follow the principles of democracy and practical know-how and interest in doing so. Profound and sustained changes in society must be accomplished with the support of broad circles—the very future of democracy depends on it.

In Bulgaria the most important changes are still ahead. The period 1989–1992 is probably the beginning of the beginning. The country is on the threshold of a profound structural reform and massive social dislocation. To predict which direction the changes will go, one needs the qualities not of an analyst but of a fortune-teller. There are, however, two important supportive factors: The first is what Adam Przeworski calls "geography"—that is, the European identity of the country; the second is time.

Appendix to Chapter 4
Basic Indicators and Chronology for Bulgaria

TABLE A4.1

Basic Economic and Social Data for Bulgaria

Population (1992)	8.5 million
Life expectancy (1989)	71.4 years
Population density	81 people/square kilometer
Urban population	67 percent
GDP per capita (1992)	US$1,066
Inflation (1992)	79.4 percent
Unemployment (1992)	15.3 percent
Gross foreign debt (1992)	US$12.9 billion
Budget deficit (1992)	4.8 percent of GDP

Source: Author.

TABLE A4.2

Chronology of Events in Bulgaria, 1989–1992

1989	Palace coup takes place in November. Zhivkov resigns. In December the UDF is created.
1990	BSP wins the first free elections in June. In November Lukanov's socialist government resigns. In December a coalition government is formed.
1991	Economic reforms are begun in February. In October the second elections are won by UDF.
1992	President Zhelev is reelected in January. Dimitrov's UDF government is toppled by a no-confidence vote in December. Berov's nonparty cabinet is formed.

Source: Author.

Notes and References

Chapter 1, "The Transition in Bulgaria, Hungary, and Poland: An Overview"

Notes

1.   We use the term "communism" in a descriptive sense, referring to political regimes operating in Eastern Europe from the late 1940s to 1989, which were dominated by the Communist party. Eastern Europe refers, for brevity, to post-Communist Europe outside of the former Soviet Union.

2.   We cannot enter into a debate on definition of "democracy" and in particular whether an unstable democracy can be treated as a "real" one. There are strong reasons, however, to accept a narrow definition (see Huntington 1991: 6).

3.   See Skocpol 1979: 33–40 and Rueschemeyer et al. 1992: 12–26 on comparative historical analysis.

4.   In fact, among the transforming postcommunist economies, so far only Czechoslovakia has avoided acute fiscal problems. After the split from Slovakia, the Czech Republic will probably be the only fiscally sound economy in the whole region.

References

Chirot, Daniel. 1989. *The Origins of Backwardness in Eastern Europe*. Berkeley: University of California Press.

Huntington, Samuel J. 1991. *The Third Wave: Democratization in the Late Twentieth Century*. Norman: University of Oklahoma Press.

Rueschemeyer, Dietrich, et al. 1992. *State and Market in Development*. Boulder: Lynne Rienner Publishers.

Skocpol, Theda. 1979. *States and Social Revolution*. Cambridge: Cambridge University Press.

Chapter 2, "The Transition to the Market and Democratization in Poland"

Notes

The completion of this chapter was made possible by the generous support of the Overseas Development Council. Previous versions were discussed at ODC meetings in Budapest in November 1992 and in Washington, D.C., in March 1993. Several Polish colleagues also agreed to read preliminary drafts and share their impressions. The author wishes to thank all those who participated in the discussions on this chapter, and in particular Władysław Baka, Tamás Bauer, Marcello Cavarozzi, Andrzej Jezierski, Deyan Kiuranov, Tadeusz Kowalik, Aleksander Łukaszewicz, Kálmán Mizsei, Joan Nelson, Barbara Petz, Ben Slay, Henryk Szlajfer, Miguel Urrutia, and Edmund Wnuk-Lipiński. Needless to say, all responsibility for opinions expressed in this chapter remains his.

1.   I use the term "communism" here in a descriptive sense, as a name of a political system in which the Communist party controls the most important aspects of social life. Some authors use other terms: "Soviet-type societies," "Leninist regimes," or "real socialism." There are arguments for this or that term, and there are inevitable ideological connotations attached to any of them. Since this is not the place to solve this issue, I choose the term "communism" in a somewhat arbitrary way.

2.   Private agriculture was strictly subject to planning through administrative prices, the obligatory selling of produce to the state, and administrative allocation of the factors of production.

3.   The analyses of Ludwig von Mises and Friedrich Hayek are unsurpassed in this respect.

4.   In June 1976, Gierek finally decided to raise food prices. That triggered a wave of demonstrations in two industrial towns, Radom and Ursus. Many participants, mostly workers, were later picked up by police, beaten, harassed, fired from work, and sentenced to heavy fines. Initially KOR activity consisted of providing them with legal and financial help and publicizing the abuses of power by whatever means possible. Later, it became an umbrella organization for various civil rights actions and for self-organizing activities on a grass-roots level.

5.   In August 1980, agreements were signed between strike committees and Communist authorities legalizing independent trade unions. In December 1981, martial law was declared.

6.   Sixty-five percent of places in the future Sejm (the lower house of the Parliament) were reserved for the Communist party (PZPR) and its allies, while the remaining 35 percent were open to the independent forces. In a newly created upper house, the Senate, all seats were open for electoral competition. The president (a newly created post; the State Council had previously acted as a collective head of the state) was to be elected by both houses of Parliament. It was tacitly understood that the office was shaped for Jaruzelski and that the person of the president would guarantee the stability of Poland within the Soviet bloc.

7.   Sugar had been rationed since the late 1970s.

8.   Enterprises were given part of the foreign exchange earned; for exports the state paid them a zloty equivalent of the export price.

9.   Already in the 1970s there were possibilities for establishing so-called Polonia

firms (founded by Poles from abroad), firms that in fact opened the door slightly for foreign capital.

10.   Rakowski is a controversial figure. For years editor in chief of *Polityka*, a liberal, proreform weekly with probably no parallel in any other communist country, he joined the cabinet of Jaruzelski in 1981 as deputy prime minister, was prime minister from September 1988 to August 1989, and after Jaruzelski's election as president became in July 1989 the last first secretary of the PZPR (disbanded in January 1990). Rakowski was disliked by the public because of his support for Jaruzelski and martial law and because of his often provocative style and tendency to personalize conflicts.

11.   Mazowiecki was a politician close to the Church and until 1981 was editor in chief of a lay Catholic quarterly. During the strikes of 1980–1981 he was one of two closest Wałęsa advisers. He was editor in chief of the Solidarity weekly, was interned under martial law, and was an important participant in the round-table talks. Mazowiecki was regarded as one of the most responsible and respectable politicians of the Solidarity camp.

12.   Balcerowicz was forty-two years old in 1989, a professor at the Main School of Planning and Statistics in Warsaw (he studied at St. John's University in New York in 1972–1974), and a member of the party until the introduction of martial law, when he resigned. At a younger age, he had also been an outstanding track and field athlete.

13.   His talk on the necessity of stabilization and reform before the members of the Solidarity parliamentary caucus was very important.

14.   Foreigners must bring in over 2 million ECU to obtain these privileges.

15.   Financing for foreign transactions was provided by two state-owned banks, and rural credit was provided by 1,500 small, single-branch cooperative rural banks, united within the Bank for Food Economy.

16.   Such a view was presented by Ian Hume, a representative of the World Bank in Warsaw, during his talk at Warsaw University on January 11, 1993.

17.   Technically, this sale would be indirect—an interested person could first buy a "certificate of share," which then could be used to buy a share in one of the funds.

18.   An enterprise to be privatized (at the joint request of the manager and the employee council, with the input of a general assembly of employees and the funding organ, and with the approval of the Privatization Ministry) is to be turned into a corporation ("commercialized," according to the Polish terminology). The employee council ceases to exist, but the employees obtain the right to elect one-third of the board of directors. Such an enterprise should be privatized within two years. The employees then lose the right to elect representatives to the board, but they can buy 20 percent of the stock at the public offering price.

19.   All these examples are from Ganowski (1992).

20.   After a wave of strikes in several large SOEs in mid-1992, the Anna Suchocka cabinet proposed that there be more employee involvement in the process of privatization (this is the so-called pact on state-owned enterprises).

21.   The percentage declines in output in the postcommunist countries in 1990–1991 and 1990–1992 were as follows: Albania: -44 and -54; Bulgaria: -40 and -55; Czechoslovakia: -24 and -45; Finland: -9 and -10; Hungary: -23 and -44; Poland: -33 and -37; and Romania: -35 and -43 (Kuczyński 1992).

22.   Two hundred permanently homeless people live in the Warsaw Central Station alone, according to press reports.

23.   Twenty-eight percent of respondents to a January 1992 poll favored authoritarian rule (*Gazeta Wyborcza*, January 29, 1992).

24.   The research done on elites has just begun; see Wasilewski and Wesołowski (1992).

25.   As this text is being finished, the election campaign is in full swing. Early August 1993 poll results show that six parties—UD, PSL, BBWR (recently created by Wałęsa), SdRP, KPN, and Solidarity—have fair chances of getting a required threshold of 5 percent of votes. Self-defense, a noisy, populist organization of disgruntled farmers, often resorting to extralegal means, has a chance of receiving votes not only from the rural electorate, but also from the urban unemployed.

26.   *Rzeczpospolita*, September 19, 1992.

27.   An extreme but good illustration is the case of Colonel Ryszard Kukliński, a member of the Polish General Staff during the 1980s, who worked for U.S. intelligence and defected on the eve of martial law. A whole ideological debate started in Poland about how he should be treated: as a hero of the fight against communism and Soviet oppression or as a traitor who broke his military oath.

28.   Six bills on decommunization and lustration are now being considered by parliamentary commissions.

29.   This is recommended by the Organization for Economic Cooperation and Development (OECD 1992).

30.   Unfortunately, "[t]he choice for quantity rather than quality in the administration is . . . [a] structural deficiency, typical for economies controlled by political parties. The general government employs 3 million people, or about 17 percent of the labor force. At the same time, salaries in the central administration are too low to retain the best individuals" (Crombrugghe 1992).

31.   In what follows, I rely heavily on Crombrugghe (1992).

32.   SOEs, overall, showed negative profits in 1992.

33.   See Crombrugghe's interesting comparisons of the expenditure structures of Czechoslovakia, Hungary, Poland, and Portugal.

34.   This is supported by data on elections. See Jasiewicz (1992), Markowski and Żukowski (1992), and Grabowska et al. (1992).

35.   This problem is recognized in the West as well. The influential magazine *The Economist* argues strongly against "the mistaken case for gradualism" (May 16, 1992). Michel Camdessus, head of the IMF, who favors "going fast," nevertheless noted, "It took my country 2,000 years to develop capitalism" (*New York Times*, April 26, 1992).

36.   To give one example, according to one poll, 25 percent of those asked did not know that Poland has a personal income tax in place, despite the fact that the system was introduced in 1992.

References

Ash, Timothy Garten. 1989. *The Polish Revolution: Solidarity*. New York: Scribners.

———. 1990. *The Magic Lantern: The Revolution of '89 Witnessed in Warsaw, Budapest, Berlin, and Prague*. New York: Random House.

Balcerowicz, Leszek. 1992. *800 dni: Szok kontrolowany* (800 days: a controlled shock). Warsaw: BGW.

Bednarski, Marek. 1991. "'Small privatization' in Poland." *PPRG Discussion Papers*, no. 7. Warsaw: Warsaw University, Polish Policy Research Group.

Bocheński, Jacek. 1992. "Zdrada panny S. Nikt nas nie uprzedzał, że będzie kapitalizm" (A betrayal of Miss S. [Solidarity]: Nobody had warned us that capitalism would come). *Gazeta Wyborcza* (September 5–6).

Chirot, Daniel. 1980. "The Corporatist Model and Socialism." *Theory and Society 9*, no. 2.

Crombrugghe, Alain de. 1992. "The Polish Government Budget: Stabilization and Sustainability." A report prepared for the Institute for East-West Studies Conference on Public Finance in the Process of Economic Transition in East-Central Europe, Prague. Mimeo.

Dąbrowski, Janusz, et al. n.d. "Stabilization and State Enterprise Adjustment: The Political Economy of State Firms after Five Months of Fiscal Discipline, Poland 1990." *Program on Central and Eastern Europe Working Paper Series*, no. 6. Minda da Ginzburg Center for European Studies, Harvard University.

Dahrendorf, Ralf. 1990. *Reflections on the Revolution in Europe*. New York: Random House.

Ganowski, Zygmunt. 1992. "Meandry prywatyzacji" (Meanders of privatization). *Życie Gospodarcze* (September 6).

Gelb, Alan. 1992. "Socialist Transformations: An Overview of Eastern Europe and Some Comparisons." Paper presented in a conference "Economic Reform: Recent Experience in Market and Socialist Economies," El Escorial, Spain, July.

Grabowska, Mirosława, et al. 1991. "Społeczeństwo polskie i jego instytucje w okresie zmiany" (Polish society and its institutions in the period of transformation). In Edmund Wnuk-Lipiński, ed., *Świat postkomunistyczny: diagnoza i prognozy* (The postcommunist world: diagnosis and forecast). Warsaw: Instytut Studiów Politycznych Polskiej Akademii Nauk.

———. 1992. "Po trzecich wyborach" (After the third election). *Przegląd Polityczny*, nos. 1–2.

Grabowski Maciej H., and Przemysław Kulawczyk. 1992. "Small and Medium-size Enterprises in Poland: Analysis and Policy Recommendations." *Transformacja Gospodarki*, no. 25. Gdańsk: Instytut Badań nad Gospodarką Rynkową.

Gray, Cheryl. 1991. "Legal Framework in Central and Eastern Europe—The Polish Case." *Transition: The Newsletter about Reforming Economies 2*, no. 11 (December).

Iwanek, Maciej, and Marcin Święcicki. 1987. "Handlować kapitałem w socjalizmie" (Capital market in socialism), *Polityka* (July 16).

Iwanek, Maciej, and Janusz Ordower. 1991. "Transition to a Market Economy in Poland: Some Industrial Organization Issues." *PPRG Discussion Papers*, no. 9. Warsaw: Warsaw University, Polish Policy Research Group.

Janowski, Tomasz. 1992. "Plajta po polsku" (A Polish bankruptcy). *Rzeczpospolita* (September 14–16).

Jasiewicz, Krzysztof. 1991. "Od protestu i represji do wolnych wyborów" (From protests and repression to free elections). In Władysław Adamski et al., eds., *Polacy '90: Konflikty i zmiana (raport z badań empirycznych)* (Poles of 1990: Conflicts and change [report of empirical research]). Warsaw: Instytut Filozofii i Socjologii Polskiej Akademii Nauk and Instytut Studiów Politycznych Polskiej Akademii Nauk.

Jezierski, Andrzej. 1992. "The Formation of the Communist Middle Class in Poland." *The Polish Sociological Bulletin*, nos. 3–4.

Johnson, Simon, and Marzena Kowalska. 1992. "The Transition of Poland: 1989–91." A paper prepared for the project "The Political Economy of Structural Adjustment in New Democracies," organized by Stephan Haggard and Steven B. Webb. Mimeo.

Kemme, David M., ed. 1991. *Economic Reform in Poland: The Afterwards of Martial Law 1981–1988*. Greenwich, Conn.: JAI Press.

Kokoszczyński, Ryszard, and Andrzej Kondratowicz. 1991. "Monetary and Credit Policy in Poland." *PPRG Discussion Papers*, no. 10. Warsaw: Warsaw University, Polish Policy Research Group.

Kostrz-Kostecka, Ada. 1992. "Prywatyzacja po polsku" (A Polish way of privatization). *Rzeczpospolita* (September 3).

Kuczyński, Waldemar. 1992. "Twarde lądowanie z komunizmu" (The hard landing from communism). *Gazeta Wyborcza* (September 10).

Kurczewski, Jacek. 1992. "Polish Middle Class at the Close of the Eighties." *The Polish Sociological Bulletin*, nos. 3–4.

Kwieciński, Andrzej, and Antoni Leopold. 1991. "Polish Agriculture during the Transition Period." *PPRG Discussion Papers*, no. 8. Warsaw: Warsaw University, Polish Policy Research Group.

Lewandowski, Janusz, and Jan Szomburg. 1990. "Strategia prywatyzacji" (The strategy of privatization). *Transformacja Gospodarki*, no. 7. Gdańsk: Instytut Badań nad Gospodarką Rynkową.

Markowski, Radosław, and Tomasz Żukowski. 1992. "Wokół wyborów: Kampania prezydencka, jej wyniki i konskwencje w świetle badań opinii publicznej" (Elections: The presidential campaign, its outcomes and consequences in light of public opinion polls). A report for the East Europe Research Group. Mimeo.

Michałek, Jakub Jan. 1991. "The Opening Up of the Polish Economy." *PPRG Discussion Papers*, no. 11. Warsaw: Warsaw University, Polish Policy Research Group.

Modzelewski, Karol. 1992. "Wobec historycznego wyzwania" (In the face of historical challenge). *Przegląd Społeczny*, no. 1 (April).

Moskwa, Antoni. 1991. "Direct Foreign Investment in Poland: Hopes and Fears." *PPRG Discussion Papers*, no. 15. Warsaw: Warsaw University, Polish Policy Research Group.

Moskwa, Antoni, and Jerzy Wilkin. 1991. "The Balcerowicz Plan." *PPRG Discussion Papers*, no. 14. Warsaw: Warsaw University, Polish Policy Research Group.

Murrell, Peter. 1992. "Conservative Political Philosophy and the Strategy of Economic Transition." *East European Politics and Societies* 6, no. 1.

Myszkowska, Maria, and Wanda Romanowska, eds. 1984. *Polska reforma gospodarcza: System finansowy państwa* (Polish economic reform: System of national finance). Warsaw: Pánstwowe Wydawnictwo Ekonomiczne.

Organization for Economic Cooperation and Development (OECD). 1992. *Industry in Poland: Structural Adjustment Issues and Policy Options*. Paris: OECD, Centre for Cooperation with the European Economies in Transition.

Ost, David. 1989. "Towards a Corporatist Solution in Eastern Europe: The Case of Poland." *Eastern European Politics and Societies* 3, no. 1.

Pinto, Brian, Marek Belka, and Stefan Krajewski. 1992. "Transforming State Enterprises in Poland: Microeconomic Evidence on Adjustment." Draft paper prepared under World Bank RPO-67758 Program. Mimeo.

Polish Policy Research Group. 1991. "The Polish Economy and Politics since the Solidarity Take-over: Chronology of Events and Major Statistical Indicators." *PPRG Discussion Papers*, no. 6. Warsaw: Warsaw University, Polish Policy Research Group.

Socha, Mieczysław, and Urszula Sztanderska. 1992. "Labor Market in the Transition to the Market Economy in Poland." *PPRG Discussion Papers*, no. 2. Warsaw: Warsaw University, Polish Policy Research Group.

Śpiewak, Paweł. 1993. "Kto rządzi w Polsce?" (Who governs Poland?). In Mirosława Grabowska and Antoni Sułek, eds., *Polska 1989–1992: Fragmenty pejzażu* (Poland 1989–1992: Fragments of landscape). Warsaw: IFiS PAN.

Staniszkis, Jadwiga. 1984. *Poland's Self-Limiting Revolution*. Princeton: Princeton University Press.

Stypułkowski, Cezary, ed. 1986. *Polska reforma gospodarcza: Samodzielne i samorządne przedsiębiorstwo* (Polish economic reform: independent and self-managing enterprise). Warsaw: Pánstwowe Wydawnictwo Ekonomiczne.

Szomburg, Jan, and Janusz Lewandowski. 1990. "Strategia prywatyzacji" (The strategy of privatization). *Transformacja Gospodarki*, no. 7. Gdańsk: Instytut Badań nad Gospodarką Rynkową.

Wasilewski, Jacek. 1992. "Od postkomunistycznej do postsolidarnościowej sceny politycznej" (From the post-Communist to post-Solidarity political scene). In Wasilewski and Wesołowski 1992.

Wasilewski, Jacek, and Włodzimierz Wesołowski, eds. 1992. *Początki parlamentarnej elity. Posłowie kontraktowego Sejmu* (Beginnings of the parliamentary elite: Deputies of the "contract" parliament). Warsaw: Instytut Filozofii i Socjologii Polskiej Akademii Nauk.

Wellisz, Stanisław. 1991. "Macroeconomic Policies in Poland in 1990 and 1991." *PPRG Discussion Papers*, no. 1. Warsaw: Warsaw University, Polish Policy Research Group.

Wnuk-Lipiński, Edmund. 1991. "Deprywacje społeczne a konflikty interesów i wartości" (Social deprivations and the conflicts of interests and values). In Władysław Adamski et al., eds., *Polacy '90: Konflikty i zmiana (raport z badań empirycznych)* (Poles of 1990: Conflicts and change [report of empirical research]). Warsaw: Instytut Filozofii i Socjologii Polskiej Akademii Nauk and Instytut Studiów Politycznych Polskiej Akademii Nauk.

Chapter 3, "Demobilization and Gradualism: The Political Economy of the Hungarian Transition, 1987–1992"

Notes

I am grateful for the helpful comments of Joan Nelson, Kálmán Mizsei, Jacek Kochanowicz, Marcelo Cavarozzi, Mária Kovács, Ágnes Pogány, András Kovács, Tamás Bauer, László Urbán, and Béla Greskovics. My thanks to Erzsébet Gém for her help collecting the necessary figures and other sources and to Charles Hebbert, who corrected and improved the English of the text.

1. The term is from Bauer (1982).
2. This section is based on Valentiny (1992).

3. International comparison with the OECD countries shows that Hungarian redistribution is the highest as a share of GDP. See Kornai (1992:495).

4. In countries like Spain, Greece, Portugal, and Ireland it was between 15 and 21 percent in 1988 (Tóth 1992:26).

5. This section is based especially on Urbán (1992a:293 and 1992b).

6. The 1991 Hungarian Central Bank Act established the bank's independence from the government.

7. There is no vote of confidence on the ministers, only on the prime minister and his program. Therefore the Parliament cannot dismiss an individual minister without dismissing the prime minister and the whole cabinet with him.

8. The German constitutional system was regarded as a model for the establishment of an efficient Parliament (electoral system) and a stable government (chancellor system). During the period of constitutional engineering in 1989–1990, the Hungarian political elite was careful to avoid the dangers of a fragmented Parliament and a weak government.

9. Given that the new parties emerged after 1987, most of the MPs joined the political parties one or two years before the elections (and many of them only during the electoral campaign), so this is a relatively low figure.

10. The six parliamentary parties as a whole improved their position in relation to the other parties. While in the 1990 elections 84 percent of the votes were cast for them, current opinion polls show that they would gain 94 percent of the votes. (Figures from a January 1992 Hungarian Gallup survey are published in *Népszabadság*, March 9, 1992.)

11. That is, the government is a surplus majority coalition. If one party withdraws from the coalition (the Christian Democratic People's party in the Hungarian case), it does not threaten the legislative majority of the government (Laver and Schofield 1991).

12. Unlike some analysts, I am not at all convinced that this is a serious drawback for Hungary. It may delay certain necessary measures and slow down the economic transition in general, but it also gives more room for spontaneous processes in the economy and makes the transition more balanced. For example, there is no single concept or direction of privatization, so a plurality of methods and channels came into being. The variety of methods distributes the economic and social risks of the whole process. Since there was no need for shock therapy in Hungary, the lack of a big-bang plan may turn out to be an advantage.

13. Results of a survey conducted by Modus Marketing Counsultancy Ltd. appear in *Magyar Hírlap*, October 17, 1991, p. 1, and *Népszabadság*, October 17, 1991, p. 5.

14. If 2 million is taken for the level of MSZOSZ membership, the proportion is 72.5 percent. If we consider 1.1 million the real figure, it drops to 52 percent.

15. See Olson (1965). Tóth (1993) uses Olson's theoretical approach for the Hungarian interest organizations.

16. A five-party bill (made up of the Hungarian Democratic Forum, the Smallholder party, the Christian Democratic People's party, the Alliance of Free Democrats, and the Federation of Young Democrats) aimed to weaken the ex-Communist unions (MSZOSZ) and favor the new "independent" unions through the redistribution of the property of the MSZOSZ to the new unions.

17. This is criticized by the ultranationalist radical wing of the ruling coalition. See, for example, Csurka (1992).

18. In July 1992 taxes on profits totaled 44.5 percent and social security contribu-

tions and other fees totaled 63.5 percent of the wage cost. Local taxes and sick benefits (for the first ten days) increased the costs of entrepreneurs still further.

19. First, the social security system was institutionally and financially separated from the budget, and the state guarantee of the system was canceled. The pension age limit is scheduled to be raised. Second, health care has ceased to be an automatic right and is based on social security contributions. Third, the financial reform of the health system has been started.

References

Andorka, R. 1990. "A második gazdaság szerepe és társadalmi hatása." *AULA Társadalom és Gazdaság* 12, no. 4:16–37.

Bauer, T. 1982. "A második gazdasági reform és a tulajdonviszonyok." *Mozgó Világ* (November): 17–43.

Bozóki, A. 1992. "Political Transition and Constitutional Change in Hungary." In A. Bozóki, A. Körösényi, and G. Schöplflin, eds., *Post-Communist Transition: Emerging Pluralism in Hungary*. London: Pinter; also New York: St. Martin's Press.

Bruszt, L. 1992. "Transformative Politics: Social Costs and Social Peace in East Central Europe." *East European Politics and Society* 6, no. 1 (Winter).

Central Statistical Office. 1991. *Magyar Statisztikai Évkönyv 1990*. Budapest.

Csurka, I. 1992. "Néhány gondolat a rendszerváltozás két esztendeje és az MDF új programja kapcsán." *Magyar Fórum* (August 20).

Economic Trends in Eastern Europe (Kopint-Datorg). 1992. Vol. 1, no. 1.

Gem, E. 1993. "The Private Sector in Hungary 1989–1992." Washington, D.C.: World Bank. Unpublished manuscript.

Gyulavári, A. 1992. "Az államháztartás kiadási oldalának kérdései." Budapest: Central Statistical Office. Unpublished manuscript.

Hankiss, E. 1990. *East European Alternatives*. Oxford: Oxford University Press.

Huntington, S. P. 1991. *The Third Wave: Democratization in the Late Twentieth Century*. Norman: University of Oklahoma Press.

Kardos, P., and A. Vértes. 1990. "Körforgás. Az 1987-89-es időszak gazdaságpolitikájának elemzése." *Külgazdaság* (May).

Kolosi, T., and P. Róbert. 1991. "A rendszerváltás társadalmi hatásai." TÅRKI Gyorsjelentések 5. Budapest: TÅRKI.

Konjunktúrajelentés (Kopint-Datorg). 1990. March.

———. 1991. March.

Kornai, J. 1992. "A posztszocialista átmenet és az állam. Gondolatok a fiskális problémálról." *Közgazdasági Szemle* (June).

Körösényi, A. 1992a. "The Decay of Communist Rule in Hungary." In A. Bozóki, A. Körösényi, and G. Schöplflin, eds., *Post-Communist Transition: Emerging Pluralism in Hungary*. London: Pinter; also New York: St. Martin's Press.

———. 1992b. "The Hungarian Parliamentary Elections, 1990." In A. Bozóki, A. Körösényi, and G. Schöplflin, eds., *Post-Communist Transition: Emerging Pluralism in Hungary*. London: Pinter; also New York: St. Martin's Press.

———. 1993. "Stable or Fragile Democracy? Political Cleavages and Party System in Hungary." *Government and Opposition* 28, no. 1. (Winter).

Kurtán, S., P. Sándor, and L. Vass, eds. 1992. *Magyarország politikai évkönyve 1992*. Budapest: DKMKA-Economix.

Laver, M., and N. Schofield. 1991. *Multiparty Government: The Politics of Coalition in Europe*. Oxford: Oxford University Press.

Lázár, G., et al. 1992. "A politikai közvélemény a Medián kutatásainak tükrében." In S. Kurtán, P. Sándor, and L. Vass, eds., *Magyarország politikai évkönyve 1992*. Budapest: DKMKA-Economix.

Mizsei, K. 1993. "Hungary: Gradualism Needs a Strategy." In Richard Portes, ed., *Economic Transformation in Central Europe: A Progress Report*. City?: Centre for Economic Policy Research.

Nelson, J., et al. 1989. *Fragile Coalitions: The Politics of Economic Adjustment*. Washington, D.C.: Overseas Development Council.

Obláth, G. 1992. "Külföldi eladósodás és az adósságkezelés makrogazdasági problémái Magyarországon." *Mühelytanulmányok* (Kopint-Datorg), no. 8.

Obláth, G., and P. Márer. 1992. "A forint konvertibilitása." Magyar-Nemzetközi Kék Szalag Bizottság, 1.számu gazdaságpolitikai tanulmány. Budapest: MTA Közgazdaság Tudományi Intézet.

Olson, M. 1965. *The Logic of Collective Action*. Cambridge: Harvard University Press.

Palócz, É. 1992. "Some Major Difficulties of Economic Transition: Hungary's Example." Paper presented at the international symposium "Adam Smith and Economic Development in the XXIst Century," Paris, May 11–12.

Przeworski, A. 1991. *Democracy and the Market: Political and Economic Reforms in Eastern Europe and Latin America*. Cambridge: Cambridge University Press.

"Survey of Eastern Europe." 1993. *The Economist* (March 13).

Szelényi, I. 1988. *Socialist Entrepreneurs: Embourgeoisement in Rural Hungary*. Madison: University of Wisconsin Press.

Thoma, L. 1992. "Szakszervezeti válság." *Magyar Hirlap* (June 18).

Tóth, I. Gy. 1992. "Jóléti intézmények, szociális közkiadások." Budapest: Budapest University of Economics. Unpublished manuscript.

Tóth, I. J. 1993. "Gazdasági érdekszervezetek és érdekérvényesitési módszerek." *Politikatudományi Szemle* 2.

Urbán, L. 1991. "Why Was the Hungarian Transition Exceptionally Peaceful?" In G. Szoboszlai, ed., *Democracy and Political Transformation*. Budapest: Hungarian Political Science Association.

———. 1992a. "A parlament és privatizáció." In S. Kurtán, P. Sándor, and L. Vass, eds., *Magyarország politikai évkönyve 1992*. Budapest: DKMKA-Economix.

———. 1992b. "A tulajdonviszonyok alakitása, a privatizáció makro-és mikrotényezöi." Budapest: Eötvös University of Budapest. Unpublished manuscript.

Valentiny, Å. 1992. "Stabilizáció és növekedés." Budapest: Kopint-Datorg. Unpublished manuscript.

Chapter 4, "The Bulgarian Transition: A Difficult Beginning"

Notes

The financial support of the Overseas Development Council is gratefully acknowledged. The author owes special thanks first of all to Joan Nelson, then to Deyan Kuranov,

Alan Gelb, Susan Woodward, John Lampe, Diana Pishev, and all the colleagues from the project for their valuable comments on earlier versions of this chapter.

1. Some of the paper's commentators (S. Woodward and J. Lampe) contested the idea of a dividing line between Central Europe and the Balkans. The author, who feels more like a historian than a political scientist, insists on the principal difference in the transitional processes of the two subregions. Regretfully, her opinion seems to be shared by the European Community, the International Monetary Fund (IMF), and Western investors.

2. Recent revelations about the existence of concentration camps until the beginning of the 1960s shocked many Bulgarians. And yet compared with the other socialist countries, Bulgaria had a negligible number of political prisoners.

3. The term "revolution" (velvet, gentle, etc.) was rarely used in Bulgaria, although some used the phrase "the reasonable revolution." The more popular term is "changes."

4. On the third anniversary of the round-table talks, President Zhelyu Zhelev underlined the special rectangular geometry of the Bulgarian round table: at the insistence of the opposition, it had only two sides—"we" and "they"—a clear demarcation line that prevented a Romanian-style National Salvation Front version of the transition, but also laid the foundation of the future bipolar confrontational model.

5. There is an interesting coincidence in the percentage of votes the Communist parties of Serbia, Albania, Macedonia, Romania, and Bulgaria received in the first round of free elections, in clear contrast to the situation in Poland, Hungary, or Croatia and Slovenia.

6. One-fourth of the deputies refused to sign the new constitution, considering it to be an inadmissible compromise with the Communists. A group of thirty-nine of them went even further; they declared a hunger strike, protesting against it and pleading for prompt new elections.

7. The example of Finland illustrates the scope of Bulgaria's problems. Finland, which had a much healthier relationship with the Soviet Union and faced no transition, also registered a sharp decline in GNP, industrial production, and trade.

8. Prime Minister Lukanov was quoted as saying, "I will not be the Bulgarian Rakowski," implying that the former Polish party leader accelerated the fall of communism in his country by starting the reforms.

9. An analysis of the schedule of the National Assembly reveals that a disproportionate share of parliamentary discussions was spent on issues like the agenda of the day, mutual accusations on current developments and the past, and technical questions.

References

Agency for Economic Coordination and Development. 1992a. *Annual Report on the State of the Bulgarian Economy*. Sofia.

———. 1992b. *Economic Stabilization in Bulgaria in 1992*. Sofia.

———. 1992c. *The Year of the Iron Sheep*. Sofia.

Crampton, Richard. 1987. *A Short History of Modern Bulgaria*. Cambridge: Cambridge University Press.

———. 1988. "Stumbling and Dusting Off, or an Attempt to Pick a Path through the

Ticket of Bulgaria's New Economic Mechanism." *Eastern European Politics and Societies* 2, no. 2.

Dahrendorf, Ralf. 1990. *Reflections on the Revolutions in Europe*. New York: Times Books/Random House.

Dimitrov, Roumen. 1992. *Tribunal ili Forum*. Geneva, Paris, and Sofia: Editions Georges Naef S.A.

Feiwel, George R. 1977. *Growth and Reforms in Centrally Planned Economies: The Lessons of the Bulgarian Experience*. New York: Praeger.

Ivanova, Evgenia. 1992. "Current Forces in Bulgarian Life and Politics." *East European Reporter* (January/February).

Jackson, Marvin R. 1988. "Bulgaria's Attempt at a 'Radical' Reform." *Berichte des Bundesinstituts für ostwissenschaftliche und internationale Studien*, no. 2.

Kaminski, Bartołomiej. 1991. *The Collapse of State Socialism*. Princeton: Princeton University Press.

Krastev, Ivan. 1991. "The Illusions of Politics." *East European Reporter* (December).

Lampe, John R. 1986. *The Bulgarian Economy in the Twentieth Century*. London and Sydney: Croom Helm.

Murrell, Peter. 1991. "Public Choice and the Transformation of Socialism." *Journal of Comparative Economics* 15.

National Democratic Institute for International Affairs and International Republican Institute. 1992. *The October 13, 1991, Legislative and Municipal Elections in Bulgaria*. Washington, D.C.

Nikova, Ekaterina. 1991. "Economic Reforms in Bulgaria in Search of the Optimum Enterprise." In *L'entreprise en Grèce et en Europe XIX-XX siècles*. Athens: SOFHIS.

Organization for Economic Cooperation and Development (OECD). 1992. *Bulgaria: An Economic Assessment*. Paris.

Pishev, Ognyan. 1992. "Extending the Public Policy Debate in Emerging Democracies: The Case of Bulgaria." Paper presented in Bellagio, Italy.

Przeworski, Adam. 1991. *Democracy and the Market*. Cambridge: Cambridge University Press.

Rothschild, Joseph. 1974. *East Central Europe between the Two Wars*. Seattle and London: University of Washington Press.

Schöplin, George. 1990. "The Political Traditions of Eastern Europe." *Daedalus* (Winter).

Vögel, Heinrich. 1975. "Bulgaria." In Hans-Hermann Hönemann et al., eds., *The New Economic Systems in Eastern Europe*. Berkeley, California: University of California Press.

World Bank. 1991. *Bulgaria: Crisis and Transition to a Market Economy*. Vol. 1. Country Study. Washington, D.C.

About the Contributors

Jacek Kochanowicz received his Ph.D. in 1976 and his habilitation in 1991 at Warsaw University, where he is an associate professor of economic history. He specializes in the comparative economic and social history of Eastern Europe in the nineteenth and twentieth centuries. In 1990–1991 he was a member of the Institute of Advanced Studies of Princeton University's School of Social Sciences. He has also been a visiting professor at the Univeristy of Washington, Seattle, and the University of Chicago. Kochanowicz chairs the supervisory board of the Bank of Social and Economic Initiatives, founded to help small businesses in Poland.

András Körösényi is a lecturer in comparative politics at the Faculty of Law and Government, Eötvös University of Budapest. Körösényi received his doctorate in sociology in 1987 and in 1989-1990 spent a year as a postdoctoral fellow at Lady Margaret Hall, Oxford. He regularly publishes in Hungarian, German, and British journals. He is coeditor and coauthor of *Post-Communist Transition: Emerging Pluralism in Hungary*, published by Pinter Publishers, London, and St. Martin's Press, New York, in 1992.

Kalman Mizsei is the Pew economist-in-residence and director of the economics program at the Institute for EastWest Studies, New York. Mizsei has been a particpant in the international project of the World Institute for Development Economics Research on East and Central European transformations. In 1990–1991 he was deputy director of the Institute for World Economics of the Hungarian Academy of Sciences, where he served as a fellow from 1979 to 1989. From 1990 to 1992 he served as an adviser to the president of the National Bank of Hungary. He was also an expert on the International Blue Ribbon Commission for advising Hungary on economic reform in 1990.

Joan M. Nelson is a senior associate of the Overseas Development Council. She received her Ph.D. from Harvard University in 1960. She has worked with the Policy Planning Division of the U.S. Agency for International Development (AID), taught at the Massachusetts Institute of Technology, and codirected a research program at the Harvard Center for International Affairs. From 1974 to 1982 she established and directed the program in Comparative Politics and Modernization at the Johns Hopkins School for Advanced International

Studies. Her publications include *Aid, Influence, and Foreign Policy* (1968); *No Easy Choice: Political Participation in Developing Countries* (with Sam Huntington, 1976); *Access to Power: Politics and the Urban Poor* (1979); *Fragile Coalitions: The Politics of Economic Adjustment* (1989); *Economic Crisis and Policy Choice* (1990); and *Encouraging Democracy: What Role for Conditioned Aid?* (1992).

Ekaterina Nikova is a senior research associate with the Institute for Balkan Studies at the Bulgarian Academy of Sciences. She received her Ph.D. from Moscow State University. A specialist on southern Eastern Europe, Nikova was awarded a Woodrow Wilson Fellowship in 1991. Her major areas of research are comparative economics and twentieth-century economic history. She has recently published *The Balkans and the European Community*. Nikova is currently a Fulbright Visiting Professor at George Washington University, Washington, D.C.

Conference Participants

Rio de Janeiro Conference

Persio Arida
Amaury de Souza
João Paulo Dos Reis Velloso
Antonio Barros de Castro
Ricardo Carciofi
Catalina Smulovitz
Juan Antonio Morales

Budapest Conference

Tamás Bauer
András Inotai
Deyan Kiuranov
Henryk Szlajfer
Edmund Wnuk-Lipinski

Index